Increasing Employee Productivity

Increasing
Employee
Productivity

ROBERT E. SIBSON

A Division of American Management Associations

Library of Congress Cataloging in Publication Data

Sibson, Robert Earl, 1925–
    Increasing employee productivity.

    Includes index.
    1. Personnel management.   2. Labor productivity.
I. Title.
HF5549.S585   658.31'4   76-20564
ISBN 0-8144-5383-X

© 1976 AMACOM

A division of American Management Associations, New York.

First Printing

To Jay and Ricky:
Wonderboy and Superkid

Preface

In the mind of management, how to increase employee productivity is clearly the number one business problem in the area of personnel relations. Any number of surveys of management attitudes have said so; there isn't even a close number two. Conversations with line management yield the same result. In the preface to my book titled *Compensation,** a comment was made that the management of executive compensation was the number two problem. Predictably, there were some inquiries: what's number one? The answer is, "How to increase employee productivity."

At the national level, increasing employee productivity is a major problem. Economists do not agree on many things, but they do agree that the standard of living is a function of the level of employee productivity. Further improvements in the standard of living in this country for a growing work force is therefore dependent upon continuing the increase in employee productivity.

As a practical matter, for reasons noted in this book, it is the opinion of the author that productivity in the United States has been declining in recent years. There is no doubt that productivity in other developed countries is doing much better than it is doing in the United States, which necessarily means that we are becoming increasingly uncompetitive in international markets. It is this combination of circumstances that represents one major reason why, in the minds of some, this country is headed toward an economic crisis in the 1980s, one that could make the 1930s look like a moderate recession. Economic difficulties of these proportions would not only represent a deterioration of living standards but also a bankruptcy of many of

* AMACOM, 1960, 1967, 1974.

our established institutions, not to mention New York City. There is little doubt that this type of economic environment, for even a short period of time, would mean changes in our basic economic and social systems.

On the opportunity side, if productivity could get back to an upward trend of even moderate proportion, say 3 or 4 percent, some very positive and profound results would occur. Almost unnoticed, and certainly not very publicized, is the fact that the United States in the post-World War II period is the first society that has achieved material sufficiency. The national income is great enough so that there is no economic reason for poverty. There may be, and still are, problems of distributing that wealth; there are many who choose not to participate; there are some strange standards of defining what poverty is; and there is a tendency in many areas to spend more than we have. But the plain fact is that the per capita wealth of this nation has raised us to a position of economic sufficiency and national well-being.

If productivity were to increase even at a 3 percent level during the next 25 years, three out of four family units in this country would go through what has been defined as "income breakpoints." This means that they would move to the next higher level of living style.

Unfortunately, the traditional methods for increasing productivity in this country are becoming less and less usable. Therefore, new methods for increasing employee productivity must be devised and implemented. One such method is the more effective management of human resources. Increasing employee productivity through better management of human resources must be applied at the enterprise level. It is therefore a management problem, and managers of individual businesses must find ways to increase productivity through better and more effective personnel relations' policies, practices, and procedures.

This book doesn't answer any of these personnel relations questions. Its objectives are far more modest than this. Even so, the nature of employee productivity is so complex and far-ranging a subject that its components are difficult to deal with.

What has been attempted is to report where we are with respect to employee productivity and to describe the elements of the problem. There are reported and discussed experiences and some methods in the area of human relations which have general applicability to most enterprises and which have resulted in increased productivity through better management of human resources.

The sources of information reported and the opinions reflected in this book are largely the result of my experiences and work. In the 15 years since entering the consulting business, it has been my good fortune to be exposed to the thinking of many leaders of major corporations, who give a great deal of thought to the subject of employee productivity. Furthermore, the views expressed benefit from in-depth exposure to the personnel activities of over 300 firms as a result of my personal work with client companies. In addition, of course, I have benefited indirectly from experience in client assignments from associates in Sibson & Company, Inc. Once again, therefore, in the writing of this book I am indebted to my clients as a basic source of information. In the consulting business, one gets all his income, much of his experience and information, and many of his ideas from his clients.

Of course I have made a thorough review of published information, but I have found that very little has ever been published on improving productivity at the firm level through better management of human resources. Information, notes, and outlines from discussions on this subject have been collected over the past 12 years. The pages of this book represent a distillation and summary of many file cabinets of information.

Robert E. Sibson

Contents

1. Productivity: Effective Use of Human Resources   *1*
2. An Organized Approach to Increasing Productivity   *17*
3. Human Resources Information Systems   *34*
4. Unproductive Practices   *54*
5. Environment   *68*
6. Staffing   *81*
7. Manpower Controls   *98*
8. Organization Structure   *112*
9. Delegative Management   *130*
10. Human Resources Development   *145*
11. Incentives   *170*
12. Personnel Management of Productivity   *186*
13. Responsibilities of the Personnel Unit Manager   *200*
     Index   *205*

1

Productivity: Effective Use of Human Resources

Management's goal in personnel relations is essentially to bring about the full or optimum utilization of the human resources of the enterprise, to see to it that employees work as effectively as possible. Human resources management involves many tasks and activities. A majority of time and effort in employee relations is spent on a variety of things that have little direct impact on productivity. All such activities may be useful and even necessary. But the essence of human resources management is to bring about the full utilization of the human resources of the enterprise, to see to it that employees work effectively to achieve enterprise goals.

Effective management of people does not necessarily have anything to do with making employees happier people, or more sensitive people, or more socially conscious people, or "better people" in any respect. Management has no special skills in such areas. One could even question whether these essentially social, psychological, and personal areas are part of the management job. Any firm would welcome and value such elements of atmosphere, but the question is whether that is the basic management job or enterprise goal. There is also some question as to whether "happier" employees are necessarily more productive employees.

Top management can consider alternative postures or different basic philosophies with respect to personnel management. The suggestion here is that adoption of the "full utilization" view is the most appropriate personnel philosophy in order to produce high levels of productivity in any enterprise. An enterprise must avoid human relations characterized by unhappy, insensitive, unproductive, or disruptive employees, but the positive or strategic goal is full utilization of the firm's human assets. This view is a fundamental philosophy of business, and underlies much of what is described and expressed throughout this book.

Full Utilization, Productiveness, and Productivity

Full utilization of human resources and productivity do not necessarily mean exactly the same thing. In the advanced thinking of personnel, "full utilization" is the broader concept. It connotes, for instance, asset utilization as well as output measures. Optimum use of human assets conceptually weighs the building of assets and the quality of these assets in terms of actual or potential deployment. Utilization also involves long-term or strategic considerations, whereas productivity infers only this year's results in terms of (income producing) output and the cost of output.

"Productiveness" is a fabricated word for business use, and differs from "productivity" in the sense that it considers the value of output. It may be viewed as qualitative productivity. Productivity represents some measure of output divided by employee input. Productiveness adds a measure in the numerator of this equation which assesses the *value or usefulness* of output.

In matters of human resources management, these three—optimum utilization, productiveness, and productivity—are parallel concepts. When dealing with matters of policy or basic enterprise strategy and concept, optimum utilization of human resources is the most useful concept. The closer one comes to designing and implementing specific actions, programs, or practices, the more relevant is the more narrow but manageable concept of productivity. Focusing solely on productivity may be an error, however, and can cause long-term difficulties. The firm may expend resources to increase the efficiency with which useless work is performed. It may be increasing productivity at the expense of quantity and quality of human assets. This would convert assets to income and might well detract from effectiveness of work in the future.

Commitment to Full Utilization of Human Resources

Most firms could increase employee productivity substantially if they simply adopted the "full utilization" view as a fundamental goal, communicated this view, and, as far as possible, made it a part of the fundamental thinking and attitude of every employee in the firm. Such an enunciation of fundamental objectives is also essential to the success of many detailed actions and practices which are specifically directed at increasing productivity.

In many enterprises, productivity is eroded or improvements in productivity are inhibited, simply because managers and employees throughout the firm see no clear commitment to optimal work effectiveness. Employees may go along with, and even support, specific measures to increase productivity, but they lack personal commitment because they perceive no enterprise commitment. They exercise no initiative because there is no apparent and clear enterprise expectation of individual or group initiative in increasing productivity. Therefore, a firm that would do nothing else except make the philosophy of full utilization a known company expectation would in all likelihood experience noticeable improvement in productivity.

For some, this is the first essential step in improving productivity—making the "full utilization concept" a part of every employee's consciousness. Evolution, articulation, and communication of a full-utilization policy requires thoughtful consideration. It involves some top-level staff time and general management time spent in reviewing considerations and in making decisions and commitments. The amount of time and cost of such an action is, however, quite moderate.

Enterprises commit themselves to various fundamental philosophies and communicate these basic aspirations throughout their organization. Some, for instance, are committed to being a "growth company." Others have a service orientation. Some strive simply to survive. All could also commit themselves just as firmly and fundamentally to a continuing philosophy of utilization of the human resources of the enterprise. Companies can, and frequently do, have multiple goals. Increasing productivity can be one of these basic goals. Like other basic goals, it can be communicated and emphasized over and over again to all employees. Relatively simple practices can reinforce this company commitment to greater productivity.

Although most firms want to increase productivity and many firms spend a lot of time and resources in order to increase productivity, few have explicitly stated a "full utilization" philosophy. What is suggested here is that a company should consider two things as the starting point in a serious, organized, and consistent plan to increase productivity. First, the firm itself should evolve a clear philosophy of employee relations, and it is an assumption here that the "full utilization" concept stated in the first paragraph of the book is the core of that philosophy. Second, the firm should "tell it like it is," that is, communicate its core personnel philosophy to every manager and every employee.

In some companies the commitment to increase productivity has been only cosmetic; the words are there, but the actions do not support the statements. Real commitment to increasing productivity requires some actions as well as communications. Four actions, none of which involve programs, are essential parts of real commitment to full utilization of human resources. Without such actions, employees are not likely to sense a commitment because supportive communication does not take place. For one thing, lower-level supervisors must observe their higher-level managers expressing their statements in their actions and consciously working toward increasing productivity.

Secondly, goals, standards of performance, and expectations must require a demonstrable improved effectiveness of work. Making the task of increasing the effective use of human resources a conscious part of every manager's job is the third nonprogramatic action step required for real commitment to better use of human resources. Assignment of this responsibility must include *allocating some time* to supervisors throughout the firm so they can better manage human relations matters.

Finally, increased effectiveness of human resources must be one of the criteria against which supervisors are measured. Part of supervisors' salary increases and bonus awards should, for instance, depend upon how well they do this job.

Adoption of a full utilization philosophy, communicating this policy to the organization, again and again, plus the four action steps outlined, represent company commitment to increasing productivity. These basic steps are in themselves an organized effort to increase productivity, without programs and at little cost. Such basic considerations are also essential to most of the more formal, complex, and costly programs, activities, and considerations which will be outlined.

QUESTIONS ABOUT THE "FULL UTILIZATION" CONCEPT

Because relatively few companies have established a clear-cut philosophy embracing the "full utilization" concept, it is important to examine why the majority have not. While no organized research has been conducted on this subject, discussions with hundreds of company executives tend to identify a number of reasons why most companies have not, first, adopted the "full utilization concept," and secondly, made it a part of the thinking and attitudes of all their employees.

For one thing, some have simply not perceived the importance of the development and communication of fundamental personnel philosophies regarding full utilization of human resources. It is their view that if they adopt programs and practices aimed at increasing productivity, they are doing the productivity job. For reasons just noted, commitment—including communications of the full-utilization concept as a part of the company goals—is critical to the task of increasing the effectiveness of the work force. Furthermore, experience as well as logic suggests that such basic policies, when well communicated, do promote the success of each specific program designed to increase employee productivity.

Some companies have not adopted a full utilization concept simply because they do not believe greater employee productivity is very important to their company's success. While increasing productivity is very important in some firms and quite important in most firms, it is (or is perceived to be) relatively unimportant in other enterprises. The company that has a market monopoly or owns patented products greatly needed or desired in the marketplace, or which enjoys other similar clear-cut business advantages, can achieve enterprise goals such as growth and profits with relatively low levels of productivity. For these firms, increasing productivity may be a relatively low business priority, at least for the time being.

There is also a question of priorities. In any operational period an enterprise, and its general management in particular, has just so much time and resources to expend. These must be prioritized. Rightly or wrongly for many, increasing productivity is not on the current year's priority list.

Some firms also lack real enthusiasm for increasing productivity. They do not necessarily quarrel with the desirability of increasing productivity. They recognize, however, that such a known policy creates a climate, and will likely precipitate some actions, which may be distasteful. Increasing productivity, for instance, may eventually involve a lot of hard work. It may also involve some risks. Certainly, increasing employee effectiveness involves the commitment of time and money resources. Adoption of the philosophy of optimum use of human resource triggers personnel attitudes and actions which may be unpleasant; for instance, the discharge of long-term associates. Thus, many firms believe that there are easier ways to increase profits than by improving productivity.

There are companies that have adopted alternative philosophies of employee relations. For example, a few in top-management ranks have seemingly adopted the basic "humanist" philosophy toward employee relations. This view, in one way or another, actually embraces the notion that the fundamental employee relations philosophy of the firm should be to somehow fulfill employees personally. There are also those who have fundamentally embraced the personnel philosophy of the "corporate society." In a sense, this philosophy views the enterprise first as a social phenomenon. These views, in essence, place the interest of employees above those of customers and stockholders. Profits are measured in terms of what is necessary to maintain jobs and the desired work environment.

Few of those who have adopted alternative personnel philosophies necessarily oppose increased productivity. They simply will not adopt or support measures to increase productivity if they impinge upon or threaten the basic tenets of an alternate philosophy. Some executives have questioned the full utilization view of employee relations on almost moral grounds. Criticism on these grounds has been expressed by employees, by labor unions, by governmental agencies, and other groups.

The general public remains unconvinced about the virtue of effective programs to increase productivity. A recent public poll, in fact, has revealed a great amount of public distrust. Many persons queried in the poll expressed the view that increasing productivity means that many people must work harder, some may lose their jobs, and the corporation benefits by higher profits. There is also concern that the basic philosophy of full utilization is exploitative. Some of those polled believed that this callous attitude toward human beings—one that views employees as pieces of equipment or machinery to be "used"—assumes that people are expendable. The fact of the matter is, of course, that employees *are* used, but only in the constructive sense that their time is to be spent productively at work. Actually, the "full utilization" view of personnel relations is not a harsh view, nor is it immoral or moral. It is simply a realistic view.

Aside from conflicting philosophies, there exist a number of constraints on management action which would discourage, if not prevent, excesses in pursuing the goal of optimum productivity. Innumerable laws and regulations govern conditions of work. Trade unions, or the threat of union organizations, represents another constraint. Employees as individuals or informal groups, particularly higher-level employees, exercise restraints by speaking out or leaving the firm. Finally, there are indirect constraints, such as public reputation.

Some feel that the full utilization approach is harsh because it requires a total commitment to work, that it somehow degrades or makes more difficult the attainment of other human aspirations. But there is nothing in the principle of full utilization that says the primary goal of life is to work or even to work effectively. It implies only that the goal while at work is to work with optimal effectiveness. The full utilization approach also implies that the manager's job is to run that enterprise. Running the enterprise with respect to personnel relations means the utilization of human resources to the optimum extent possible.

As a practical matter, there is not anything at all contradictory between the ideas that people should work effectively and that people can and should lead well-rounded lives and be happy. Quite the contrary. Many studies by sociologists and by psychologists suggest that the full utilization philosophy promotes and is consonant with "the good life." Also, higher productivity means higher real income and material standards of living are part of the "good life." Furthermore, most people are happier doing a job efficiently than they are doing a job inefficiently. Most people want to go home at the end of the day knowing that they have done a good job and that they have contributed their share. People do take pride in their work when their work is done well. Most people do want their talents used effectively.

LEVELS AND TRENDS OF PRODUCTIVITY

Questions regarding management of employee productivity require insights as to the level and trend of output per man-hour. For the manager and staff specialist, this includes information on national, industry, and then company productivity. The only concrete measures that are publicly available and which indicate just how effectively human resources are being utilized is found in productivity statistics. These comprise indexes that show, for broad sections of the economy or for selected industries, a measure of labor output divided by labor man-hours.

General Productivity Data

Government statistics on productivity show modest improvement of about 3 percent per year over the past 25 years. Reported productivity data is summarized in Table 1. Such data as these lead the press and the seven o'clock newscasters to report that productivity has been increasing—in some years as much as 5 percent. And data such as these, and the reporting of them, lead most people, including many business leaders, to believe that productivity in the United States is increasing. This kind of reporting is about as misleading as it is to say that the cost of living increased by about 11 percent in 1974.* The information is factually correct in a technical sense, but is misleading in practical application. The fact is, as Table 1 shows, that productivity reported in this instance is for the "total private economy." For

Table 1. Productivity data for the total private economy.

Year	Productivity Increase *	Year	Productivity Increase *
1950	8.6%	1962	5.0%
1951	3.5	1963	3.5
1952	2.4	1964	4.1
1953	4.0	1965	3.4
1954	2.0	1966	4.2
1955	4.2	1967	1.9
1956	0.2	1968	3.0
1957	2.8	1969	0.4
1958	3.0	1970	1.0
1959	3.3	1971	3.6
1960	1.6	1972	4.6
1961	3.3	1973	0.9
		1974	2.7

* Change in productivity over prior year.
Source: Bureau of Labor Statistics.

* The prices of goods and services typically purchased by a factory worker with a family of four living in an urban community increased by about 11 percent. Actually, even for this group, the *cost of living* as contrasted to the prices of goods and services increased by only about 7 percent.

this segment of the economy, data in the form of an index showing the change of a particular measure of output per man-hour indicate that productivity has been increasing.

There are many questions as to the technical appropriateness of "national" productivity indexes. For example, Table 1 shows that, for some years, employee productivity increased more in periods of full employment than in periods of high unemployment. Every business manager knows that employee productivity actually decreases during periods of high employment and increases in periods of low employment. The fact is that such government data are the best measure available and no one yet has come up with anything better. It is misleading, however, to array such data and conclude or infer that productivity in the United States has increased an average of 2.7 percent over the past ten years. There is no productivity index for the United States. At best, therefore, the productivity index can only say that over a full business cycle, a particular measure of productivity for a limited segment of the economy has increased somewhere between 2 and 3 percent per year. Government data suggest that even on this basis the increases in productivity has experienced a slightly declining rate of increases since the middle of the 1960s.

While there are no data that really answer the question "what is the trend of employee productivity in the United States," analysis suggests that productivity probably leveled off during the 1960s and has probably been declining in the 1970s. Estimated productivity figures for the United States overall are shown in Figure 1. The overall decline has been small and its extent unclear, but the rate of decline may in fact be increasing.

The most important reason for the decline in productivity is the change in the work force. A higher and higher percentage of workers, for instance, are employed in professional business and in professional units of commercial business, where productivity is significantly less than in the industrial segment of the economy. Even more significant is the fact that a larger and larger proportion of the total work force is being employed by government, where productivity is extremely low and declining.

One other important point about national productivity: Every indicator suggests that in the past 25 years the rate of productivity in other developed countries has been increasing much faster than it has been in the United States. In the European economic community the rate of increase in output per man-hour has been approximately 6 percent, or double the rate of increase for the "private sector" in the United States. In Japan, productivity has been increasing at the rate of 10 percent.

This summary suggests to the business manager some very important things about productivity. Productivity measures reported are unreliable and in some respects misleading. Employee productivity in the United States has

Figure 1. Estimated percent change in productivity in the United States (1964–1974). Estimates based on various government data.

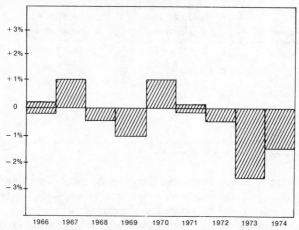

leveled off, and is probably declining. Because productivity in the major developed countries abroad is still increasing, American business is becoming less competitive in international markets.

Company Productivity Data

The primary view of productivity by the business leader must necessarily be parochial: What has happened to productivity in this company and how does it affect this firm's current and near-term competitiveness? Furthermore, productivity is managed at the individual business level, not at the national level. Therefore, national and international trends are interesting and have broad economic relevance. But the primary focus on managing productivity must be at the individual enterprise level.

Obviously, trends in productivity vary greatly between industries and between different companies in the same industry. Over the past 25 years, for instance, productivity has increased at the rate of 7 to 10 percent in such industries as radio and television manufacturing, hosiery, air transportation, and petroleum pipelines. But, on the other hand, productivity has increased hardly at all in some industries, such as nonferrous metals, can manufacturing, footware, and steel.

Few firms have valid and accurate productivity information, and it is very difficult to compare data that do exist. When information exists at all, it is usually in terms of partial measures of productivity in a factory, some warehouses, or some field-office operations. Only recently have companies refocused attention on providing productivity information for management's

Table 2. Company productivity measures based on comparable electrical manufacturing firms.

Company	Annual Change in Productivity, %	Period of Measurement, Years
S	11	5
B	9	4
M	6	5
G	6	3
A	2	5
R	0	5
W	−1	6

Source: Sibson & Company, Inc. 1975.

use in managing human resources. Therefore, comments on company productivity must be based largely on a very few in-depth studies, gross measures, observations, and the judgments of operating management.

One study of productivity within an industry is summarized in Table 2. The data in this study were difficult to obtain, were subject to considerable statistical error, and were considered confidential by participants. Even so, the study illustrates that these seven companies of about comparable size—who competed in the same product and labor markets, and were subject to similar general economic circumstances—experienced very different trends in employee productivity.

OPPORTUNITIES FOR IMPROVED PRODUCTIVITY

Studies by the National Commission on productivity suggest what businessmen already know: Substitution of capital for employees accounts for almost one-half of improved productivity over the past 25 years. Better methods and procedures of work account for 30 or 40 percent of improved productivity. Improved effectiveness of workers (better utilization of human resources) have contributed at best a minimum amount to increased productivity. Individual company studies raise the question as to whether or not labor-controlled productivity has increased at all, or whether in fact it has been declining.

Perhaps of greater significance in business enterprise are the questions: "What are the opportunities for improving productivity in the future"? "What is the current level of productivity and what can it be"? Meetings probing these questions have been conducted with operating managers in almost 50 companies over the years. Their impressions and judgments consistently indicate that the opportunities for productivity improvement are very great in every firm where such interviews were conducted. Collectively, the judgments of these operating managers—who are close to their operations and in the absence of data are the best source for such information—suggest that better management of human resources could significantly improve levels of productivity.

If one were to take 100 percent productivity as optimum, the most human beings could effectively produce consistent with a work pace and environment that is proper for health and reasonable comfort, then the judgments of operating management suggest that productivity is at about 80 percent of optimum in factory positions overall. This 80 percent average for production workers includes mechanized and automated operations (for example, automobile production) and batch processing factories (for example, chemicals) where the work pace is controlled by machinery. In these types of operations, labor productivity is probably 90 percent or more of optimum. But the average factory figures also include some factories where productivity is as low as 50 percent of optimum.

In office operations, where the numbers of employees are gradually increasing, productivity is probably not more than 60 percent. The average 60 percent labor-productivity figure for office workers includes a sizable number of jobs that are machine controlled or where work is so routine that it is subject to industrial engineering methodization and work-measurement systems. In these jobs, productivity in the office is probably close to that in the factory, which means that labor productivity in a great many office jobs is less than half of what it should be.*

Productivity among "middle group" employees is somewhere between 60 and 75 percent, in the judgment of operating managers interviewed. This middle group includes all those whose pay is above office and factory levels, but below management level.† This middle group is important in terms of productivity because it is a large group and the most rapidly growing part of the work force in many firms. Furthermore, the middle-group worker has an important effect on the work of others in the organization. This group includes supervisors, who obviously affect the productivity of others, and also "technologists"—those running computers, designing products and even designing systems, methods, and practices that determine work methods which others follow.

For those who like the dramatics, an ample number of cases can be cited which would put form and shape to statistics. For instance, a business equipment manufacturer stated in a recent annual report that the company in-

---

* Productivity in government agencies is probably less than one-third of optimum.

† Productivity figures for management are not even presented. In these jobs, the question "Is he doing the right thing?" is so much more important than "Is he doing it efficiently?" that the whole concept of traditional labor productivity has little relevance, and management must be viewed in terms of productiveness.

creased its sales by 15 percent and at the same time reduced employment by 20 percent. Productivity in warehousing in the retail food business was estimated by executives in the chain grocery industry as low as 40 percent. If productivity could be raised to the 70 or 80 percent level, consumers would pay 5 percent less for groceries.

A study of 20 "peer group" manufacturers showed that, during the recession of 1966–1971, when sales volume had fallen 10 percent in constant dollars, the administrative work force had actually increased. In perhaps less dramatic fashion, every business has experienced creeping growth in the size of administrative and staff positions, a growth not justified by business volume or explainable by the increased technology of business.

Residential construction productivity is far less than one-half optimum. Homes are still built essentially the same way they were 100 years ago. Union controls and building codes prevent the construction of homes by more modern methods. If mass-production methods were applied to the construction of home units, the cost of housing might be cut by more than half. This may be *the way* to *really* provide for low-cost housing.

POTENTIAL IMPACT OF GREATER PRODUCTIVITY ON BUSINESS RESULTS

Increased productivity can have important impact on business results. For the commercial business, this means greater profits. Table 3 for instance,

Table 3. Potential impact of greater productivity on profits.

Payroll Expense as Percent of Sales	*Percent Increase in Pretax Profit* * *from Improvement in Productivity of:*			
	5%	*10%*	*20%*	*40%*
20	20	40	80	260
30	30	60	120	240
40	40	80	160	320
50	50	100	200	500

* Assumes a return on sales of 5 percent.
Source: Company financial statements.

shows the impact of improved productivity on earnings per share for firms of varying capital intensity. If these firms could achieve one-third the potential improvement thought possible by the operating managers, the pretax profits referred to would double. This result would not likely be achieved in one year, but is more likely to occur over a five-year period. That kind of earning improvement would put any firm in the "growth" company category, and would likely be leveraged for stockholders. Earnings growth might result in a higher price/earnings ratio in the stock markets, and so stock prices might increase by more than twofold.

Such increased productivity might result in lower retail prices. It is extremely difficult to estimate the relationship between improved productivity and ultimate consumer prices, but even if only a modest part of potential improvement in productivity resulted in lower prices, it would represent a damping effect on their upward movement. Some relief in rising consumer prices over a five-year period would be most welcome.

The fact is that increased productivity would likely manifest itself in a number of ways. Greater productivity of even moderate amounts, say 10 or 20 percent, would increase profits and stock price substantially. It would at least damp the upward trend in consumer prices, and it would make available more capital for further development of the business and the economy. This, in turn, would help provide jobs for those now unemployed, for those displaced by greater productivity, and for additional employment needs of a growing population.

No doubt greater productivity at the individual firm level might be effected by having fewer people required to do a given volume of work. If repeated throughout the economy, this would mean a great deal of job displacement. Even a 20 percent increase in productivity by this policy could result in 10 million unemployed. Economic history teaches us, however, that this approach doesn't work like that. Rather, increased productivity ultimately means more jobs.

Besides more jobs, the increase would have other less direct or visible economic benefits. Investment of funds made available through greater productivity in research may lead to new products that would not be otherwise developed. To the extent this happens in industries like pharmaceuticals or foods, there might be great public benefit. Moreover, growth and company success generated by greater productivity would mean better jobs for some and could contribute to job enrichment.

The principal benefit from greater productivity is, of course, better living standards. Economists don't agree on many things, but all agree that improved living standards are dependent absolutely on increasing productivity. This is particularly true when, as in the United States, the ratio of workers to nonworkers is declining substantially.*

How well human resources are managed will become an even more critical element of enterprise success in the future than it has been in the past. The management of human resources will therefore become a relatively more important part of the management job. For some businesses, success or failure in handling the employee relations problem—how well they utilize

* This ratio has declined from 3.5 in 1950 to 2.0 in 1974.

human talent—will represent a "go" or "no-go" situation. That is, it will determine the success or failure of the enterprise. This is a judgment shared by most top management people as well as by senior personnel specialists.

The complexities of managing human resources effectively will increase greatly for enterprises of all types, and will be particularly greater for commercial enterprises. This is an inevitable consequence of trends and developments currently taking place in businesses and in the economic and social environments that surround businesses. For example, the demand for general management personnel in commercial enterprises will probably double in the next 15 years; that is, there will be twice as many management jobs to fill as there are today, but the supply of qualified general management people available to commercial enterprises will likely not increase at all. Thus, greater skills are going to be required to extend or leverage management over a broader span of the company.

The job of managing human resources will also increase simply because of the continued development of technology. More advanced technology is obviously taking place in physical sciences, social sciences, and other recognized academic disciplines that are used increasingly in most enterprises. Business technologies (for example, computer sciences and administrative areas) are also growing. Such a growing proliferation of technologies and specialists makes the coordination, control, and communications between interdependent sections of an enterprise more and more complex.

As these areas of technology increase, the people who work in them become progressively more critical to the future success of the business. These technologies require specialized knowledge, not possessed and generally not very well understood by general management personnel, and are therefore extremely difficult to manage. Also, the very nature of the work involved in the various kinds of technologies does not lend itself to the analytic process or control of traditional budgeting, costing, work methods, and other procedures. Thus, not only the increase in the various types of technologies, but also the difficulties of managing people who perform work in these areas, contributes to increased difficulty in managing human resources and increasing productivity.

These examples are among the elements that are likely to make the job of increasing productivity more difficult in the future. Others will be noted as the specific issues in optimum use of human resources are examined. Both the nature of the problem as summarized and the difficulty of people management clearly suggest a new urgency in evolving management techniques, practices, and styles that will more effectively utilize the human talent of the enterprise. Personnel staff has always had, as its major role, assisting management in increasing the effectiveness of people at work. What companies need now, in addition to a conscious policy of and commitment to increasing productivity, is a serious and organized effort to increase productivity.

INCREASING EMPLOYEE PRODUCTIVITY

Most managers agree with the need for increasing employee productivity in their companies. Most accept the supposition that increasing employee productivity will become progressively more difficult in the future. Managers who have had the opportunity to examine the issue in their own firms also agree that there is today a new urgency for evolving management techniques, practices, and styles that will more effectively utilize human talent.

Having agreed to such propositions, assumptions, and conceptualizations, the general manager then asks: *How do we increase employee productivity?* No one has yet discovered a single technique or gimmick that answers this question. Every company says it is different, and indeed it is. As long as every company is unique, then the answer to any basic question, such as how to improve employee productivity, must be customized to that company's specific situation.

Experiences of the past few years in instances where improved productivity has been approached in a serious and organized way does suggest, however, that there is a process which may appropriately be followed, that there are certain characteristics of work involving better utilization of human talent, and that there are some areas of opportunity which are common to many companies.

Part of this process has already been outlined. It involves formulation of policy and commitment to full utilization of human resources. After this has been done, certain basic action steps are possible without adoption of a program. These include assigning responsibility for increasing productivity to supervisors throughout the organization; giving them time to do that job; and evaluating their performance in part on how well they do it.

Beyond that, programs or activities involving substantial commitments of resources must be made. Determining what programs or activities are appropriate requires a rather precise and definitive articulation of both needs for increasing employee productivity in a particular firm and realistic opportunities. These cannot be generalities or platitudinous statements. They must pinpoint the needs and opportunities; they must define in concrete ways how increased productivity will help achieve business objectives.

Such an analysis or audit would ideally be a normal part of the strategic analysis and planning of the firm. If not, it can be conducted as a separate effort, which in effect would be a feasibility study. A feasibility study on improving productivity need not be an elaborate or prolonged project. The key is to know what to look for. Management can provide the inputs necessary to make the analyses needed for broad policy guidelines in improving employee productivity. Most information required for a feasibility study of productivity improvement resides in the firm. A feasibility study or audit should be restricted to gathering existent relevant information and arraying it in a way that facilitates management decision making.

Certainly, part of the audit or feasibility study should identify how the firm has increased employee productivity in the past. It would obviously be an error, however, to assume that what has been done in the past should be done in the future. What has been done in the past must be evaluated in light of current and likely future conditions. In addition, there must be identification of other practical avenues of approach that could be seriously considered in increasing employee productivity. The identification of all areas or activities that might be considered not only provides management with the type of information needed to draw policy conclusions, but also represents the next step in the process of increasing employee productivity. These identified areas are the potential component parts of an organized approach toward increasing productivity in a particular company.

2

An Organized Approach to Increasing Productivity

Increasingly, companies will need to have an organized approach, as contrasted to an informal or transactional approach, toward improving the use of human resources. Among other things, this means a careful identification of the ways in which employee productivity can be improved. Once potential areas for improvement have been identified, then an analytic evaluation of these areas will pinpoint those that represent, for that particular firm in the foreseeable future, the most promising and practical targets for improving productivity.

A TRANSACTIONAL APPROACH TO IMPROVING PRODUCTIVITY

Most work on productivity in business over the past 50 years has been highly transactional. Some clear or apparent problem has confronted a business and management has reacted. People worked inefficiently because their methods were poor, so methods engineers redesigned jobs. For example, when some machinery manufacturer designed a piece of equipment that could save a great number of man-hours, the user firm purchased that piece of equipment. More recently, many professional people have clearly reacted against some personnel practices, even to the point of organizing into unions, and new personnel practices have evolved.

A transactional approach to problems has its virtues. It assures, for one thing, that a business is reacting to real problems. On the other hand, by assuming a transactional role in the area of productivity, management has more often dealt with productivity matters that have been brought to their attention. This can lead a firm to react to the apparent rather than the important and to deal with what are *perceived* as needs rather than needs that may be more significant even though they have little visibility. A transactional approach to productivity has the defects of a piecemeal approach to an important problem. It almost inevitably means that efforts are random and the firm is not concentrating on targets of greatest opportunity.

A transactional view of productivity by management has, to some extent, transferred the leadership in increasing productivity from management to the technologists. The technologists have worked hard to convince companies that they should adopt programs which deployed the knowledge possessed by the technologists. The industrial engineer urges methods work; the behavioral scientist urges organization development (OD).

Company efforts to improve productivity can be very uneven without a systematic and organized effort. In one year there may be a major effort to increase productivity in order to reduce cost and increase earnings per share that year. In the next year, with optimistic profit forecasts, efforts to improve productivity may be abandoned. Improving productivity is not really a "this year" problem. It is a continuing and long-term or strategic need for most firms. To turn productivity on or off depending on this year's budget is a little like gearing up an R & D effort in the year a firm needs a new product.

PRODUCTIVITY—A SYSTEMS PROBLEM

Increasingly, better use of human resources will require direction and leadership by general management. It will require affirmative action, not just reaction. Work to improve productivity must be a continuing effort rather than a series of efforts on narrow and scattered fronts. Significant improvements will require recognition of the fact that productivity in most firms today is a true systems problem.

Productivity improvement is, in a sense, a systems problem because there are many facets of company work and company activities which impact employee productivity. There are, as indicated, a number of areas of work which can improve productivity. There are also many department and staff functions that need to be organized. The need is to identify all elements, or at least to be aware of all facets, of activity which influence productivity significantly. This, in turn, requires structure of an organization so that it represents the process by which productivity will be improved. Only then can specific steps be taken confidently which will have the greatest value/cost relationship and the optimum effect on improving employee productivity.

In the great majority of American enterprises there is seldom a single activity, technique, or method that provides the only basis for meaningful improvement of productivity. It is even rare that there is a single technique or method which is the principal opportunity for increasing productivity in a given company. Generally, there are a number of techniques and methods in combination which provide the most efficient means of significantly increasing productivity. The key to formulating the problem consists of three steps: identify just which activities have the greatest relevance and greatest potential impact for improvement of productivity for the individual company; set priorities; and deploy resources in the areas of priority at the proper time and in the proper manner. The resolution of these steps represents the essential elements of a systems problem.

This means that a firm looking for a single answer or some canned program is likely to be disappointed. It means that copying what some other company did will probably deploy techniques that are less effective than those selected on a custom basis. The most effective approach is to consider all possible activities and techniques that can improve productivity and analyze their adaptiveness to the needs and characteristics of that particular business.

METHODS OF IMPROVING PRODUCTIVITY

Many of the key techniques, methods, and areas of work that can effectively improve productivity are illustrated in Figure 2, which diagrams the essential four broad areas of work that have significant impact upon levels of productivity. The first area is the substitution of machinery for human effort. A second broad area involves activities directed at determining and applying the most appropriate methods of work. A third, and frequently overlooked opportunity for increasing productivity, is removal of unproductive practices that in effect inhibit or detract from productivity. The fourth area of activity for improving productivity essentially involves personnel methods designed

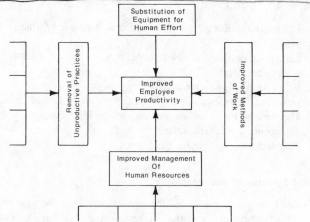

Figure 2. Methods of improving employee productivity.

to help management utilize more effectively the human resources of the business.

In each of these four broad areas there are a variety of more specific techniques. Methods work, for instance, may require time and motion study, setting better work methods, or designing more effective work layout and procedures. Additional equipment may cause actual displacement of people by machinery, or may provide new tools so that they can work more effectively, which may in turn mean fewer people doing the same volume of work. There is also a high degree of interrelationship between many of these areas. Use of better tools, for instance, would likely require development of new work methods or, in the area of human resources management, new training activities.

SUBSTITUTING MACHINERY FOR PEOPLE

There is no method for determining the true causes of increases in employee productivity which have occurred over the past 50 years in the United States. Most managers, students of business, and the President's Commission on Productivity agree that about half of the productivity improvement in this period is the result of firms finding ways to substitute machinery for human effort in whole or in part. Almost every company that has been in business since the end of World War II has deployed enormous amounts of capital for the purpose of substituting mechanical effort for human effort, and thereby increasing employee productivity.

The substitution of equipment for people is, of course, a broad category or area of activity that may be considered for increasing productiveness. More specific activities within this broad area would include:

- ☐ The purchase of a piece of equipment to do the job formerly done by people.
- ☐ Equipment designed to assist people to work more efficiently or to facilitate their work.
- ☐ Better location of facilities.
- ☐ Design of facilities and equipment for optimum scale of operations.
- ☐ The various forms of automation, which represent simply a further dimension of mechanization.
- ☐ New technologies that facilitate work.

Capital Investment per Employee

The capital committed to increasing productivity over the years has been enormous. Government statistics suggest that the capital investment per

worker in the private sector has more than doubled in constant dollars over the past 25 years, although the data are unprecise because of changes in product mix and other business characteristics. More precise data in selected industries are given in Table 4, which shows that in four peer-group companies, capital per employee has increased 70 to 95 percent in ten years. It is interesting to note that investment per employee is quite similar in each of these very different industries. Data for individual firms in each of the peer groupings also show quite similar figures.

Table 4. Investment per employee: four cases.

Comparable Group	Number of Companies	Assets per Employee (000)		
		1975	1965	% Change
Diversified machinery and metal firms	19	$37.3	$19.1	+95
Chemical firms	12	36.4	21.2	+72
Pharmaceutical companies	15	35.6	19.6	+82
Diversified communication firms	16	32.1	18.8	+71

Source: Part of a study by Sibson & Company, Inc., 1976. Based on data from company financial statements.

During this 25-year period, industrial engineers and accountants have developed for management rather precise and analytic ways for assessing the economic feasibility of substituting machinery for human effort at a given interval of time. These procedures provide management with rather factual and reliable information for deciding the cost effectiveness of any particular investment in capital to replace human effort. There are also analytic methods that help management to assess alternate opportunities for investing in capital for the purpose of increasing productivity. Improving productivity in this manner has become a well-known and standard part of the management process. Enterprises know how to do it, and they have the analytic inputs to do it effectively. They also have a long history of success in improving productivity by substituting equipment for human effort.

Future Use of Capital Substitution

It is natural to consider whether this basic method will serve the purpose of increasing productivity in the future. It is certainly logical to look to the proven method first. In the future the opportunities for increasing productivity through the substitution of machinery for human effort will vary between firms in terms of how much real opportunity there is and the types of opportunities that exist. *On balance for many enterprises, the opportunity for increasing productivity by substituting equipment for employees is the least promising stratagem for improving productivity in the future.* It is the area of

least promising opportunity for many firms because they have exploited this opportunity for increasing productivity so much in the past. Furthermore, the economics of substitution are becoming less favorable in most firms and unfavorable in many. This means, as a generalization, that *this principal method for increasing productivity in the past will be progressively less usable in the future*.

Some firms, of course, are already so highly capital intensive that they may well have reached, or are approaching, the point of diminishing returns with respect to further substitution of capital for people. Others may face considerable risks associated with excessive capital investment for the purpose. The introduction of more capital may restrict the flexibility of operations and impede opportunities to adapt to changing market conditions. In still other firms, additional capital investments may involve such large amounts that it may strain their financial resources. These and other technical considerations indicate that previous successes of improving productivity by substituting machinery for people have reduced the opportunities for meaningful improvement in the future. The more a company does in this area, the worse the economics of substitution become.

The declining ability to increase productivity by this traditional method is a crucial issue for business and for the economy overall. It is the primary reason why firms must turn to other methods for increasing productivity, such as improved management of human resources. This issue must therefore be carefully examined by each firm.

Economics of Substitution

Capital investment per employee averages about $30,000 throughout the economy. In manufacturing positions, where opportunities to improve productivity through substitution of equipment is most relevant, the average investment exceeds $40,000. The investment per employee in 1975 and 1965 for the 15 largest industrial firms is shown in Table 5. These firms, which together employed almost 3.4 million workers in 1975, increased their investment per employee over 90 percent in the past ten years. Per-dollar productivity for these firms in the same period doubled. While these are the largest industrial firms and are dominated by automobile and oil interests, their investment per employee is fairly representative of all large firms. A group of 15 firms with sales close to $2 billion increased investment per employee by 95 percent in the same ten-year period, and also doubled the per-dollar productivity of employees.

There is, for many firms, the serious issue of whether the additional cost of capital is as great as the cost savings from increased productivity. The average capital investment per employee of the companies listed in Table 5

Table 5. Investment made per employee by the fifteen largest industrial firms in 1975.

Company	Assets per Employee (dollars in thousands)		
	1975	1965	Percent Increase
Exxon	$235.6	$88.3	167
General Motors	27.9	17.1	63
Ford Motor	30.5	20.8	47
Texaco	224.8	93.7	140
Mobil Oil	192.5	64.7	198
Standard Oil of California	294.6	93.8	214
Gulf Oil	237.2	94.3	152
General Electric	23.2	14.3	62
IBM	48.0	27.1	77
IT&T	26.1	10.1	158
Chrysler Corporation	26.3	18.7	41
U.S. Steel	41.2	26.1	58
Standard Oil of Indiana	189.2	85.5	121
Shell Oil	189.7	74.4	155
Western Electric	27.6	13.6	102
Average	120.9	49.5	144

is over $120,000. Assuming the average payroll for jobs where substitution of equipment is practical is $8,500, this means that the cost of capital to replace a job is *now* equivalent to the payroll dollars saved by substitution. Such analyses, on a more detailed basis in specific company situations, have led some to believe that the money deployed to increase employee productivity must return at least 20 percent, and preferably 25 percent, each year to be economically feasible. The opportunities for increasing employee productivity in this magnitude are diminishing.

The economics for machinery substitution are complex. A number of factors are working against future application of this method. For one thing, additional capital for substituting machinery work for man's work results in incrementally smaller increases in employee productivity because each dollar of capital typically buys less productivity improvement. Secondly, there is a tendency for each additional unit of equipment to become more complex and therefore more costly. Companies prudently buy first the most economic piece of equipment to achieve productivity objectives. Additional equipment becomes more costly. Some areas of work obviously lend themselves more to equipment substitution than do others. As firms deploy capital toward the more marginal position, the cost effectiveness of substituting equipment for man-hours also declines.

There are other emerging economic problems in substituting equipment for people. Replacement cost of such equipment is obviously rising, not only because of inflation but also because this year's model is far more complicated and technologically advanced than the one produced 10 to 15 years ago. Also, as such equipment becomes more specialized, the risks associated with special-purpose equipment becomes greater. The risk of obsolescence is also an increasing factor as another supplier sells your competitor new, better, or faster pieces of equipment.

Even if firms had opportunities to substitute equipment for people on an economically sound basis, there is also the problem of financing such additions to capital. Funds are costly and, in recent years, in periodic short supply. In order to continue the rate of investment of the past ten years into the next ten years, the firms shown in Table 5 must raise over $250 billion. These numbers represent enormous financing needs. Whether a company can eventually expect to raise this much more capital must be determined in each firm. But the 15 firms shown in the table would likely not have sufficient earnings (less dividends) to invest $250 billion unless their current earnings increased substantially.

Companies must, of course, always be alert to emerging new technologies. The opportunities for increased productiveness through the substitution of machinery for people can change dramatically with major advances in technology. As noted, for instance, most firms that are highly people-intensive, particularly if they have a high number of knowledge workers, now have a limited number of opportunities for increasing productivity significantly by capital investments. The development of the computer represented substitution of machinery for people with specialized knowledge. In the near future, it may be that there will be the development of other "machine tools for knowledge workers" which for many firms could represent major opportunities for further increasing productivity through substitution of equipment for man-hours of work.

DEVELOPING BETTER METHODS OF WORK

The modern era of work methodization started in the 1920s. Since that time it has been the second greatest contributor to the increasing productivity of the work force in this country. Methods work can encompass a number of more specific activities. Design and implementation of the most effective method by such techniques as MTM is one specific area. Setting of work standards through such techniques as time and motion study is another technique. Facility layout, work-flow analysis, and time-and-activity analysis are other examples of specific techniques logically included under the broad category of improving methods of work. The contribution of methods improvement to greater productivity has been and can be enormous. There are cases where improved methods resulted in increases in productivity of 200 or 300 percent.

Much of the work done in improving productivity through methodization involves a group project or contributions from a number of areas in the business. In more and more situations it is no longer a simple matter of using time and motion study, or MTA manuals, or analytically working through a better method. The industrial engineer certainly should be one of the participants in any such undertaking. So should the employees themselves, particularly when they are technical people who are applying technologies largely unknown to others. Personnel specialists also need to take part in this work. And, of course, line supervisors should not only be involved, but should also have the basic accountability for proper work methods.

Participation by a number of sections of the firm suggests the need for thoughtful review of the organizational structure, to ascertain how their activities can be coordinated with the methods work to be done. The traditional simplistic answer of assignment of responsibility to an industrial engineering department does not fit the realities of the modern enterprise. Some form of combination of multiple organization, usually involving matrix organization and project groups, is necessary to assure optimum productivity through better methods. That very situation makes even more important a careful identification of authority, which logically rests with line management assisted by a number of staff areas.

A considerable amount of well-developed analytic techniques for measuring the results of methods work on productivity have been developed. In methods work, as in capital substitution, management has rather precise and highly useful guides and information inputs for decision making. Furthermore, businesses have had a vast amount of experience utilizing the technologies of methods work to improve productivity. There is not only a vast amount of technology, but also considerable experience in how to manage that technology. Failing an unforeseen and hard-to-imagine breakthrough, however, significant further improvements in methods technology or its management is unlikely.

Improved productivity through use of improved methods has the virtue of involving relatively moderate capital investments. Usually, the cost associated with this area of improving productivity is the salary and overhead costs of specialists who design and teach the methods. Investments costs involve such items as equipment, fixtures, tools, and supplies, and are usually moderate. Annual operating expenses for continuing improvement and maintenance of methods work are also typically moderate. The ratio of equivalent full-time methods experts in all staff areas (including personnel) to total employment seldom exceeds one-half of 1 percent; and in large, well-established operations the percentage is less than one-tenth. Furthermore, these expenses can be handled on a business-unit or investment basis, with total expenses weighted against costs savings through improved methods.

The time span required to produce demonstrable productivity improvement is typically very short. From the start of a methods activity to implementation of a new practice, time is generally measured in weeks. Also, the risk of implementing new methods is very modest. If, in fact, a new method proves unproductive or no more productive than the one it replaces, it can be modified quickly. There are exceptions, but the expenses of methods work are typically moderate, results impact operations quickly and involve very little capital expenditure, and there is a high degree of certainty in projecting positive results before the work starts.

From every point of view, therefore, methods work is an ideal approach to the productivity problem. In spite of this, opportunities for further improvement of productivity through better methods of work are becoming limited in most firms. This is true because so much methods work has been done that operations are already highly and effectively methodized. Methods work in many firms is therefore essentially a maintenance job, and requires developing new methods only when products, equipment, material, or other factors affecting operations change.

In fact, in some firms, work has been overmethodized. In many cases, work has been so simplified that it could be done by trained monkeys. Employees have reacted to such situations, not only because of the monotony and boredom of highly routinized work, but also because such automated work is dehumanizing and more than the nervous system can tolerate. In these cases there is a trend toward the "demethodization" of work. Demethodization is more in line with the human capabilities, and the engineering of jobs to people as well as people to jobs is what "job enrichment" is all about. But the net effect, in some instances, of job enrichment is *lower* productivity from demethodization.

Job enrichment, by its very nature, usually involves demethodization of work, and results in a less efficient work method. It does not, however, necessarily mean lower productivity. Actually a less efficient method applied and carried out conscientiously can mean a net increase in output. Job enrichment or, as some now call it, "increasing the quality of work life" has other potential advantages. More diverse responsibilities provides experience that broadens skills and knowledge. This can mean greater flexibility in work assignments and development of employees for future responsibilities. Job enrichment can build more positive work attitudes, which may, for instance, result in better quality of work. It may also contribute to more positive work environment, which in the long run may result in a more productive work force.

Where these possible advantages are not possible, then job enrichment may be necessary anyway, simply to design jobs so that they can be tolerable, to avoid trouble. In this instance, there is no offset to demethodization of work, and the net effect is lower productivity. Job enrichment efforts should be designed to exploit opportunities, as well as solve problems, and bring about increased employee productivity.

There are substantial numbers of middle-level positions (including methods engineering) where work has not as yet been methodized. Existing systems of methods technology are not very appropriate for most of these positions. In fact, methodization, proceduralization, and institutionalization are frequently antitheses of effective work in middle-level positions, and an increasing proportion of workers is in this group. If appropriate methods techniques could be devised for these types of positions, then a major opportunity for productivity improvement would be created.

In summary: There is diminishing opportunity for further productivity improvement through better methods. Thus, two pillars of productivity improvement in the past, substitution of equipment and better methods, are likely to be less and less applicable in the future.

UNPRODUCTIVE PRACTICES

While business enterprise in the economy overall was increasing productivity at a respectable rate over the past 50 years, largely through the substitution of machinery for people and improved methods of work, many types of unproductive practices crept into work systems and became entrenched, not only in manufacturing but also in commercial enterprises. Rather than any large single restrictive practice or a number of significant identifiable ones, there have been many, each rather small in terms of their impact on any one business. Cumulatively over the years, unproductive practices have become a major factor that detracts from the effectiveness of work. The result today is that unproductive practices of different types have proliferated to the point where they are seriously affecting production in most enterprises and in the economy overall.

Generally, the introduction of these unproductive practices was highly transactional. For example, a group reacted to some circumstance, perhaps some abuse, or what it perceived to be an abuse, and forced or evolved some restrictive practice to deal with that situation. Most of such restrictions, therefore, do (or at least did) benefit some individual or some group of individuals. Regardless, they all represent a cost to business. The major impact of the cost is lower productivity.

Since the opportunities for increased productivity are diminishing, at least in the traditional areas of substituting machinery for people and improved methodization of work, the problem of unproductive practices must be reviewed. This problem is bounded by very complex considerations. For instance, it may have to deal with opposing attitudes of a company and its employees concerning the relative merits of increased productivity versus decreased employment security. It may require a trade-off between productiveness and safety. If may even involve more productive work rather than more satisfying work.

Generally speaking, there are three sources of unproductive practices that have impacted many enterprises in a significant way. Probably the greatest single source of unproductive or restrictive practices has originated in collective bargaining. Union-negotiated provisions for the benefit of members have significantly detracted from the effectiveness of work. The second greatest contributor to restrictive practices that reduce productivity is the government. Third is a significant list of self-improved unproductive practices that enterprises themselves have injected or have permitted to happen.

Correction of unproductive practices involves virtually no capital expenditures. There is, therefore, also no risk of obsolescence or other cost/risk dimensions. Even annual expenses associated with greater effectiveness of work from this source are minimal. Results are immediate, or very short term; removal of unproductive practices in some instances can be implemented in hours, days, or weeks. Even risks of mistakes are minimal; mistakes can be identified quickly and corrected. Obviously, all elements for increased work effectiveness are favorable. It is an area of opportunity which should be examined by every company. When potential opportunities are high, it may be the first priority in a serious and organized effort to increase productivity.

The inevitable problem facing a firm that sets out to correct unproductive practices involves dealing with vested interests, tradition, and protectionism. These handicaps make it difficult to reject any unproductive practice that detracts from productivity when it is in fact, or is perceived to be, of some value to some persons. The issues are not always factual or legitimate, but are frequently emotional or subjective matters to be dealt with.

Removal of unproductive practices mostly entails human resources management policies and practices. It is identified as a separate area for increasing employee productivity, and is discussed in Chapter IV before subareas of human resources subjects are examined. This has been done mostly for convenience and because dealing with unproductive practices does involve somewhat unique considerations, particularly in the area of group relationships.

More Effective Use of Human Resources

The fourth area of activity which can result in significant increases in productivity is the better management of human resources. This requires more effective utilization of the talent the company has, that is, better personnel management. It is essentially the application of the idea of full utilization of human resources. In many enterprises today, increased productivity through better management of human resources may represent the number one opportunity for productivity improvement. Frequently, this is accomplished through default; that is, the company has reached the point of diminishing returns with respect to the substitution of machinery for people or through improved methodization of work, and it is limited in its ability to remove unproductive practices. Therefore, the only remaining opportunity of significance available in the foreseeable future is to increase productivity through better management of human resources.

There are enterprises where increases of productivity through better utilization of human resources is the number one opportunity of the firm because of the nature of the operations. This is particularly true of highly people-intensive operations and professional businesses. In other firms, effectiveness of personnel management has been very low in the past. This may have promoted low levels of productivity. In these cases also there would be very great opportunities for increasing the effectiveness of work through better human resources management policies and practices.

The increase of productivity through better utilization of human resources is, of course, the focus of this book. This should not suggest that increased productivity through better management of people is the only opportunity, or even the principal opportunity for increasing productivity in every company. Traditionally, it has not been the way in which productivity has been increased. But much of what has been examined and many studies that have been made suggest that this area is an area of increasing importance with respect to improving employee productivity.

There is no single personnel technique or practice which in itself brings about greater productivity through better management of human resources. Sensitivity training, for instance, is certainly not necessarily the most important opportunity for better management of human resources in all companies, or for all people in any company. Even where there is an opportunity for improving productivity through sensitivity training, that narrow technique (or any other) in itself will not bring about significant improvement in productivity.

It is essential to examine all opportunities in human resources management, and specific practices in each, as an early step in an organized approach to increasing productivity. Each company is truly unique, and divisions or sections within a firm would be likely to benefit from different areas of human resources management opportunities. Thus, it is necessary to treat each organization as a separate case, and to identify exactly where resources and time should be deployed in order to increase productivity. Frequently, improved effectiveness of work through better management of people will be one area. It is, however, a relatively new area, with few usable tools available.

Some of the efforts to increase productivity through better utilization of human resources represents new thinking. Frequently, however, the methods used simply mean better use of knowledge and experience already available. There have been cases where major increases in productivity were achieved quickly at low cost by using techniques and methodology of personnel management which have been in existence for many years. With time, and from results of work now being done to increase productivity, new methods and better human-resource information will probably evolve.

The more prudent plan for increasing productivity by better personnel management starts by doing what is known. When work is under way in known areas, it may be that new practices, information, and management guidelines will evolve in the course of the organized program. Such an approach is designed to assure results, but it also accepts the premise that (at least in human resources management) innovation is frequently the result of involvement. Important new information and personnel practices have evolved from work on improving productivity. Some have come from success and others from failure.

Some students of business see the economy today as going through the same basic type of management revolution, or evolution, as that experienced when occupations changed from agricultural to industrial predominance. Today there is a transition from a manufacturing-dominated economy to a professional-work economy. If this view is correct, then it is logical to deduce that there is enormous opportunity, need, and indeed pressures for fundamental breakthroughs in management practices and techniques in the area of human resources management.

The techniques involved in better management of human resources involve relatively minor capital commitments. All human resources activities in which a company might invest during the course of a year are likely to cost less than the expenditure for one facility. Also, the practices and techniques employed in personnel management for increasing productivity are not fixed pieces of equipment—besides no capital commitment, there is no rearrangement of physical equipment, which can be changed or modified, or even eliminated, when usefulness passes. In other words, risks inherent in work aimed at higher productivity through better management of human resources are relatively modest, if for no other reason than mistakes (if properly monitored) can be quickly corrected and programs that become obsolete can be terminated.

The problems of investment in personnel management are twofold. First, results to date in most firms have been extremely disappointing to management. Basically, personnel work aimed at increasing employee effectiveness has been characterized by gimmicks or canned plans, and these have not worked. Secondly, management does not have analytic tools available to assess or make judgments with respect to the investment in personnel activities for increasing productivity, such as they have in the purchase of capital or the adoption of better methods. Nor do they have the same analytic tools to monitor progress or measure returns on these investments.

METHODS FOR INCREASING PRODUCTIVITY: PERSONNEL MANAGEMENT

As in each of the major areas of opportunity for increasing productivity, there are more specific functional activities associated with increasing productivity through the better use of human resources. These cover some of the traditional functional areas of personnel administration. Before identifying them, however, it is advisable to mention two basic areas of consideration in the human resources management area which have some impact on, or relation to, much of what is done in increasing productivity by more effective personnel management. These are consideration of basic environmental factors affecting employee relations, and data or information usable in effective employee relations.

There are five major areas of opportunity in the traditional functions of personnel administration which have the most direct relevance to increasing productivity. These are discussed below.

Selection: This includes both selection of new employees and proper placement of current employees. Selection of new employees is in effect asset-acquisition management, and must weigh strategic considerations as well as near-term requirements. Placement of current employees has more direct impact on productivity in the sense of optimum asset utilization.

Manpower Controls: Reducing the denominator of the productivity equation, man-hours of work, obviously enhances use of human resources. Control of manpower, assuring an appropriate number of employees with needed background, on a continuing basis is also part of the manpower control job.

Organizational Structuring: Organizational structure is the vehicle through which company work is accomplished. If the organizational structure is a cumbersome, outdated, or inappropriate vehicle, it will certainly impede effective work. The more important aspect of organization work, which directly and significantly affects productivity, is whether organization *facilitates* more effective work and smoother working relationships.

Human Resources Development: Training, or providing the knowledge and skills required to perform current job assignments effectively can have a most direct and immediate impact on productivity. Development activity promotes continuing productivity growth by providing knowledge and skills for tomorrow's jobs or by developing greater or more diverse skills required by the enterprise.

Motivation: Any practice that motivates, encourages, or otherwise induces employees to work more effectively rather than unproductively can be a key part of a program to increase effective work. This includes the use of proper financial incentives.

Just how well the personnel function is managed also affects productivity. The degree of planning is an important facet of personnel management. Personnel input to company operational and strategic plans is essential to effective general management. The personnel staff should be a key source of information, guidelines, and support to management in improving employee productivity. Therefore, the organization and utilization of personnel staff is another contributive element in a system approach to increasing effectiveness of work.

It has already been noted that two relatively simple actions or practices can contribute to improved productivity. First of these is the conscious adoption and communication of a company policy and commitment to improve use of human resources. Secondly, the firm can take certain direct and low-cost actions to help implement that objective. Beyond such steps, companies that set out in a serious and organized manner to increase productiveness through better management of people must think in terms of a major project. Any such major effort must recognize that both the areas of opportunities identified and the specific activities in each are interrelated. For instance, the purchase of a new piece of equipment to increase productivity:

May impact restrictive practices
May effect and require reworking of layout or work flow
Would require new methods
Would require selection of employees to do the new jobs, and transfer of
  others
Would require training of employees to do new jobs
May involve changes in organization

Thus, one set of actions to increase productivity impacts other areas that affect productivity. Furthermore, it may start a whole chain of actions. Resultant new methods and layout might make opportune the purchase of still other equipment; changes in organization or work relationships may require job redesign; there may be need for new communication; the training effort required may redeploy effort from other personnel activities; and changes in compensation may result. It is the interrelationships of these activities, as well as the presence of multiple opportunities and involvement of a number of staff and line persons, which make improvement of employee productivity a systems effort.

In order to realize significant accomplishments in increasing productivity, a company should think in terms of a three-year project. It should also assume that the time-cost investment involved in such a project would be between a tenth and a half percent of payroll. Over the three-year period this means a total "investment" of time-cost for improving productivity of about 1 percent of annual payroll. This, of course, includes all elements of out-of-pocket expenses; costs of outside consulting help; incremental time-costs of top personnel and top management executive time; and expenses of travel, equipment, reports, and training. When translated into dollars for a company with 10,000 employees whose average income is $10,000 per employee, the investment required in a productivity improvement program would involve expenditures and incremental time-costs of approximately $100,000 per year.

These are significant expenditures, but they are moderate when compared with the costs that management spends routinely on substituting machinery for people, for improved methods produced by industrial engineering and other staff necessary to design and implement methods, or the costs of unproductive practices. If successful, the leverage effect on earnings per share for even modest improvements in productivity can represent enormous returns on this investment. The company that experiences even a 2 percent increase in productivity might increase earnings per share by 10 percent. The $300,000 investment over a three-year period could quite reasonably result in a million-dollar improvement in business returns over a finite period—here assumed to be three years. Some results are permanent and others may at least continue for a number of years. Seldom do companies have opportunities from which they can obtain such a high return on their investments.

3

Human Resources Information Systems

Human resources information systems represent a new area of work in the field of human resources management and promise to be of very great value. The term "information systems," as used here, refers to work directed toward development and use of information to assist management in its decision making in the area of human resources management. Development of these data serve a number of important management objectives.

For one thing, information and guidelines can assist both line and staff management in evaluating the "state of the health" of employee relations in a company. To the extent that it does this, it provides a measure of the effectiveness of current human resources management policies and practices. The "state of the health" of basic employee relations has indirect but potentially very positive impact upon levels of employee productivity. It can be of great value to a company in establishing its human resources needs and priorities so that effort can be concentrated on the most essential areas. For example, if data were to show a trend toward excessive costs and elapsed time in hiring critical personnel, this might identify a high priority need. In turn, this might focus attention on important changes in labor market supply and demand, on need to reevaluate recruiting processes, or on need to review compensation levels and practices.

Certain components of an information system provide a basic measure of enterprise performance, for accounting systems do not measure productivity or how well human assets are utilized. Financial statements measure how well capital is utilized, but give no measure of how well human talent is utilized. Some management executives argue that as long as business results, as measured by financial criteria such as earnings per share or return on assets, are satisfactory, then personnel management may be measured to be satisfactory. The fallacy of this argument is that employee relations problems don't show on the yearly financial report. By the time personnel mismanagement affects profits, it may be become disastrous. Even if it is identified before it reaches this point, immediate correction is practically impossible. Corrective solution of basic human relations problems may require considerable time, which in any case certainly exceeds the one-year period of a financial statement. For all these reasons, management and company directors need some ongoing measure of the effectiveness of human resources management, and human resource information systems can provide such measures.

Human resources information systems may also alert both line and staff managements to specific employee relations problems so that they can be eliminated in a timely manner before they become major and while corrective action can be taken at moderate cost. This early warning system has great value because small, easily corrected problems are prevented from developing into major ones. Timely diagnosis of employee relations essentially avoids trouble. It contributes to greater productivity by avoiding conditions or circumstances that would cause deterioration of productivity. Timely information, for instance, about the extent and nature of deteriorating employee attitudes could avoid unionization or future difficulty in collective bargaining if a union were involved.

Also, human resources information systems may provide general management and top staff people with data and guidelines to make key business decisions. This potential contribution of data and guidelines has immediate application in the managerial process in most firms. In effect, it could be a logical basis for a more analytic, systematic approach toward making employee relations decisions of critical importance to the firm. Such an approach is likely to result in sounder decisions and more predictable results. To the extent that human resource information systems do contribute to better management decisions, they will contribute proportionally to better utilization of human resources.

Finally, human resources information systems can aid materially in better management of the human resources management function itself by helping to develop a more effective personnel group. This directly benefits the personnel operation, and indirectly has a beneficial effect on personnel administration throughout the company.

Availability of Human Resources Information

There is relatively little data or information available for personnel decision making in companies today. Although there is sufficient compensation survey information for higher-level positions and for operations-level positions, the data for middle-level positions is inadequate. There is a great deal of information with respect to employee benefits, including types of plans, levels of benefits, and costs of such benefits. All these data represent human resources information that relates to the objectives already identified and which particularly serves as guidelines for business management decisions.

Except for compensation and benefit information, however, much of the data and guidelines are not now in forms that are usable for more effective human resources management. To be sure, companies do keep and report additional data. Most companies report in one form or another such information as employee census data, turnover, and safety records, but most of this is no more than bookkeeping information. It provides facts, but it does not usually present them in a manner that serves business objectives. These reports fail to include comparative data for evaluating the effect of employee relations on performance, identifying an early warning of emerging problems, or contributing to better decision making in the area of human resources.

This state-of-the-art in human resources information contrasts sharply with the type and quality of information management has for critical decisions in other important functional areas. In manufacturing, for instance, there are methodologies and data available for determining to the nearest penny the cost/effectiveness of a new piece of equipment. There are even computer programs that tell on a daily basis the unit cost of production—for a company overall, for departments, and frequently for every individual work station. In marketing, some consumer companies can predict the dollar value of sales for a new product plus or minus 5 percent, based upon very limited market research samples. In the area of facilities planning there are computer programs and models that can tell precisely where to build a new warehouse, how large it should be, and what the basic configuration of that warehouse should be. Even in the area of materials, some of the chemical process industry, for instance, have computer models that *make* the decisions as to where materials go and how they should be processed.

It is unlikely that human resources data will ever be developed to the same degree of specificity and usability as those just outlined. But if people are indeed a firm's most important asset, or even *an* important asset, and the effectiveness of people at work has both an operating and strategic impact upon business success, then management must have at least some usable data and information guides in making important people decisions. However crude such data and guides may be, it is difficult to see how human resources can be better managed without some information and guidelines. It is difficult to know how to increase the effectiveness of work of people unless the cost and/or value dimensions of an activity can be evaluated. And, of course, how can one talk about increasing productivity unless a company has the ability to measure productivity?

There is no important area of the business where management is called upon so regularly to make key business decisions of vital importance to the business largely on an intuitive basis, or on the advice of staff "experts" who also lack data. Intuitive decision making is extrinsic to the managerial process. Modern managers in complex businesses simply cannot take the risks associated with key decisions unless they are based in some way on data and information guidelines, and unless the results of such decisions can be monitored in some objective manner.

Management decisions may actually be counterbalanced by the presence of analytical information and guidelines in most facets of the business and the absence of such guidelines in human resources management. In allocating funds, management would be inclined to invest in areas where returns are measured on a quantifiable basis; that is, deal with the known rather than the unknown. There may even be a tendency to allocate more top management time to subjects where data and guidelines exist so that time can be spent usefully.

Types of Human Resources Information Work

The work that has evolved in the area of human resources information systems has taken a number of distinctly different directions. There is a significant amount of work being done in all these areas. All have value, but their objectives are also quite different. Simply for clarity, then, it is of some importance to identify and make more specific the areas of work being undertaken.

There is, for instance, and has been for a number of years, considerable interest in what might appropriately be labeled "human resources accounting." Work carried on for a number of years at the University of Michigan, for example, aims at developing a complete human resources accounting system. The ultimate goal is to have both a balance sheet statement and an income and expense statement on human resources. Commitment of resources in this area have been major.

The accounting problems associated in developing a method of valuing human "assets" seem insurmountable. Liabilities in the area of human resources are difficult to even identify. Present accounting knowledge cannot cope adequately with human resources expenses. "Uniform accounting principles" for costing such expenses in detail or even for establishing a "chart of accounts" is not available. Finally, the job of developing a method of determining "income" from human resources seems at this point in the work to be impossible. For these reasons the probability that this work will ever develop into a reasonably complete and meaningful accounting system of human resources is very slight. The work is, however, worthwhile and appropriate for the academic environment of a university. Like so much academic research, it may well uncover some core knowledge that can be translated into usable information for better management of businesses.

The second type of human resources information system work involves what might be labeled "human resources bookkeeping." The first objective of this work is to identify the information that must be kept or should be kept. The second objective is to collect and have available for retrieval such information on a cost/efficiency basis. This usually means computerization of obtainable data. Many companies are engaged in this work, but the cost of developing and implementing a human resources bookkeeping system is quite high. The values are also high in terms of lower cost of handling information and more timely reporting of data. Certainly, the collection and efficient handling of human resources information seems just as important as the collection and reporting of other major expense information relating to the business.

The third and newest area of work, labeled "human resources information systems," involves the development of data and guidelines for more effective management. This is a very pragmatic approach and far more limited in scope than human resources accounting. It aims at identifying specific data of high importance in the area of management. Its purpose is to develop specific information, such as basic data, guidelines, comparative data, and other material of direct relevance and usefulness to both top executive management and staff management in making important human resources decisions.

These three areas of human resources information are obviously interrelated. Human resources *accounting* and *bookkeeping,* particularly the computerization of data, facilitates the use of information in human resources management. It makes possible a timely and appropriate display of information and special analysis. Theoretically, work on human resources *information systems* should be done before human resources bookkeeping because information analysis can indicate to a company what information should be put into its bookkeeping or computer system. Otherwise, the programs and procedures may have to be revised later at considerable cost in order to accomplish the ultimate objectives of supporting better management of human resources.

BASIC WORK AND GENERAL GUIDELINES

In developing human resources information systems, two preliminary steps must be taken. The first is to determine what data are now recorded and available. The second is to determine what information is required or desirable for more effective decision making. Most companies now keep enormous amounts of personnel data. One group of companies involved in a human resources information system project has kept, on the average, data in 126 areas of human relations, and maintains about 500 or more pieces of discrete personnel information. From this experience it can be deduced that the starting point is to determine what data are to be kept and what data have potential use, either in their present form or with minor modifications, for the purpose of human resources management.

At least 90 percent of personnel information is kept for accounting use or to meet government requirements. With respect to the latter, there are 40 categories of data that must be kept for various periods of time to meet the requirements of 16 federal laws and on the average 10 state laws. Equal employment opportunity requirements alone account for about 25 percent of the data currently kept by some companies, and it has been estimated that it costs each company more than $150 per employee per year simply to collect and maintain personnel data.

This data analysis serves a number of important purposes. For one thing, it serves as a checklist of personnel data that companies actually do collect for any reason. In turn, each company can then compare the data it keeps against data other companies keep, to answer two questions. First, is it not now keeping information that others have perceived of value? Secondly, if it is now keeping data that others do not keep, is such data necessary?

Most important is that the review of data kept provides a starting point by determining how personnel data now collected has potential use—either in its present form or with minor modifications—of value in management planning, control, and decision making in human resources management. Companies that have made these analysis have found about four dozen items that could be used for management decision-making purposes. In some of these areas the data as now kept would be sufficient. In most instances, however, minor modifications, once made, would not require or involve additional costs, and would serve the specific purposes of human-resource information systems work.

Work done so far also indicates some general principles or guidelines applicable to human resources information systems. These can be illustrated by three distinct guidelines. One involves use of benchmark data; another, the precision necessary in data reported; and a third, the useful ways in which data can be reported.

Some human resources information for management purposes needs to be recorded by benchmark positions. Benchmark positions for this purpose can be far broader than they are for employee relations. For instance, turnover need not be kept for each office job. Turnover experience for office operations jobs, as collected and reported for all such positions or for three or four specific jobs in the office, serves as a guideline for office positions generally. Benchmark job groupings in this broad categorization have been identified for:

Operations positions, factory
Operations positions, office
Technical positions
Supervisory positions
Knowledge-worker positions
Operational general management positions

The second general guideline has to do with how the data are used. Human resources data for management purposes need not be precise. Certainly there is no need (and probably no possibility) that such data will be as refined as financial reporting information. Data that are accurate within plus or minus 20 percent can have relevance. This is particularly true if the data are reported in terms of trends or indices. Data can also be extremely valuable when used on an internal comparative basis. An example would be productivity measures in a number of similar field operations. Comparing the productivity of one against others is a very useful management information technique. There has also been some useful external comparison data (for example, comparison of a company's turnover versus the turnover in other firms of similar nature). Ultimately, the evolution of some models—what the manpower ratios *should be*—will be of considerable value, and work so far has indicated that useful models are practical.

Wherever external measures are made, it has been found necessary to develop a "standard business classification" system as contrasted to the traditional "standard industry classification" (SIC) system. The latter, as is well known, includes many disparate types of companies, and comparative human resources data have therefore little value in SIC terms. The categories in the "standard business classification" compare companies with similar operating and economic characteristics. They identify true "peer group" companies. Peer group comparisons based on similar economic and operating characteristics are the criteria in human resources information systems. Size of operation is less relevant; six broad categories of size are usually all that is required. Within such a broad scope of categories, there is no difference in most human resources (HR) measured.

MANAGEMENT DECISIONS

Another basic area to explore is the identification of the types of decisions that general management actually makes in the control of human resources. Companies that have undertaken this exercise have found it to be a rather difficult process. There are a number of types of human resources decisions. One involves personnel decisions, which are self-evident. Many of these are in fact not made by general management. Other employee relations matters are essentially business decisions. These involve use, in one way or another, of human resources. The difficulty with these is in identifying those business decisions in which human resources considerations affect a major part of the overall decision, and in which human resources information, guidelines, and data should therefore be an integral part of the decision-making process.

Management makes many decisions involving human resources. Every year executives must consider the major cost impact of salary levels, benefits, and other forms of remuneration. This has not only great cost impact but also direct relation to the question of the company's ability to attract, retain, and motivate the numbers and types of employees required. Management makes major decisions as to the number of employees, not only the overall census, but also numbers in different operating units in the company. It is called on constantly to decide the size of training and development budgets, the expenditures of time and money on communication, and specific training activities. It must also decide frequently on policy relative to labor relations, not the least of which involves the limits to which the company will go before it faces a strike. For any company, these illustrate areas representative of a very long list of personnel-related decisions with major business implications. Part of developing a human resources information system for implementation in a specific company requires an identification of these personnel-related decisions *particularly relevant to that firm*. These need to be evaluated both in terms of their importance to the business and the degree to which management needs data, information, and guidelines in making such decisions.

There are also examples of general business decisions where human resource considerations are an important factor. For instance, companies are constantly planning to deploy financial assets to the development of new businesses or the extension and growth of existing businesses. Human resources capabilities in these areas are a critical part of planning decisions. Yet, typically, management has little if any useful information, data, or guidelines with respect to this important dimension of business growth strategy. Management frequently will make major general management decisions regarding its distributive system. For instance, information as to the ability of the current sales force to meet new objectives or to adjust to new distribution methodology is critical to that kind of decision. Management also makes site location and acquisition decisions where human resources questions are critical. These are but a few examples of general management planning in which personnel play a dominant role, but decision makers have little if any useful human resources information input to assist them.

One highly successful chief executive officer goes so far as to describe the essence of his position simply as "strategic thinking and resource alloca-tion." Human resources use and allocation are in his mind the essence of top management. But it is only in this area of employee resource allocation that management is without the data or guidelines to do the job in a rational and analytical manner. At all levels of the organization the same problem confronts the modern enterprise. Supervision *means* effective use of human resources, and planning and directing the work of employees to obtain op-timum productivity. At lower levels of the organization the decisions are not so visible, nor do any of them have great business impact. Cumulatively, however, they largely *determine* productivity with the existent equipment, methods, and practices. Yet, supervisors throughout the organization lack data and guidelines to make such personnel decisions.

Finally, management makes decisions about personnel management operations, as contrasted to decisions regarding management of personnel. These involve such questions as which recruiting source to use in filling a given job, should a position be filled from the outside or by promotion, and what type and how much training is required in a given case. Even with re-spect to such technical and procedural personnel questions, there is a dearth of human resources information.

FACTORS OR AREAS

Evaluation of data, personnel-related management decisions, and general business decisions with major human resources dimensions leads to an iden-tification of specific factors or areas where a company should concentrate its efforts in developing human resources information. For example, such tradi-tional areas of personnel information as turnover, absenteeeism, and frequency of accidents would be focuses in gathering information. There is for any firm a considerable list of such areas or factors, but at any given period it will be obviously limited in its ability to develop meaningful data and procedures for using the data.

Identification of specific elements in human resources information sys-tems is guided by two criteria. The first is the importance or value of the data to the company—just how much will the information contribute to bet-ter human resources decisions and what would be the likely impact on busi-ness results. Second is a practical value judgment based on answers to three questions: In what areas does a company now have data? In which of these does the company know how to use the data and is confident of its reliability and validity? In which of these can the company be assured that, in the near term, investments in human resources information analysis will result in tan-gible benefits in the decision-making process?

Companies, in fact, are well advised to select some data with high value and some that present considerable difficulties, unknowns, and other factors readily manageable but having limited value. In this course of action there would be some areas where the data are available and usable, and where there is assurance that there could be, in a reasonably short period of time, a result that would become part of management's decision-making process. By selecting a few factors of this nature, the company can be assured that at the end of a year it will have had a return on its investment, which could exceed the investment itself and be the basis upon which future investment would be made.

At the same time, work could be focused on a few additional areas that the company knows are highly developmental in nature. There are no data for these, of course, and so it is not known whether such work would be successful. But these developmental factors, or areas, if successful, would have major impact upon the decision-making process and the ability of the company to reach its objectives.

Work to date has indicated more than three dozen areas where the ideas and principles of human resources information systems would have applicability in most firms. These fall into somewhat discrete categories in terms of how the information is primarily used. Naturally, most areas or factors serve multiple purposes, and there is overlap, but work so far has identified a sufficient number of common attributes that a system of categorization has been possible. The categories proved to be helpful are:

Defensive information
Cost-related information
Monitoring or auditing information
Evaluative information
Information of strategic value

Defensive information includes data and guidelines involving compliance with government requirements and regulations. Illustrative of such areas or factors are:

Equal employment opportunity data provide information to answer questions or charges by the government with respect to compliance; to implement company policy in this area; and to carry out affirmative action programs.

Health and safety information and data can help answer government questions or charges initiated by third parties under the Occupational Safety and Health Act (OSHA).

A number of areas are partially cost related. These include:

Safety data are designed to provide guidelines for making important decisions to protect employee health or safety and to control related insurance costs.

New hire costs provide comprehensive cost of hire data, which may be broken down for better management of the employment function.

Turnover data serve both as an early warning system to identify problem areas and as an instrument for pinpointing decision areas.

Cost of management data include information of relevance to the board of directors but are also useful as a tool of organization planning.

Budgeting and bookkeeping information may provide a more finite and useful "chart of accounts" for employee expense reporting.

Time-cost data comprise a system for assessing the people cost of alternate practices.

Some areas or factors tend to have primary value as measurement information. These include:

Attitude information provides a measure of the climate of the organization, pinpoints problem areas, and measures the value and effectiveness of various personnel policies and practices.

Labor contract information can provide analytic information and guidelines to make key labor-relations decisions and to formulate collective bargaining policy and strategy. In nonunion organizations, parallel information would be kept on policy matters.

Productivity data are crucial in improving productivity and can help to evalute specific programs and activities designed to improve productivity.

Critical positions analysis involves the identification of those positions which are either critical to the success of the business and/or are of a nature that requires special focus in personnel decision making.

Census data not only provides accounting information, but also serves as measurement data for various other human resources information.

Other areas are essentially evaluative and analytic in their application. These include:

Compensation progress data serve as complementary information in compensation administration and as a monitoring tool to control appropriate pay levels.

Manpower ratios provide basic inputs to effective manpower controls.

Organizational ratios serve as basic decision-making and control guidelines in organizational structuring and also provide important information inputs to the design of organizational structure.

Individual performance ratings—not for the purpose of development but more specifically as conclusions information—can be used as a critical input to a number of important human resources management decisions.

Finally, there are some areas or factors used primarily in strategic analysis or planning. These include:

Performance potential information accomplishes the same purpose as performance ratings on current jobs, but relates more to job-succession decisions and the determination of future staffing needs.

Investment spending analysis involves the identification of payroll expenditures that truly involve investment spending and also applies to systems for measuring the returns on such investments.

Future environmental information includes a variety of areas critical to future planning. It is also important as an information basis for making today's decisions compatible with tomorrow's realities.

Even the identification of this list, which is necessarily a partial list based upon factors or areas where human resources information analysis work has been conducted, suggests that no one company at a given period can undertake significant efforts or hope to achieve significant acomplishments in all possible areas of human resources information analysis.

This has led some companies to join with other firms in a group project to accomplish some of the work. On a group basis there is a sharing of research and development cost. There is also value in exchange of information and experience. Individual firms can then focus on application of a selected few factors or areas that have particular relevance to their own operations.

ILLUSTRATION OF FACTOR INFORMATION AND GUIDELINES

While the work in human resources information systems is a relatively new area in human resources management, much has already been accomplished. To detail these accomplishments would require a separate volume, and would also compromise information that companies regard as proprietary. Some detailing can, however, illustrate the nature of human resources information systems work and outline the specific values that can accrue from such work in human resources management planning and decision making. For this purpose three particular factors have been selected: new hire costs, productivity, and investment spending.

New Hire Costs

This work involves identification of all elements of new hire cost, and the development of total cost of hiring information by benchmark positions.

This factor is characteristic of human resources information systems where data now exist or can be recorded and retrieved at little cost, where the level of understanding the data is high, where data have validity, and where there is a predictable and useful result.

The first step in new hire cost analysis is to identify all elements of cost. There are a considerable number of distinct areas or elements of new hire costs. They include such bookkeeping items as employment advertising, search fees, employment agency fees, and reimbursement of travel expenses for employee candidates. They also include identifiable administration costs, among which are space cost, personnel staff time expenses, and testing costs. A considerable part of employment costs is allocated to time costs of personnel staff and line managers. Finally, there are many substanial indirect expenses such as the time a new person requires to come up to job standard. In all, approximately two dozen specific items of employment cost must be considered.

The second step is to identify company records where elements of employment cost are typically kept, or could readily be kept, and then to determine actual expenditures. The recorded expenses typically represent about one-third of the total cost of hiring. The critical procedure here is to identify on a case-by-case analysis the ratio of nonbookkeeping to bookkeeping costs so that total cost of hire can be extrapolated. This should be done for the overall business operation and for a series of benchmark positions.

Another critical area of activity is identification of factors that affect new hire cost. The prevalent economic environment is an obvious factor that influences the cost of hiring employees. Labor demand and supply characteristics to be considered for a given benchmark job category also affect costs and may not correlate with economic activity. Employment methods and practices have a pervasive effect. The number of persons to be recruited in any given job category, and the time leads permitted for recruiting significantly affect new hire costs. The complete identification of all these factors is necessary so that models can be built to reflect true or reasonably accurate total costs of hiring under different circumstances.

As in many of the human resources information elements, data can be analyzed and arrayed in a number of significant ways. For example, the total gross-cost data for a group of companies is shown in Table 6 by benchmark job category. Such data gives a reasonable estimate of the *true* cost of adding people to the payroll. This can have great significance with respect to business plans relating to the growth of a given area or function of the business. It can have an evaluative value if historic indexes are developed; this helps to identify whether new hire costs are being well managed.

This type of information is further enhanced if data about the experience of peer group companies and their new hire costs are obtained. Where a number of similar company operations hire local employees, location against location comparisons within a company can be made. This in turn can pinpoint those operations that, at least from a cost point of view, are managing the employment function effectively. Further analysis of these areas can then lead to identification of methods used in some areas of the business, which can then serve as models to improve the employment function in other operations.

Very few companies keep accurate new hire cost information, which represents a major expenditure and should be treated like any other major expense. These costs cannot be treated with the detailed precision of financial accounting, but can provide data sufficiently accurate for important managerial decisions such as the formulation of operating budgets, preparation of long-term business forecasts, and planning of growth strategies. Hire

Table 6. Example of total new hire costs.

Benchmark Job Category	Average Total New Hire Cost
Secretary	$ 600
Accountant, Intermediate	1,500
Engineer (five years experience)	5,000
Middle Level Manager ($25,000 salary) →	7,500
Business Unit General Manager ($40,000 salary)	15,000

Source: Human Resources Information Project, 1974.

cost information has already had an effect on the plans and actions of some companies. One company, for instance, had planned to expand very greatly in a business area, but canceled the project when it saw the true cost of hiring the number of persons necessary in order to achieve its objectives. This cost alone changed a profit projection into a very questionable breakeven operation.

Cost-of-hire information has given companies insights into whether or not these important costs were competitive, and how they were trending. It has also assisted a number of companies in making decisions with respect to the employment function. These include pinpointing the cost efficiency of various recruiting sources under various circumstances for different types of positions. These data also provide insight into the most effective use of staff versus line personnel in various parts of the employment screening process.

New hire cost information also provides interesting details on very specific and detailed questions with respect to management of the employment function. Data provide guidelines on employment ratios, such as the optimum number of candidates per new hire. They reveal the contribution of different steps in the employment process to the final employment decision, and provide specific information such as the appropriate number of days after final interview that an offer should be made.

Productivity

Productivity is obviously important human resources information. It is basic to policies, programs, or practices designed to improve productivity. How can a firm manage productivity unless it knows what it is? What actions can be taken to increase the effectiveness of work unless there is some way to measure whether or not such actions have been successful?

The fact of the matter is that, based upon sample surveys, half of the companies in the United States today cannot measure productivity anywhere in their operation. Half of those that *can* measure productivity anywhere do not. The few firms that do measure productivity at all have done so only in a few offices, factories, and/or field offices.

Absence of productivity measures also raises the question of how management can be asked to adopt a given training program or a specific personnel policy. How can management be asked to make decisions with respect to a new organization (or to anything else) unless there is some way to measure employee productivity? Even more fundamental perhaps is the question of why companies should expend major amounts of money either on a piece of equipment or on human resources management practice to increase productivity if there is no way to measure results or where the productivity of that firm may already be greater than its competitors?

Is it now possible to measure productivity? Work in the area of human resources information systems clearly answers that question affirmatively. It is rare, however, that productivity in its traditional form can be measured. Traditionally, productivity was measured by dividing physical output by man-hours of work:

$$P = \frac{\text{physical output}}{\text{total man-hours of work}}$$

This was a productivity measure that was appropriate for its time, when the typical business was a shoe factory or a single-product steel mill. It is rare that businesses are so simplistic today. As a result, the concept of the "key productivity index" has evolved. This productivity measure does not attempt to measure all physical output. Rather, it measures either output of a few products or services that represent a majority of the operation, or output of a few products or services that in turn are indicative of overall output. Some insurance companies, for instance, measure the productivity of their claims department by the number of claims handled per man-hour of work. In factories, industrial engineers have designed statistical models for at least a number of key products in order to measure essential productivity norms. The formula is:

$$KP = \frac{\text{output of product A } + \text{ output of product B } + \ldots +}{\text{total man-hours of work}}$$

Dollarized productivity is another useful proxy measure of employee éffectiveness. Oversimplified, dollarized productivity is expressed simply as dollars of sales divided by payroll dollars. It is, in effect, the method used by the federal government in reporting national productivity. Such information on a historic index basis can at least show the company whether or not this proxy measure of productivity is increasing or declining for the overall business and for various sections of the business. It can also serve as an internal peer-group comparison index. Finally, some valuable work has been done on comparing dollarized productivity among truly peer-group outside firms. The formula is:

$$\$P = \frac{\text{total sales}}{\text{total payroll}}$$

Ultimately the measure of productivity in today's contemporary business is qualitative. Qualitative productivity measures have been labeled "productiveness," as contrasted with productivity. Productiveness measures (see the preceding equations) first the value or appropriateness of what is done; secondly, the efficiency with which the work is done (productivity); and thirdly, the degree to which it has caused disruption to other elements of the business. This productivity measure is still very much in the conceptual state. The formula is:

$$PV = \frac{\text{correctness of action } + \text{ measure of output } - \text{ disruptive effect}}{\text{hours of work}}$$

Investment Spending

In most segments of the business there are distinctions between expense spending and investment spending, but every dollar in the area of personnel is treated as an expense. Actually, in a number of clearly definable areas, the increased payroll dollars or other personnel expenditures accurately reflect investment spending. One example is the salary increase granted for improved performance. Such pay increases do not represent increase in expense but rather expense reduction. The improved performance, whether it is reflected in more effective work or in a fewer number of people doing the same work, actually represents net income, which almost always is far greater than the increase in payroll dollars expended. Similarly, incentive awards for output above reasonable expectation represents an investment. One could also argue that much of training expenditures really represent investment.

The return on personnel investment spending can be extremely high. Returns can range up to and, in some cases, exceed 100 percent per year. The interesting thing about this type of investment spending is that the company makes the investment *after* it gets the return. Unless it gets the *return*, it makes no investment.

There is a need in human resources management to develop analytic methods for measuring the return on personnel investment spending. Even the mere identification of investment spending items would clarify and assist human resources management thinking and decision making. Because returns from personnel investment spending are great, such analytic measurement methods will open new opportunities for deployment of company funds. Investment-return analysis need not be precise in human resources management in order to be useful. At this stage in the system, gross measures on return would be highly useful.

Another type of personnel investment in human resources management can best be described as "supportive personnel actions." These represent personnel activities that are an expense related to some specific personnel need or some required activity. If these activities are so structured that they get secondary value, then that value represents an investment. For example, the development and application of many management incentive compensation plans have resulted in far more effective forecasting. The work that resulted in improved forecasting was a by-product and represents zero expenditure; values from improved forecasting are an investment return. Certain types of compensation plans also have a very real financial value; the financial values are fallout. This would include an employee compensation plan using company stock, which helps company financing or supports the market for company stock.

SURVEY INFORMATION COLLECTION AND REPORTING

Those involved in human resources information systems find that the primary value of such work is in developing ideas and applying information guidelines inside their own company. It is the application of information that is usable in increasing the productivity of the work force and in improving human resources planning and decision making which represents *the* payoff for investment of time and money expended on these information systems. The collection of information on a standard basis from a number of comparable or relevant companies and the reporting of this information to all companies is a valuable information *input* to the overall human resources management undertaking. This is quite analogous, of course, to compensation surveying. Human resources information "surveys" cover such areas as:

New hire costs for a sample of benchmark positions
Turnover rates
Compensation progress data, for a number of job families
Cost of management information
Manpower ratios
Productivity ratios
Distribution of individual performance ratings and performance
  potential ratings
Organizational ratios

Such reported information first provides important insights to all survey participants. Reported data provide comparative information, both in terms of magnitude and trends. Such information represents guidelines for all survey participants as to what is appropriate and what is achievable. The collection and dissemination of this information also provides new insights into the in-company uses of human resources information data. Lessons learned through such surveying can improve the quality of each company's human resources information. Finally, experience at this early developmental stage of human resources information has shown that activities inherent in the survey work has itself provided insights into how to manage and use this data, and has occasionally been the source of innovation.

There is an important second aspect of information exchange on a group-participating basis. This permits the exchange of experiences. The nature of developmental work involves some success and some failures, and some trial and error. Comparing information on a case basis makes it possible for each participant to learn by everyone's experiences.

MULTIPLE INDICATORS

Data and information in any one of the human resources information areas has a value in that subject area. In some cases, however, it is the combination of data that has the greatest relevance. Many examples could be cited. Certainly, for instance, the combination of turnover data and individual performance ratings has definite value. Similarly, multiple indicators that combine compensation progress and performance ratings are applicable. In fact, more than two dozen multiple indicators have been identified, and a number of these are now in use in a selected number of companies. These companies have found that it is the combination data or the multiple indicators that in some circumstances have the greatest value in providing insights into the employee relations function, in identifying areas in which employee productivity can be improved, and in supporting human resources management decisions.

Multiple data can be used in another way that involves their use in business analysis. For example, if individual performance improves then theoretically this should result in greater employee productivity and/or lower levels of manpower. If there is greater productivity and/or lower manpower, the business results should improve. The fact is that this logical sequence doesn't always happen because the information itself is sometimes faulty and because multiple analysis pinpoints the validity of information going into the human resources information system in the first place. But combination analysis also may indicate far more substantive business problems. It might, for instance, indicate that people are achieving a higher level of productivity by doing the wrong things.

PROCEDURES USED IN HUMAN RESOURCES INFORMATION ANALYSIS

In the work that has been done on human resources information systems, a great deal has been learned about effective procedures and processes. Using the right methods in this work is important in terms of what is likely to be accomplished. This is particularly true in the early stages. Inherently, the early stages of human resources information analysis involves a great deal of developmental work. The developmental process typically includes learning about effective procedures. These in turn provide a sound ground for work in the future; that is, for increasing the productivity of human resources information analysis itself.

One lesson learned is that it is important to explore, consider, and investigate a large number of factors that are essential to human resources information analysis. This aspect of the work is important because so much of what has been done in the area of human resources information is developmental, and therefore may include presumptions as to which of these areas have the greatest impact on the business and at the same time the highest probability of success.

There is a considerable amount of time cost needed to explore 20 or more areas of work on a concurrent basis. Also, as has been noted, part of the developmental work benefits from data exchanged, information inputs, and reporting of experiences of others. For these reasons, most companies involved in this work have concluded that, on the basis of economics alone, at least part of the work should be conducted as a joint venture with a number of other firms.

Application of human resources information guidelines within a company is best done on a very selective basis. The pressure of day-to-day requirements in the field of human resources management, and dealing with near-term problems and opportunities leaves, at least for most firms, relatively little time for developmental work of any kind, regardless of how important it may be to long-term success of the business. Also, the application of these ideas requires considerable amounts of time-cost investment. Finally, in any given enterprise, there are identifiable areas that relate specifically to company problems or plans. For all these reasons, company application usually requires concentration on a few areas of human resources information and the development of those areas to the point where they are usable and integrable with the management process. Experience has indicated that the time necessary to develop any one of these usable factors is usually a one-year cycle.

Another important guideline in developing human resources information systems is the plan of work in terms of manageable pieces. An open-ended project would involve enormous expenditures and might not have demonstrable values for many years. That type of activity or investment is difficult to justify because it is risky and because the results are uncertain. In human resources information analysis work, however, it is possible to identify on a year-by-year basis the specific objectives that can be accomplished each year. At the end of each year the results can then be compared to the objective and the investments necessary to work in the next year's objectives can be evaluated.

The really important step is that, once *some* conceptualization, guidelines, and information evolves from the developmental work, application deep in the organization is undertaken. To continue developmental work and conceptualization until a complete and final result is achieved is unrealistic, and inevitably will result in an open-ended, never-ending project. Furthermore, the yearly period of developmental work is a closed-ended loop of activity. With each degree of accomplishment, a basis is created for continued progress.

4

Unproductive Practices

When considering areas of opportunity for increasing productivity, the first place to look should, for most firms, be the substitution of machinery for people and improvement of methods. These are the areas that have produced best results for most businesses in the past, and as a winning game plan they shouldn't be abandoned. A systems view of increased use of human resources provides a more rational and comprehensive approach toward examining alternatives, and the existence of human resources information systems provides an analytic basis for evaluating alternatives. If this examination suggests that continued substitution of machinery for human effort or further improvement of methods remains the best course of action for further improvement of productivity, then obviously that course should be followed and perhaps will be the only action appropriate. These courses of action involve bodies of knowledge and procedures that are not considered in this book.

Earlier analyses suggest that many industrial firms and most people-intensive enterprises have reached the point where the opportunities for increasing employee effectiveness by capital substitution or methods improvement are diminishing or have already become impractical. For these, elimination of unproductive practices may be an immediate opportunity for major improvement of employee productivity. This area of productivity improvement to a very large extent involves human relations management techniques, a special category of improving productivity by better management of human resources.

TYPES OF UNPRODUCTIVE PRACTICES

The term "unproductive practices" as an area of opportunity to increase productivity is used in a very broad sense. Unproductive practices include work that contributes little to the achievement of enterprise objectives. This type of work practice is inherently restrictive in that it prohibits or makes difficult a high level of productivity. Specifically, restrictive practices refer to those rules, regulations, requirements, or simply traditional operations that present roadblocks to effective work or impede increases of productivity. In some firms, efficiently performed work might be labeled "disproductive" because it is actually counterproductive to achievement of enterprise objectives. Even if disproductive work is efficiently performed and has useful application, it may cause an overall loss of productivity because of its disruptive effect on other work.

Reorganization of a company is one example of a disruptive action. The change may be necessary and appropriate, but any change in organization structure has some disruptive effect because it disturbs established working relationships. It takes some time before these relationships can be reestablished. The resulting loss of productivity represents a disruption cost. It frequently means that for some time after reorganization, work is done less efficiently overall. Companies must realign organizational lines from time to time, but consideration of disruption effects is a factor that should influence the extent of change, how often the structure should be changed, and the most appropriate change.

Unproductive work includes any unnecessary activity or one that has a value less than its cost. Unproductive work always results in lowered productivity. Employees might simply do things that are not necessary to the achievement of enterprise goals— they waste time. It doesn't matter how efficiently they waste time; efficiency merely means fewer people are wasting time achieving the same useless objectives.

Poor quality of work is an example of disproductivity. The very likelihood of poor-quality work requires extra man-hours of effort to check, inspect, and audit work. The better the quality of the work built into the process in the first place, the fewer checks or audits will be necessary. Work improperly done and errors made usually mean that man-hours of related work are wasted. For instance, the poor product is passed on to other workers who add something to it. Work improperly done and errors made, therefore, usually mean that these man-hours are lost, including those for work done preceding the error and work added afterward.

Unproductive work of all kinds has a leverage effect on lowering productivity. When employees do the wrong things or useless things, or produce poor-quality work, they generate work for others, which is wasteful of more time. A simple example is an employee who conducts some study that is not really needed or useful. The time spent on the study is unproductive and lowers productivity. In addition, the study creates disproductivity because it takes staff people to support such work—people in personnel, accounting, bookkeeping, etc.

Any work, including an unnecessary study, takes supervisory time and at least some measure of managerial time as well. Furthermore, such work may result in some action by others. A written report, for instance, must be read by others. The time it takes to read the report detracts from the productiveness of the readers. Useless or irrelevant proposals or ideas may have to be debated, discussed, and perhaps rejected, and all that takes a great amount of time from many persons. Thus, the work itself is unproductive, and the distraction from other work, which might otherwise be productively deployed, magnifies that unproductiveness.

These distinctions are useful in analyzing how productivity can be improved through the removal of what has been generically labeled unproductive work. Dealing with increased productivity through the removal of unproductive practices, whether restrictive practices, disruptions, or disproductivity, is a discrete approach among numerous other basic methodologies (which will be outlined subsequently) for increasing productivity through better application of human resources management practices. Dealing with unproductive practices generally involves the *elimination,* or modification, of activities, methods, or procedures. Its objective is to tear down barriers that prevent more productivity.

In the years when the economy overall and many companies were enjoying rapid increases in productivity through the substitution of machinery for employees or through better methods of work, many unproductive practices became a part of the work system. As long as productivity was increasing rapidly, companies could afford such unproductive practices. In fact, some of these unproductive practices crept into the process of operations directly or indirectly as a result of substitution of machinery or development of improved methods of work; they were a part of the cost of improved productivity made possible by these methods. For instance, many restrictive practices were designed to provide employment security or job security for employees as productivity was increased through the substitution of machinery for people or through better methods of work.

As the opportunities of increasing productivity further through the substitution of machinery for people or for improved methods of work decline, the justification for protective unproductive practices logically dissipates also. More importantly, as these traditional methods fail to produce continued increases in employee productivity, new methods for increasing the effective use of human resources must be found. Abolishing or neutralizing unproductive work practices is one such method.

Estimates made by a few firms suggest that the removal of existing unproductive practices in a company would increase productivity by one-third, but many of them, as will be noted, could not be jettisoned. Of those that could be managed, all combined were estimated to represent about 10 percent potential improvement in productivity. These studies also showed just how difficult it is to project with any degree of specificity the potential for increasing productivity by removing unproductive practices. It may be enough, however, to know that the opportunities in most firms are considerable.

The important thing is to work on removing unproductive practices. The simplest and most effective way to do this is to identify unproductive work. This list of expendable areas need not be exhaustive, but just long enough to work on. In most firms it isn't very difficult to find such areas, providing there is a commitment to at least identify potential areas of unproductive work, even if some represent some very sacred cows. In making such a list it is helpful to include for each item the source of or reasons for the unproductive practice.

Generally speaking, there are three sources of unproductive practices. Collective bargaining contracts and union policies represent for many firms the principal source of unproductive work, particularly restrictive practice. For every firm, the federal, state, and local government laws, rules, regulations, and activities represent another major source of unproductive work. Finally, every enterprise will find in its own operations the presence of self-imposed restrictive practices and activities that are unproductive, disruptive, or disproductive.

COLLECTIVE BARGAINING

It is hard to estimate the overall loss of productivity in a given company or in the economy overall because of collective bargaining provisions and practices. Those employees best qualified to estimate may be biased. But it is also difficult to find any union leader who wouldn't say that contract provisions and practices significantly impede productivity; in fact most management representatives say that productivity losses caused by collective bargaining are enormous. There really hasn't been a definitive study or detailed analysis of the cost of collective bargaining or its impact on productivity. A listing of unproductive practices under union contracts alone makes it clear, however, that whatever the pluses of collective bargaining may be, one minus is a very substantial cost in terms of lower productivity.

Examples of Unproductive Contract Provisions and Practices

There are a number of ways in which union contracts and contract administration inhibit productivity. Certainly one is that most contracts require more employees than are necessary to do the work. Many major industries have accepted union contract provisions that require keeping employees on the payroll doing unnecessary work. For instance, in the railroads a few years ago, a study estimated that there were 40,000 excess union employees, particularly firemen. This group of employees had little or nothing to do with the equipment that was then being used. The technology had changed, but the firemen still stayed on the trains.

Other rules stated in union contracts make it difficult to let people go when they are no longer needed. Many contracts with municipal employees (for instance, the sanitation workers in New York City) make it impossible except under extreme conditions to let people go within the framework of the contract during any contract period, whether they are needed or not. Less dramatic, but cumulatively important in lowering productivity, are the more typical contract provisions that make dismissal of employees for marginal or substandard output a cause for contention.

Any number of collective bargaining provisions restrict output in one way or another. Provisions dealing with the setting of work standards fall in this category. Typically, union contracts restrict output by setting work standards below optimum. One case will illustrate the result of bargaining for lower standards over a period of time.

A moderately sized electrical manufacturing company with 1,500 factory employees moved from a New England location (which was union organized) to a Middle Atlantic location (which was unorganized). In New England the employees had been working under an incentive plan—which is supposed to result in greater productivity. When the firm moved, it operated in the new location without a union and on day-work payment, and took the opportunity to review work standards. After reexamining and resetting standards, the company found that the former work standards under the incentive plan were 20 percent of what they should have been. Within a few months employees at the new location had achieved the higher standards and without complaint. Total labor costs of manufacturing were reduced proportionately. In fact, the total cost of relocating that factory operation from New England to the Middle Atlantic states was paid for by lower factory costs in the first 11 months of operation after the move.

Another type of collective bargaining provision, which has major impact upon productivity, is the one that restricts work to a given trade. Only electricians can do electrical work; only a carpenter can do carpentry. At higher skill levels, of course, this presents no problem; a carpenter isn't likely to be able to do very complicated electrical work anyway. It is at the lower or intermediate skill levels that such restrictions reduce productivity unnecessarily. The amount of downtime alone in waiting for the next tradesmen to proceed on the next sequence of work is very costly and results in a considerable amount of unproductive work.

Some union work rules are even more unproductive than the foregoing examples. The electrical workers, for instance, in some cities have rules that not only prohibit efficient production of products or components, but also require rework. In some cases the rules require that products or components that are factory produced on an efficient basis have to be disassembled when they arrive at location, and must then be reassembled before they can be installed. This is disproductivity.

A variety of other provisions in union contracts seriously inhibit management's right to manage the business effectively. These include the right to assign people to work they are best qualified to do. Sometimes there are restrictions on whom the employer can hire. More typically, management is restricted in transfer, promotion, and work assignment. All such restrictions limit the ability to assign work to the best qualified person. Such restrictions obviously tend to reduce productivity.

Unionization also means strikes and disruptions of work. These actions represent the extreme of unproductiveness. In some cases, strikes and disruptions occur because of jurisdictional disputes or intraunion struggles. Here, loss of output has nothing to do with conditions of work, but the union activity detracts from productivity just the same. Finally, there are many subtle detractions from productivity under collective bargaining. For example, because of contract requirements, management may be unable to take timely actions to solve production problems, and this restriction can significantly lower productivity.

These illustrations are only a few of the ways in which union contract provisions restrict productivity. The very process of collective bargaining is itself a considerable detraction from productivity. Enormous amounts of time are spent in yearly negotiation of a contract. In many firms it is necessary to repeat that process in dozens of contract negotiations. Even more costly in terms of detractions from productivity and unproductive work is the time spent in day-to-day operations, in discussions with union stewards, handling of grievances, and getting union stewards' agreement to take necessary actions. These are all elements of operation inherent in a unionized situation that calls for time off from work; all are unproductive. The cost associated with this unproductive work is very substantial.

Unions and Productivity

The focus here is on employee productivity and not collective bargaining or the pros and cons of unionization. Nothing reported is meant to imply censure of collective bargaining or even to suggest that the unions are at fault for lowered productivity under collective bargaining. These are important debatable issues, but the fact is that collective bargaining and union contract provisions and administration necessarily reduce productivity, primarily by unproductive rules, regulations, and practices. Just about any union leader will agree that this is true, and it is a relevant point in this book.

A side remark, but one still worth adding, is that just about any business leader will also agree that many of the restrictive and unproductive practices in union contracts came into being because of some real or perceived employee needs resulting from management actions. Many were adopted because jobs were threatened when new machinery was brought in to replace people, or when new methods required fewer employees. These restrictions were imposed to protect employees from what were, or what were thought to be, arbitrary or self-serving actions by management or individual supervisory persons. Union rules were frequently concerned with issues of marginal importance from a business point of view, but which had major effects on employees.

As a practical matter, union leaders rarely oppose improved productivity. Generally, they view the improvement of productivity to be the job of management. There are many instances at the national and local levels where union representatives have worked hard to increase productivity, while at the same time protecting the interests of their members.

Productivity Bargaining

It doesn't do much good, of course, to merely identify areas of unproductiveness in union relations. In terms of increasing productivity through better utilization of human assets, management must establish an "affirmative action" program. For many firms, such a program must be something other than more of the same or success resulting from a near-term bargaining advantage. Companies have sought to eliminate unproductive practices and to reject new unproductive provisions from collective bargaining for a long time, applying great skill and effort. Their failures have resulted in a great number of unproductive practices that significantly reduce productivity. An affirmative action program to increase productivity under collective bargaining generally means a planned program for "productivity bargaining."

The first management step toward productivity bargaining should be to identify all those elements of the union contract which indeed inhibit or reduce productivity. This is a relatively direct action which may result in quite a list of items. Each of these unproductive practices should then be costed and developed into an analytic framework for estimating the potential improved productivity if these practices were eliminated. There also needs to be an assessment of the importance of these practices to the union and its constituency, and of how alternative provisions can meet essential requirements of employees and their representatives. These alternatives must in turn be analyzed and costed.

A great deal was heard about productivity bargaining a few years ago, but not very much has happened. Companies had great enthusiasm, but tended to approach productivity bargaining solely from a businessman's viewpoint. There was, on the part of some companies, an assumption that the overwhelming logic of increasing productivity through the reduction of unproductive practices would by the sheer force of reasonableness induce unions to accept in whole or in part what would seem mutually profitable and so eminently proper. But this management-oriented approach obviously overlooked the fact that the unions have their problems and their interests. Thus, in many cases the productivity bargaining failed simply because it did not involve a two-way discussion.

Productivity bargaining in other instances failed because of an almost stereotyped labor-relations attitude. The company objectives were identified. The company representatives then engaged in productivity bargaining as a contest, a battle of wills and strengths. This is not only a myopic approach but also a presumption that union representatives have no interest in productivity bargaining. Rarely have union leaders opposed productivity bargaining. Some have expressed a desire to see productivity improve and have demonstrated willingness to work for it under collective bargaining. They don't want their members to lose jobs to foreign competition. Some want greater productivity because they see in the new jobs less demanding work or more interesting work. They frequently favor productivity increases, and therefore productivity bargaining, because the results may represent opportunities for their membership to progress to higher jobs and earn more money.

To be effective, productivity bargaining must be more than collective bargaining. It must be a joint venture. The parties must sit on the same side of the table. Productivity bargaining, as contrasted to collective bargaining, is not a matter of trading points, concessions, and compromise. It's more a joint undertaking to achieve common objectives.

THE GOVERNMENT

The government is another major source of unproductive work. It is difficult to estimate exactly just how much productivity is impeded or reduced because of government actions and requirements. One can, however, identify the ways in which government requirements and actions detract from productivity. First, the government itself requires a lot of work, much of which is unproductive. Secondly, the government establishes many regulations and requirements. Thirdly, in cooperation with other organizations, they engage in practices or establish requirements that also contribute to unproductive work.

It has been estimated that approximately one of every 20 employees in enterprises today work for the government. The work these employees do has little if anything to do with the efficient or successful conduct of the enterprise, but is done solely because the government requires that it be done.

The work done to satisfy government regulations includes a great deal of bookkeeping and accounting work, and the filing of an enormous number of reports, many of them dealing with employees. It involves a considerable amount of time in conferring with government officials on an endless variety of subjects. In a sense, of course, these employees work for the government. They are, in effect, one of every 20 "employees in the private sector" who really are not employed by the private sector at all. They are paid for by the private sector, but they work for the government. They are part of the cost of government. They represent a form of indirect taxation on working men and women.

What work should be done for the government represents a point of view. Clearly, if government is to function, there must be employees directly employed by the government as well as employees in the nongovernment sector who are indirectly working for the government. The cost of these workers, direct and indirect, is reflected in the standard of living for the country overall. To the extent that the volume of their work can be reduced, however, national productivity increases.

There isn't much that companies can do about this required work for the government. They can, of course, do it as efficiently as possible. They should also recognize that a company's success in being more productive with respect to this unproductive government work is, in effect, being more productive than its competitors. Certainly a company should see to it that while it meets all government rules and regulations, it does no more work than it is required to do, as well as doing that work as efficiently as possible.

There is a second area of government impact on productivity. This involves laws, regulations, and requirements imposed on business in terms of how the business conducts its affairs. Here, again, companies must recognize these rules and regulations as a fact of life. They aren't really problems, and they certainly aren't opportunities; they are "givehs." As in the case of work required for government reports, work associated with government rules and regulations must be performed. A company should avoid overcompliance, but should meet requirements as efficiently as possible.

All these rules and regulations represent government actions designed to accomplish some social objective. Whether or not the social objectives are good or bad is a political issue with which companies cannot deal other than in individual citizen roles. But companies must recognize that many of these objectives have the effect of reducing employee productivity. The government has, in effect, enacted regulations for some usually worthwhile purpose, which is paid for in part by lower productivity and therefore necessarily in lower living standards. Work done to comply with these requirements also represents another form of taxation.

The Equal Employment Opportunity Act (EEOA) is an example of government-imposed, nonproductive work. It has always been in the interest of business to hire the best qualified person for each position. The person who is best qualified over a long period of time is not necessarily the person who scores highest on some tests or in other ways meets some of the preconceived notions of eligibility for a position. Clearly, it is unproductive for companies to eliminate better qualified persons simply because of their race, sex, color, creed, or national origin.

The EEOA as it has been administered and implemented, however, has created a paradoxical interpretation of this business philosophy. It has in many cases been described as the *unequal* opportunity law in the sense that it represents truly reverse discrimination. Companies must now preferentially select less qualified and less productive employees in order to meet the requirements of the law. They must also, of course, commit significant resources in order to be in compliance.

The Occupational Safety and Health Act (OSHA) is another important area affecting employee productivity. No one can quarrel with the objective of providing a safe work environment. The way in which these regulations are being implemented, however, suggests the likelihood of requirements for large capital expenditures, the diversion of many man-hours of work, and the adoption of less productive work practices and methods. More safety at the cost of lower living standards is a value judgment. Whether the government's dictums are right or wrong, the result of the way in which enforcement of legislation is being administered seriously detracts from productivity. It is another very major area of unproductive work which must be managed.

Governmental bodies have also enacted rules and regulations in consort with some private groups. They have, for instance, enacted building codes, usually with the urging of craft unions. Many of these result in highly unproductive work. Government has responded to environmentalists by establishing various rules and regulations affecting company operations, which also reduce productivity.

There is no intent here to engage in social commentary or express views on such matters. Actually, the author favors equal opportunity and safety, but like most people, he doesn't like bureaucratic government. The only point is that much of the government rules and regulations affecting the conduct of the business results in unproductive or disproductive practices and substantially reduces productivity. These are the facts, and the most important potentiality of improving productivity is by removing unproductive practices, whether they originate in government, union, or other group policies.

As in the case of work required by the government, work done in compliance with governmental rules and regulations must first be structured to meet requirements as efficiently as possible. Some companies have found it helpful to isolate these procedures as much as possible so that they do not corrupt the main stream of company activities. To the extent possible, the company should physically isolate people with such jobs and functions. They certainly should identify them in the accounting system so that they can keep track of this unproductive work and manage it as effectively as possible. Finally, companies are finding it necessary to have staff persons knowledgeable in dealing with the bureaucrats and enforcers.

SELF-IMPOSED UNPRODUCTIVE PRACTICES

Organizations of almost all types have imposed upon themselves a variety of unproductive and restrictive practices. This is particularly true of large, mature, and necessarily bureaucratically structured organizations. These restrictive practices, of course, are not required by some outside organization or force. The company puts them into place. The company can eliminate them.

The difficulty with self-imposed company restrictive practices is that they are not obvious and sometimes not very visible. Certainly, nobody puts these practices into place to lower productivity. Many of them seemed like a good idea at the time, or even if they didn't, they at least didn't seem to be terribly harmful. Self-imposed unproductive practices are frequently procedures, programs, or traditions: the way a company does business. Generally speaking, they involve such things as unnecessary meetings, protectionist practices, and what might be called "business protocol."

Some companies that have looked at the subject closely have estimated that up to 5 percent of their exempt employee payroll costs are represented in meetings, most of which are not really necessary. They could therefore reduce their payroll and increase productivity significantly by eliminating unnecessary meetings. Meetings, of course, are far more unproductive than just the time spent at the meeting. Usually, considerable amounts of preparation time are spent before the meeting. Frequently, each meeting also generates other unproductive work, such as the next meeting.

Another target in removing self-imposed unproductive work consists of practices designed solely or primarily to create prestige. People in high places frequently get involved in matters that really do not concern them, or they review activities simply for the purpose of enhancing their image or their prestige. Such practices illustrate a type of self-imposed unproductive work. A related unproductive practice might be labeled business protocol. Matters are reviewed by people or they are informed about them simply as a matter of courtesy. But each such communication involves a cost. It involves time, which is unproductive time. If, as a matter of protocol, the person involved acts or causes additional work, then the unproductive time is compounded.

Some elements of business protectionism also represent restrictive or unproductive practices. Other procedures are designed to make sure that people do not make mistakes. That is a good idea, but a business can be supersafe. There can be so many reviews and so many inputs that the stream of directives is highly unproductive, and the result not necessarily any better. Other procedures seem designed to obscure responsibility for mistakes so efficiently that accountability for incorrect actions or decisions is diffused and can never be traced to anyone.

In many cases there was originally a good reason or a need for some of these self-imposed unproductive practices. Although the need may no longer exist, the practice continues. Company practices and traditions are like law in that they are easier to implement than to eliminate. In many cases there may still be some logic or value to a practice, but the cost in terms of productivity exceeds the value. Another difficulty is, of course, that all such practices as individual instances or activities are not obvious, and many such unproductive practices involve relatively small amounts of time and cost. Therefore, each cannot be viewed as a significant contributor to declining productivity, but cumulatively they can be significant in any company.

Self-imposed unproductive practices probably reduce productivity less than unproductive practices from collective bargaining or the government regulations, but its impact is very substantial. Companies are free to remove self-imposed unproductive practices, and there is some merit to the view that an employer should put his own affairs in order first. Obviously, this involves less work and fewer complexities than removal of unproductive practices from other sources. From every point of view, therefore, the logical place to start work on removal of unproductive practices seems to be a company's internal operations.

Such a course is not without its difficulties. The work starts with identification of self-imposed unproductive practices. Many of these, however, are difficult to identify because they tend to be only small components of an unproductive practice. These apparently insignificant trouble spots are seldom formalized in written procedures, and so many are accepted as normal business practice. A second problem with self-imposed unproductive practices is that they so often are matters of interest to higher-level managers or represent someone's "sacred cow." Experience in this area has turned up hundreds of cases of self-imposed unproductive work, but in not one instance has someone failed to advance reasons why these unproductive practices were proper or essential.

Action is largely dependent upon a company's degree of commitment to better utilization of human resources. Real commitment plus a few direct and highly visible actions induce the entire organization to search out and eliminate unproductive practices. Commitment also implies willingness to assume small risk for the sake of higher productivity, risk that some of the unproductive practices eliminated may in fact turn out to be necessary.

Success has been achieved in removing unproductive practices by taking some action steps. Even correcting only a few unproductive practices can start a chain reaction throughout the company. In one firm, a division head eliminated some meetings and focused considerable attention on the effective conduct of those meetings that continued. Since there is a considerable body of knowledge and experience on how to conduct meetings in the most productive manner and in the minimum amount of time, he could conduct his meetings effectively, which saved time. As a result, other supervisors within that organization were soon doing the same thing.

Managing Unproductive Practices

The area of unproductive practices is a subject that has not really received a great deal of well organized planning or concentrated effort. There is a natural and well-advised reluctance to twist the tail of the government or raise new issues with the union. Many self-imposed practices involve sensitive issues, sometimes with higher-level persons. Overall, the relations risks associated with meaningful work in removing unproductive practices may be significant. There are also uncertainties: Once a firm starts on such a course of action, the ensuing chain of events or reactions cannot be foreseen. But businessmen are risk takers by nature. When the productivity stakes are high enough, when increasing productivity is important enough, and other methods for improving productivity are less available, there will be innovative ways to remove unproductive practices.

It would, of course, be unrealistic to expect to remove all unproductive practices in any firm. Some serve a function, such as necessary review or control. Others involve legitimate and essential interests of people. Removing half of the unproductive practices may, however, be a reasonable goal. Thus, in the typical industrial firm, it might be possible to increase productivity by as much as 10 percent by removing unproductive practices, which is certainly a worthwhile objective.

Some analysts have pointed out that removal of unproductive practices is a finite objective. When they are removed, the problem is solved. This is only partially true. Once existing unproductive practices are eliminated, the job then is to avoid adoption or evolution of new ones. This requires constant monitoring because many of the activities of an enterprise inherently breed unproductive work. Most projects, or application of new systems or programs, for instance, go through distinct phases. The first involves developmental time. The second involves an implementation phase. After implementation there is a maintenance phase, which usually requires far fewer persons than implementation and generally uses fewer man-hours of work with the passage of time. Such phase-down of work is difficult to accomplish, at least in a timely manner. In addition, people are more perceptive to the needs for more work than they are to the needs for less work, and increased activities develop a built-in momentum in any enterprise.

Removal of unproductive practices as an area for increasing productivity has some unique advantages. There is seldom any capital investment required. Risks of mistakes, as contrasted with relations risks, are relatively easy to identify and correct. There is generally little likelihood that productive as well as unproductive work would be eliminated, at least not for long. Finally, visible results can be achieved in a relatively short period of time. These characteristics recommend removal of unproductive work as a fruitful area in any organized effort to utilize more fully the human resources of the enterprise.

5

Environment

Increasing employee effectiveness through better management of human resources directly—as contrasted to substituting machinery for people, establishing better methods of work, or removal of unproductive practices—covers a number of areas. One approach common to many firms is to deal effectively with "environmental" factors. This includes all those situations and conditions that surround the work and have influence upon workers' effectiveness. Effectiveness of people at work is influenced by their total environment; everything that affects a person can in some way influence how well he performs his assigned duties.

The things that affect any particular worker are obviously unique and will vary for each person to some extent through time. But it is the total environment of the person at any given time which affects behavior on the job. Obviously, the job itself, the employee's training and knowledge, and the enthusiasm with which he attacks his work will affect his productiveness. Not so obvious, however, are the ways in which the environment surrounding the worker influence work effectiveness. These include such external factors as the employee's intelligence, attitude and temperament, home environment, community environment, and the overall social environment. There are also internal environment factors, those created by the employer, which include personnel policies, physical conditions or work, general climate, the business image, and levels of expectation.

It isn't critically important to measure just how much the environmental factors influence work; it is sufficient to recognize that many factors other than direct work considerations have a distinct influence on effectiveness of work. Cumulatively, these environmental factors can have a very significant impact on the productiveness of the work force.

For any given company the environmental factors that affect the work productiveness are not only numerous, but also unique to each firm. There are, however, enough environmental elements common to many enterprises to illustrate what some of them are, and to suggest the overall effect they can have on employee productiveness. These commonalities also indicate some of the ways in which companies can "manage" environmental influences and thereby contribute to greater productivity.

Many environmental factors are difficult to deal with because they are not peculiar to any single firm. Companies are basically organized and structured to deal with parochial problems, those that affect their own markets, facilities, etc. But they are not well structured to deal with external forces. Increasingly, however, it is the external forces that determine business results. Local industry and other employer associations may be effective either in dealing with specific regulatory agencies or acting as lobbying groups, but are not well organized otherwise to deal with conditions that impact businesses generally. Part of this is due to the fact that laws make cooperation in some cases difficult. Further, companies hesitate to spend significant resources to benefit all businesses, including competitors, many of which may not pay their fair share. Essentially, therefore, firms have trouble in dealing with external factors because they are designed, structured, and oriented to focus on the unique problems of their own business.

Enterprises generally devote little time and resources to dealing with environmental factors, mostly because they have enough problems directly connected to the work place to occupy their time, attention, and resources. Also, the relationship between environment and work effectiveness is frequently tenuous. Companies also tend to be cautious about dealing with at least some of the environmental factors because they fear reactions to activities directed toward managing environment. Some managers also think that they are not well qualified to deal with some of the environmental factors that affect work. Finally, companies perceiving that individual environmental factors have lesser impact on work effectiveness than do direct elements of work will assign these factors to a low order of priority and will frequently never get to that level. They do not realize that, cumulatively, these environmental factors can have a major impact on work effectiveness.

THE EMPLOYEE AND HIS HOME

The person's home environment, own personality, attitudes, and everything about him or her as a person have some effect on both work life and productiveness at work. This includes how much the employee drinks and whether or not he or she takes drugs. It certainly includes the state of the employee's health, and basic social attitudes and philosophies. Similarly, the health, background, and attitudes of the worker's family as well as their demands on him and his time must affect a worker's productivity. The whole maze of these personal factors can have a very important impact on the ability of the person to perform effectively at work.

A few companies have developed programs and activities to deal with some of these matters. A large mining firm, for instance, has a direct phone service to which employees or members of their families can call and receive social counseling and sometimes psychiatric counseling at no cost. Some companies develop and maintain fairly complete dossiers of employees, compiled not only from published reports, newspapers, and other sources, but in some cases from reports obtained from private investigation agencies. One of New York City's leading banks recently hired a firm to observe employees and inquire into many basic attitudes on personal matters.

Those who conduct such activities believe they are developing insights that provide a basis for action to increase the effectiveness of people at work. Such beliefs are unproven, and their investigative activities raise three types of questions. One is the moral question of whether or not a company should carry on such activities. The second is a more practical question of whether or not they are effective. Finally, there is the question of whether the results are commensurate with the inherently very high risks associated with such activities.

Companies do have the right and the need to gather direct work information about each employee, such as his training, experience, and work record. The firm has every right, and the need to follow very closely its employees' performance, attitudes, and behavior *while at work*. This information can be obtained quite easily with little risk of employee resentment or legal complications, and can be employed most effectively in making personnel decisions. But to gather information surreptitiously or to take positive action steps with respect to current employees as human beings and with respect to their personal habits, their home life, their community activities and personal views is questionable, extraordinarily risky, and generally very ineffective.

It is doubtful whether a firm needs to "manage" the private lives of employees even if they could. What a company *can* do is to be perceptive and observant about an employee's performance. It has the ability to identify and understand what work-related factors may be affecting performance and attitude. What is not identifiable on the job can just be assumed to be an external cause. A company can't control an external environment, but it can control internal operations by taking proper personnel actions. To the extent that an employee's ineffectiveness is caused by *work* environment, then perhaps the company can deal with it. If it is due to unknown factors, perhaps inherent in the person or his home life, the company can only react and make appropriate decisions. In other words, the company cannot manage the *cause* of personal negative environment, but it can consider the manifested *results* in making personnel decisions.

THE COMMUNITY

Companies can change elements of external environment in other ways. They can, as members of the community, exercise proper influence. Employers can, for instance, consider the question of whether or not the community in which they are located is the kind of environment that will attract and retain the types of workers they need, and whether the community has a favorable impact on employee productivity. New York City "leads" in a number of respects; one is the degree to which the environment has led hundreds of firms to move out. High taxes on employees (as well as on employers), poor transportation, poor educational facilities, undependable municipal services, and many other factors can create an environment that makes high productivity impossible and high employee costs inevitable.

Community location is particularly important for enterprises with a high percentage of specialists and managerial workers. In fact, some of these companies are thinking of strategic ways to help create the right kind of community environment, one that can be a positive factor in productivity. Some are going so far as to think in terms of building new towns specifically designed to attract, retain, and motivate knowledge workers.

Once in an adaptable community, a company can regard a reasonable degree of participation in legitimate community affairs as part of the cost of doing business. The firm is not managing the community in any sense. Rather, it is supporting those segments of the community that create the environment to enhance productivity. This contribution may be direct financial support or a grant of employees' time and talent to community affairs, at least partially on company time. These expenditures of company resources constitute a form of voluntary tax on the enterprise. Selective allocations of money and time to community affairs, directed at creating the proper environment for work, can indeed have an important impact upon worker effectiveness. There are many examples of how a firm may effectively allocate resources that contribute to a community environment that is conducive to a more effective work force. For example, support of the educational process may help assure that there is a continuing flow of reasonably well educated persons needed by the firm locally.

Another important consideration in selecting a community is the excellence of local transportation. Time spent going to and from work may not count as work time, and certainly doesn't contribute to more effective work, but it is part of the employee's workday. For instance, employees in the city of New York spend a larger portion of their day devoted to work than in almost any other community, but they spend fewer hours actually working on a company's premises. Better transportation facilities also have a tendency to expand and enlarge the company's labor market. Other areas of community concern include community recreational facilities, appropriate zoning provisions, eating and shopping facilities, etc.

The foregoing examples show how companies can legitimately and constructively spend time and money to influence community characteristics by special emphasis on compatible community relations. Traditionally, community relations is essentially a "company giving" activity. Members of management or a committee review numerable requests for donations and, based upon uncertain and sometimes highly personal criteria, make grants that frequently have little relationship to the conduct of the business. Companies should rethink community activities along a much more pragmatic line of reasoning. Time and money expenditures should be *invested,* and the primary purpose of such investments in community activities should be to develop the type of environment that contributes to a more effective work force.

GENERAL SOCIAL ENVIRONMENT

Because business is an integral part of society, it follows that major changes and trends in the social environment may have some impact upon workers in the company. It follows also that some of these influences on people might eventually affect productivity. As is the case of environmental factors related to home and community, many sociological influences have some effect upon the productivity of people, but few have a very obvious relationship to employees' work habits. Yet the relationships are real, and they have great cumulative impact upon how well human resources are utilized in the enterprise. A few examples should be sufficient to illustrate the point.

There are pockets of racial tension throughout the United States, and the stresses that manifest themselves in the community and on the streets reflect on the work place. Any factor that deters people from working effectively and cooperatively together will have a negative impact upon the productivity of people at work. Racial tensions are no exception. There is also among young people an increasing disinclination to make the knowledge investment necessary to do higher-level work. They want the "knowledge" jobs, but many don't want to make the study investments necessary to perform these jobs effectively.

The apparent deterioration of the formal educational system in the United States is coincident with declining employee effectiveness at work.

At both the primary and secondary levels as well as higher education, the continuing trend toward substitution of social goals for career goals, combined with the increased inability of school administrators to manage effectively, is resulting in a crop of graduates less well equipped with basic learning tools. And they are less well equipped to deal with the growing complexity of the technological and business worlds.

While credentials of those in the work force become less commensurate with the knowledge requirements of work, industry and business expectations of worker capability become higher. The imbalance between employee and employer expectations therefore creates an unrealistic common goal. Young men coming out of business schools expect to manage, even though they know nothing about the things they want to manage, and little about management itself for that matter. Others go into the investment world and expect to make a quick fortune. The person who finishes college generally expects to do college-level work, even though at the time there may not be enough jobs in his or her field to go around. And the unskilled laborer expects to make $4.00 or $5.00 per hour. All these cases emphasize a level of expectations among people generally, which is not only very high but also unrealistic, beyond the economic capacity of even the richest nation on earth.

Not even the largest firm can meaningfully change the social environment. It can only structure its activities to deal with social issues as effectively as possible. The most promising approach is through the recruiting process. Recruiters can pick the most appropriately qualified, most highly motivated persons with the most realistic expectations. Companies can also deal with the social elements by building a knowledgeable first-level supervisory group that is adept in communications. Only a supervisor having direct contact with working men and women throughout the organization can deal with manifestations of social unrest and conflict at the work place. This in turn demands considerable requirements for supervisors in terms of knowledge and skill, and vests in them an accountability and responsibility at every level in tomorrow's business environment. It also requires an organizational structure and management policy that matches supervisory accountability with authority.

GOVERNMENT

Government affects employee productivity in three ways. It creates unproductive and restrictive practices, as outlined in Chapter 4. Legislated regulations designed for political and social goals impose restrictions on the conduct of business and the lives of workers, none of which may be direct but which have a very real impact on productivity. Another indirect effect of the government on productivity in enterprises is the impact of its image on the business community.

Government at every level is assuming an intrusive posture to be dealt with by enterprise and by every worker. It touches almost every facet of business. It is increasingly becoming an all-pervasive influence on the success or failure of individual enterprises. Naturally, we assume that government will, and should, set the rules for conducting business in a way that is compatible with national goals and social objectives. However, it is also assumed that rules formulated by bureaucratic government would be balanced, applied in an even-handed manner, and implemented fairly and impartially. Government agencies haven't done much of that for a long time, and do not any longer even pretend to be even-handed. Whether their posture is right or wrong isn't the issue here. What does concern the business community is that their rules, and more importantly how they apply those rules, detract in major ways from work effectiveness.

It is extremely difficult to estimate the result of all government regulations on employee productivity. It is particularly difficult because one must measure the *cost* in terms of dollar expenditures plus the dollarized cost of lower productivity against the *values* measured by entirely different criteria related to social goals of health, safety, fair treatment, etc. These evaluations are complicated by the fact that each political or social action has some identifiable need, value, or virtue, and the cost of any one seems infinitesimal in relation to the overall national product. It is the cumulative impact of all regulations of federal, state, and local governments which seriously reduces productivity.

These regulations are very difficult to deal with from a management point of view. Obviously, companies must obey each of the hundreds of laws that affect their operations. For most firms this concurrence has been a defensive activity; that is, they comply as much as possible, as efficiently as possible, and with the least amount of disruption in normal operations.

At present, the deteriorating government image has fallen to a critical level because the public has lost respect for the *bureaucracy of government*, which most people label as the "establishment." Bureaucratic "authority" touches everyone's life, and usually in a very distasteful way. Experiences with bureaucratic bodies are almost invariably unpleasant.* The general view of working men and women is that government operations are not only

---

* Many discussions with groups of working people at the operations level suggest that the only bureaucratic group that has a universally high profile is the fire department. The only other group with a profile more plus than minus is the police department. All other agencies that deal with people have a negative profile, with the Internal Revenue Service and the welfare agencies at the absolute bottom of the list.

inefficient, but are also frequently incompetent and are occasionally inflexibly dictatorial. The result is generally a negative image of "authority" and the "establishment," and because business hierarchies represent a form of authority, they generally get tarred with the same brush.

When employees come to work they seem to find another form of bureaucracy, and it is only natural that they should transfer to employer bureaucracy much of the hostility they feel toward government bureaucracy. Even when the company is efficient, competent, and fair, employees view it negatively because of what they have experienced with, or have been informed about, government bureaucracy. There isn't much a company can do about this prejudice. It merely warns business that it must be careful not to acquire the characteristics of a government bureaucracy. The company must make sure that employees understand the difference between its organizational policies and those of government bodies.

EXPECTATIONS OF EXCELLENCE

A number of environmental elements are internal, which the company sets largely by itself or which are inherent in the nature of the business. The expectations of the business in terms of employee performance is part of the environment which it creates for itself and which affects employee productivity. Generally speaking, the companies that expect high performance have better than average employee effectiveness. Those that accept mediocrity tend to get mediocrity.

Levels of expectations, or standards of performance, are set one way or another by every enterprise. People are sensitive to what is expected. A company can set high levels of expectation for employee productivity in two dimensions. First of all, it can expect improvement. Furthermore, most businesses and many units within each business can set external criteria of success. They can get some measures of how effectively their competitors are doing or how well companies like them operate. Then they can adopt levels of expectations accordingly.

High standards can be set for companies that are very large and for enterprises that grow only with the trends of the population or the economy. It is also possible for a company to "grow" and to experience increased productivity without getting bigger. Even companies in declining industries can create an environment of excellence and personal growth by simulating a growth environment. So, almost any enterprise, whether it is a commercial business or a not-for-profit organization, can set high levels of expectation.

Every enterprise can also adopt work standards for units of the firm as well as for the business overall. This is important because levels of excellence at the overall enterprise level represent goals for relatively few people within the organization. Therefore, levels of expectation must be set for each operating unit so that the people within that unit have a standard that is visible and meaningful to them.

Simply setting standards can have a dramatic effect on productivity. Expectation of excellence encourages excellence. Such a climate tends to be self-reinforcing. Excellence creates pride and confidence, which encourages further striving for excellence. To accomplish this, however, the standards must be understandable, attainable, and perceived to be reasonable.

Standards are more than words; the employees' understanding of standards of excellence are determined also by what the worker sees and experiences. The firm which in fact ships only products of the highest quality, or accepts only quality work from each work place, creates an atmosphere in which people tend to expect quality in their own work. Thus, not only companywide standards, but also standards established in each division, department, and unit of the firm determine the ultimate degree of excellence.

The immediate supervisor also contributes to observance of standards of excellence. What the supervisor says and does, what he expects, and how well he receives standards set by higher authority all make up the *real* standards perceived by employees. The supervisor's constant attention to quality and his acceptance of the standards are part of the *enterprise* standards. How the supervisor communicates the need for excellence and how he expresses his enthusiasm for it define the quality expected. In many ways, of course, the supervisor *is* the company and his standards *are* the company standards. All of this has much to say about the job of the supervisor, his accountability and authority, and his capability, training, and experience necessary for effective supervision. It also suggests his value to be far more than "10 or 15 percent above the highest paid person supervised" and relates to the efficacy of organizational structure and managerial style.

PHYSICAL CONDITIONS

Physical conditions of work also affect employee productivity. Employees obviously need the proper equipment and facilities if they are to work effectively. The machinist needs tools, jigs, and fixtures; the secretary needs a typewriter, desk, and appropriate work space; the technician needs laboratory equipment, etc. Such needs seem obvious, but providing optimum conditions for efficient work in every position is not so simple in practice. This is extremely difficult because the optimum physical conditions will vary for different jobs, and even for different employees doing the same job. Most companies, particularly larger firms, believe it necessary to establish rules and procedures that determine uniform physical surroundings for employees, but this often conflicts with the need to customize equipment and facilities for employees whose jobs are unique.

There is a minimum amount of equipment and facilities below which employees cannot produce to high standards. When this minimum is not maintained, each dollar of equipment and square foot of space is an expense that must be weighed against the values of greater work effectiveness. Determining this cost-value relationship is difficult for a number of reasons. For instance, if estimated for each employee, the cost of multiple analyses might be greater than the resulting value. Also, the value of incremental facilities may change with an employee over time.

Even less clear, but nontheless real, are the values of physical surroundings, such as color, decorations, and music. More appropriate physical surroundings are not necessarily more expensive. On the other hand, what is "more appropriate" is unclear, and will likely differ among individuals. Various studies show that physical surroundings do influence workers' effectiveness, but the relationship is tenuous and sometimes transitory. Furthermore, there is a difference between what employees like and how their preferences impact productivity. Employees frequently like music at work, but for some it may be an irritant that *lowers* productivity.

"Plush" working conditions, overdone or overemphasized, may detract from effectiveness. Grandeur and opulence is not only costly but also can be counterproductive. Some feel that ornate corporate headquarters distract corporate staff people from reality, warp their views of their own roles, and sometimes cause resentment in operating people "out in the trenches." If surroundings tend to make people inflate their own importance so that they neglect their responsibilities, their work effectiveness is impaired. If conditions lead people to interpret success by size of office, space in the parking lot, and type of rug on the office floor, these trappings of affluence become a form of disproductivity.

BUSINESS IMAGE

The image of the business may raise or lower work effectiveness. Many firms need to consider how their practices and policies affect employee attitudes and inclination to work effectively. The type of business success record, general business objectives, manifested attitudes toward cost, some accounting practices, proper and legal conduct of the business, and executive work habits are but a few examples of business practices that are visible to employees. Employee perceptions of such matters create an image that can have a significant impact on productivity.

The nature of the business itself is an important part of the business image and the environment that impacts productivity. Some businesses by nature lack glamour, and work conditions are necessarily unpleasant. On the other hand, there are businesses, such as some highly technological firms, where work seems glamorous; businesses, such as those in the news media, which seem exciting; or firms engaged in environmental control, which would be perceived by many to be useful and socially desirable work. All these and similar areas of business will tend to have a positive impact on employee enthusiasm and effectiveness.

The success of the firm can also influence employee attitudes. Successful firms are more exciting, offer greater employee opportunity, and have high standards. There is excitement and pride in being the best, and a fast-moving pace focuses employee attention on the important goals and creates a sense of urgency. All these elements tend to provide a positive environment in every section of the firm, which promotes higher productivity. Success may not breed further success, but it is self-reinforcing.

Business practices may have some impact on attitudes and effectiveness. Even normal and entirely proper practices may be viewed very differently from the factory floor than from the Board room. For instance, many companies engage for financial reasons in what is euphemistically called "managing earnings." This means reserving funds, or expending money, or writing off items in one year so that a constant earnings growth or predetermined earnings growth can result. It is all very legal, proper, and in some ways necessary. Such accounting practices may or may not impress the investment community, but it directly impresses employees to whom it is visible. The impression it makes on employees may not be a good one from the point of view of employee productivity. They may infer that false standards are the expectations of the business rather than substantive standards of success. It may suggest to them that it is all right to give false reports of success, and that this policy also applies in their own area of work.

Some business intrigues also have impact on employees. Whatever the real story or circumstances—illegal election campaign donations, concealment of the real nature of energy problems, bribes to foreign customers, and other revelations of improper actions—the business image is generally impaired. The result tends to be a low-confidence profile applicable to all businesses. Those companies caught in the act can do little but repent, but others must somehow persuade their employees of their innocence.

When employees rightly or wrongly perceive inefficiency or wasteful expenditures at the top, the message is communicated throughout the organization and cannot help but detract from the effectiveness of people at work. This is not to say that certain types of executive or managerial benefits and perquisites are inappropriate. Quite the contrary. In fact, employees tend to care less about the amount of managers' compensation than they do about whether they are worth it. Companies must realize, however, that if employees think top management pay, benefits, or perquisites are frivolous or excessive, this will make employees believe that reasonable control of cost or careful use of time is not regarded by the company as terribly important. Anything that suggests that management is not serious about work standards is bound to find its way down through the organization and detract from the effectiveness of workers.

Finally, the standards of performance that management sets for itself, and the effectiveness with which it applies them, are important in shaping the business image. Work attitudes and habits of key managers have a ripple effect down through the organization and simply must permeate the attitudes and habits of others. There is also the important, though difficultly defined, element of leadership. Whether top management leads the firm in the right direction, successfully develops the best game plan, and makes the few truly crucial decisions that guide the future of the firm are, of course, essential. But so far as worker productivity is concerned, it is the overt display of leadership which is critical and which consists partly of example, partly of appearance, and to some extent charisma.

Personnel Policies

Part of the environment a company creates for itself is the climate, attitude, and framework established by personnel policies. When personnel policies originate from considerate and thoughtful decisions of top management, they can serve a number of extremely useful purposes. If properly structured and articulated by the key decision makers in the company, they serve as guides to bring a controlled and orderly process into decision making on personnel questions.

A second objective of establishing personnel policies is to have them represent a basis for delegating personnel decisions far down in the organization. This does two things. First, it saves top management time, which can then be allocated to matters that only top management can deal with. It also results in better personnel decisions. When personnel decisions are made at lower levels in the organization, for instance, the decision maker not only has the policy guide, but also has intimate knowledge of the relevant facts and circumstances. Making personnel decisions appropriate to each situation tends not only to satisfy the work force, but also to increase its productiveness. This system of distributing personnel authority allows decisions to be made more rapidly and with better understanding of circumstances at the appropriate or lower level in the organization, all of which logically contributes to higher productivity.

Formulated personnel policies serve a number of other important functions. One of these is that they can guide top management in judging the performance of subordinate management. Personnel policies themselves are part of the internal climate the firm sets for itself. Policies perceived to be rational and fair create positive attitudes on the part of employees. Policies that suggest a quality firm, high standards of excellence, reward for achievement, and a mutual commitment by the company and its employees all help set a tone that encourages effective work.

Policy making of any kind is a formidable job. It is a job that few managers like to tackle unless it is absolutely necessary; and it is a job that seldom seems urgent. Most managers have their time pretty well committed to problems at hand. Policy making facilitates the management job tomorrow; many feel hard pressed to deal with things present today. Urgent matters usually get priority over important matters. So, policy making is an intellectual exercise of the highest order with potentially enormous long-term benefits, but which has little apparent or immediate benefit for today's operations.

As a practical matter, companies need few personnel policies with respect to the question of effectiveness of people at work. Generally, a dozen top-management policy statements are sufficient. These would deal with such questions as fair employment, employment security, promotion, and job placement, grievance handling, compensation, communication, and the development of people.

It is not necessary to make a major project out of policy formulation unless an enterprise faces problems in this area of major proportions. It is unwise to establish within a personnel staff group a section or unit whose assignment is to devise policies. Policy formulation is not a quantitative problem, but a qualitative problem, and it is not a race. It does not matter nearly as much *when* the company gets its policies formulated as *how well* they are formulated, the processes by which they are formulated, and how well they are communicated and used throughout the organization.

Policy making of any kind is a formidable job. It is a job that few manticulate what the policies currently are in fact. Second, it requires input from the employees, from supervisors throughout the organization, and from staff. Third, it involves an evaluation of the alternatives that are available to the company, in terms of each major personnel policy. Fourth, recommended policies or policy changes must be postulated, and the reasons for these policy changes must be well documented for management.

Finally, approval of the policies or changes in policies must not only be communicated, but must also be made part of the decision-making process of the company.

6

Staffing

Staffing in its broadest sense involves management of the human assets of the enterprise. Management of human assets entails the acquisition of the talent and skills required by the firm; the proper deployment of these assets; and replacement of employees who leave for any reason. One of the basic problems of effective staffing is that it has been viewed too narrowly, essentially as a job of filling outstanding requisitions. Staffing in the context used here has a very broad meaning. It includes bringing new employees into the company, placing these employees in their proper position, and severing the employment of others.

Acquiring human assets obviously is essential to the operations of the company and the effectiveness of the work force. If it were possible simply to select potential employment candidates who would be highly productive from those who would be less productive or unproductive, then employee productivity would not be the problem it is. This is exactly the objective of the staffing function. Similarly, correct placement of employees within the company affects employee productivity. If employees are in positions where they are more highly productive, then their effectiveness is increased accordingly. Finally, the control of severance policy and tactics designed to discourage resignation of highly productive employees also contribute to greater overall employee productivity.

BUSINESS ECONOMICS OF STAFFING

While there is a great deal of material and rather precise analytic guides with respect to the acquisition, utilization, and disposition of physical assets, there has been relatively little usable analysis of a similar nature with respect to human asset acquisition and utilization. The economics of human resources asset management versus physical resources asset management is different in a number of respects that have important implications to general management policies and decisions, and to technical and procedural questions relating to the operation of the employment function.

Replacement of physical assets, for instance, is invariably at a higher cost. In fact, replacement costs inevitably exceed funds that have accrued on the books for replacement under depreciation. "Replacement costs" for human assets are not higher; if anything, they are generally lower. Human asset acquisition expense is usually thought to be simply the cost of recruiting. In fact, the net cost of human asset acquisition is a resultant of employment costs, net compensation differences, and differences in the effectiveness of workers involved.

If dollarized values were put into this human asset acquisition equation, the *general* case would be that the expense involved in the hiring of a new employee is offset by the lower compensation costs of the new employee compared with the level of compensation of the employee replaced within a year and a half. Results will vary among actual cases, but a new employee's pay is *generally* less than the pay of the employee replaced. Compensation and expenses can be measured so that this part of the human asset acquisition analysis is factual. If lower compensation costs and recruiting expenses do net out, then the key to the cost of human resources asset acquisition is the productivity of employees hired compared to that of employees replaced. *Generally,* new employees are initially less effective than those replaced; this is a learning period or a start-up cost which adds to the front-end expense of employment. Once the new employee goes through the period of adjustment and learning, a period that may vary from a few days to a few months, then the productivity of the new employee versus the employee replaced is measured by his capabilities and application.

The expense of recruitment is illustrated in Figure 3. Initially, the expense of acquisition is significant because it represents employment cost and productivity loss. Over time, however, lower compensation cost of the new employee and greater productivity as he comes up to speed in his new job results in minimal expenses, zero expenses, or actually net income. The direct variables are net compensation differences and net productivity differences. In many situations, net productivity differences must be at least partially judged rather than measured.

Actual models of human resources acquisition costs must take into account whether there was a replacement or an addition—as well as placement expense, net compensation difference, and net productivity difference—and whether employees replaced in turn replaced others. When a replacement occurs by employment and triggers a series of job moves, the cost savings of

Figure 3. Net cost of human resources acquisition.

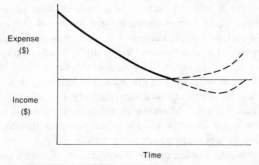

all must be considered. From a strictly financial analysis it would be more appropriate perhaps to spread the cost of employment over the working life span of the employee. It might also be more correct to figure compensation differentials over a long period of time and to build in retirement or termination costs. The bookkeeping techniques in the area of human resources asset management, however, simply are not up to this accrual type of analysis. However, it may not make any difference. A few cases where such detailed analysis has been attempted indicated that the resulting conclusions are essentially the same.

Such analysis first illustrates the type of investigation useful in increasing the effectiveness of human resources management through staffing. It is a tangible illustration of the value of human resources information system. It shows that human resources acquisition, if properly managed, may involve no cost or, at worst, small expense compared with the cost of acquiring or replacing physical assets.

Some other very interesting business aspects of the employment activity have an impact on productivity. One relates to the rate of turnover; that is, separation and replacement rates. These figures vary a great deal among companies, but if one were to strike an average for all business, the turnover rate among operations-level workers is between 25 and 50 percent a year; for middle-level workers, between 15 and 30 percent per year; and for top-level people, 5 to 10 percent a year. For all employees this averages, in a typical firm, a turnover of between 20 and 30 percent of the work force each year. Within five years the cumulative turnover might be 75 percent or more. To the extent that this represents a strategic planning period for a firm, the enterprise is effactually replacing three-fourths of its human assets every five years. This, of course, can be contrasted with replacement of building and equipment, which requires a far longer time span for turnover. The business implication is, of course, that it takes a relatively short time to replace human assets simply through normal turnover. Therefore, a firm can potentially change substantially (for better or for worse) the quality of its human assets at relatively low cost and in a relatively short period of time.

The working life of human resources—the number of years a recruited employee will remain with the company—is another important aspect in the acquisition of human resource assets. Surprisingly, few firms track even this single area of human resources information. Employees may be with the firm for weeks or months, or over 40 years. The longevity or working span of human assets for each individual varies greatly and is largely unpredictable. Yet it makes a great difference in the business economics of staffing whether human assets are employed for a short time or a lifetime, and where in the company they perform one or many jobs.

Another illustration of the unique characteristics of human-asset acquisition management is the fact that human resources are far more multifunctional than any physical asset. Even a so-called multipurpose piece of physical equipment has a very limited number of uses. To redeploy it to a new purpose takes both time and expense. Each employee, on the other hand, may do many jobs. Frequently, employees can change jobs instantaneously, with almost no training. Employment activities can be structured to make the work force more or less multipurpose, depending upon the needs of the business and the long-term growth prospects of the firm.

Other aspects of staffing have relevance to better use of human resources. A physical asset is usually never more effective than when it is new, but employees appreciate in value (not depreciate) during most of their working careers. They perform many functions during their working life, some not even contemplated when they were first recruited. Furthermore, the current year's applicants (models) are not essentially different from those of earlier years. All these examples of business aspects related to the staffing function can potentially influence productivity. The business economics of staffing need to be better understood and should be analyzed—quantitatively and not just subjectively—at least on a case, model, and sample basis. There is a new focus as well as importance to these matters. Simply stated, if companies cannot increase productivity by substituting machinery for people, there are opportunities to increase it by more effective substitution of people for people.

EMPLOYMENT

While the term "staffing" is used here in its broadest form (that is, the hiring, placement, and separation of employees), the word "employment" is used to mean hiring of new employees. Employment is virtual human assets acquisition. Procedurally, employment practice includes identification of new hire needs, recruitment, identification of satisfactory candidates, screening of candidates, and selection. In each of these areas there are management as well as technical matters, both of which affect the recruitment activity and determine the appropriateness of human assets acquired.

The determination of employment needs is essentially a matter of manpower planning and operational knowledge. Manpower planning aims at setting guidelines as to the number and types of jobs required at a given level of activity and in terms of enterprise objectives. Within general guidelines such as these, requirements specified in requisitions must be set by immediate supervisors, based upon detailed knowledge of the jobs to be filled and knowledge of local operating requirements. Determination and articulation of correct recruitment *needs* are critical to the acquisition of a productive work force. They comprise the first requirement of effective manpower control. Correct specification of requirements for employment is also the basis for subsequent recruitment, screening, and selection.

Time and money spent on employment where needs and requirements are not correctly specified represents unproductive work and detracts from productivity. Resources expended on employment for unnecessary jobs represents disproductivity. Employment activities expend significant amounts of resources. Time costs, as illustrated in Chapter III, are quite substantial. Effective management of these costs is keyed first to the correct identification of employment needs.

Recruiting

Recruitment activities raise a number of questions about methodology. One such question relates to the choice of recruitment source. The alternatives are rather finite, essentially involving the use of search, agency, advertising, direct recruitment, or response to individuals who contact the company. The selection and management of these recruiting sources depends on cost effectiveness, the productivity of the recruiting source, and how the productivity of the recruiting source selected can be optimized. The cost effectiveness of different recruiting sources need not be judged entirely on an intuitive basis. Principal elements of cost from different recruiting sources can be analyzed for different types of positions. Cost is not merely a question of out-of-pocket expenses spent by members of the personnel department. Total costs must be managed, including cost aspects of management time expended, and the time necessary for the new employee to become acclimated to his job and come up to work standards.

As indicated in Chapter 3, human resources information systems can measure the cost of recruiting. The *reliability* of the recruiting source and the possible costs of unfilled positions must also be considered. For example, during a critical period of reorganization a large financial institution successfully completed less than half of the searches initiated. Here the cost of completed searches was reasonable, but the cost of all searches was excessive. Thus, not having essential work done at a critical time was a key factor in subsequent severe business problems. Unfilled critical positions can be an expensive and vital factor in a firm's success or failure because they handicap all employees, and thereby lower effectiveness.

The value of recruiting sources is difficult to measure. Each type may be proficient in several ways but not in all. Recruiting must consider not only reliability, but also the time it takes to get employees into the organization and the degree to which they meet operational needs. Above all must be considered the degree to which the recruiting source presents qualified candidates for consideration.

Some firms have found recruitment cost and effectiveness to be so critical to a firm's success and recruiting sources to be so costly and ineffective that they have set up in-house company recruiting activities to handle fulfillment of critical positions. A large, diversified consumer goods firm makes it a part of every manager's job to report names of high-performance marketing people in other firms when he has the opportunity to do so. These names are fed into an inventory system, which is tapped whenever there is an opening in the marketing organization. Many professional businesses do the same thing.

A number of large industrial firms have established their own in-house recruiting firm. One even permits the captive recruiting source to handle assignments for other (noncompetitive) firms on a fee basis. As a result, its net cost of recruiting for its own needs is zero. In-house recruiting units have generally been established to lower the cost of recruiting. Most firms have found, however, that such operations are also more reliable and, more importantly, deliver better qualified candidates.

Recruiting is a particularly difficult problem in middle-level management and staff personnel. Communication to recruiting sources and staff personnel of information with respect to needs is difficult. Job descriptions can be written only in generic terms because understanding of specifications requires knowledge of the technologies involved. Experience requirements are rarely fixed and specific. Often, the knowledgeability in a professional or technical field and skills in applying technology are the critical qualities. Recruiting specialists are not likely to be able to recruit or screen in terms of such qualities.

Screening

The screening of candidates for selection is the second critical step in the employment process. Selection techniques have been thoroughly described and detailed in the literature pertaining to the personnel field. Companies also have an enormous amount of experience with different selection techniques. It is not, therefore, very useful to repeat what is widely known and experienced. But it is certainly worth noting that how well these selection techniques are applied has an obvious impact on whom is brought into the company, and ultimately influences employee effectiveness. If a company consistently applies these techniques successfully and thereby recruits higher caliber people into the organization, it will have a greater "human resources asset base," the basis for greater employee productivity.

For most firms what is needed is not more or fancier selection techniques. What is really needed by most is to apply the basic techniques in a more effective manner. For instance, the interview is a critical and very traditional screening procedure, and is essential to the selection process. It is difficult to conceive, for instance, of any employee selection that would exclude an interview. Research suggests that well over half of the evaluative information useful in making a hiring decision is derived from the personal interview. Yet the people with knowledge of work requirements are scattered throughout the organization. They are not inherently very well qualified either in the techniques of interviewing or in the evaluative process, since supervisors are usually untrained in these arts. For instance, training sessions on interviewing skill show typically that for every hour of an interview, 10 percent or less of that time is used by untrained line managers to gain information that is not available from other sources relevant to the selection decision. Interview training (see Table 7) doubles the productive

Table 7. Allocation of interview time.

	Personnel Specialists		Line Manager	
	Before Training	After Training	Before Training	After Training
Getting information relevant to the selection decision not available from other sources	31%	38%	9%	20%
Giving information relevant to the selection decision not available from other sources	16	17	11	22
Getting or giving information already available	17	12	24	18
Repeat subjects	9	8	16	9
Casual conversation	16	14	26	19
All other	11	11	14	12
	100	100	100	100

time managers spend in getting or giving information relevant to the selection process. As would be expected, a personnel staff, already trained in interview techniques can be much more effective.

A great deal of activity in personnel administration has been directed in recent years toward the development and use of more advanced and sophisticated techniques of selection because of the critical importance of employment. An example would be the use of psychological assessment. No doubt these more elaborate and sophisticated systems enhance the selection process if used by well-trained professionals who also understand the business. But they are not terribly useful unless they have additive value, and may actually detract from candidate evaluation unless the basic selection techniques, such as interviewing, are used and utilized well.

Human resources data relating to selection can also be the basis for improving the selection process. For instance, it is a rather simple bookkeeping procedure to record the number of candidates who are approved or eliminated at each step of the selection processes. It is possible to analyze retrospectively some of this experience and to formulate guidelines for cumulative scoring of candidates at each step in the selection process. This aims at eliminating prospects before time is spent on complete screening. Such information is valuable to a firm in further improving the process and avoids the cost of nonproductive time.

There are a number of related management concepts very useful in the application of the selection techniques within a company. One of these involves the concept of sufficiency. Frequently, supervisors or managers like to see a number of well-qualified applicants in order to choose the candidate who is *best* qualified. There is some logic and rationality to such a view. It is, however, extremely costly, frequently reflects the absence of well delineated job specifications or criteria for selection, and may result in basing the final selection decision on questionable criteria. Evidence from case studies suggests that in fact such a process adds very little to the effectiveness of the employee selection. The concept of sufficiency is applicable in many areas of employee relations; in the area of recruiting it suggests that when a candidate meets the requirements of a job, he or she should be offered the position, regardless of incidental personal characteristics.

Strategic Needs

Another important factor as far as productivity is concerned is the consideration of near-term and strategic or long-term recruiting effectiveness. Those recruited into the organization are usually brought in to fill a specific job. The ability of the candidate to fill that job is of near-term critical importance. Typically, the employment and recruiting process is designed solely to make sure that a properly qualified person is recruited to fill a particular job. Experience requirements, knowledge requirements, and selection process all tend to be geared to evaluating the candidate's suitability for the immediate job opening.

Many employees recruited into a company are with the firm a number of years. Over the years they fill a number of positions besides the job they originally were recruited to perform. Typical recruiting processes do not take this important fact into consideration. Selection procedures and selection criteria should evaluate the longer term needs of the firm and the likely positions the employee might fill in the future, as well as the candidate's qualifications to fill the immediate opening. The degree to which the company is building its human assets to meet not only its near-term needs but also its long-term needs obviously has an effect over a long period of time on the level of work effectiveness in the company.

One case study showed that, on the average, salaried persons brought into a firm in middle-level exempt positions remained for seven years. During that seven-year period, they filled three distinctly different positions. Thirty percent of the employees stayed with the firm for fifteen years or more. During that period of time they filled seven different positions. In both cases the position for which these employees were originally hired was performed by them for an average period of about two years, although selection processes had been geared only to the near-term needs of the company, since the candidates' abilities were evaluated for the first jobs they filled when hired.

There should, therefore, be a balance of criteria in the selection process for evaluating candidates against the near-term needs of the job and in the more strategic long-term criteria. Employment decisions then consider the potential productivity of candidates over their entire estimated work life in the organization. To measure long-term service requires not only additional selection criteria, but different evaluative systems as well. Screening against long-term needs requires data and information with respect to the prospective employee's record of length of service and the number of positions that that applicant is likely to hold during his entire tenure if accepted. It would also require some historic data about the normal career paths that have stemmed from the job which is being filled immediately. This provides guidelines for evaluating candidates against long-term capabilities and requires consideration of the more basic personal attributes such as intelligence and motivation.

Companies that evaluate strategic or long-term employment criteria find it necessary not only to add these criteria to the list of candidate qualifications, but also to modify their employment procedures. For instance, those best qualified to evaluate near-term criteria and judge qualifications to perform the first job filled are the first-level supervisors and personnel staff people who know that particular operation well. These persons are frequently very poorly qualified to evaluate the strategic criteria and make evaluations as to the potential long-term productivity and motivation of the individuals. Long-term qualifications may involve levels of knowledge and skill not possessed by the first-level supervisor, require a broader perspective than that held at a local operating-unit level, and involve a balancing of near-term and long-term projections that lower-level management cannot be expected to make.

Equal employment opportunity requirements place a third set of evaluation criteria and selection requirements on the employment process. In addition to considering near-term qualifications for the immediate job being filled and the long-term or strategic requirements, a company must now consider compliance and affirmative-action programs in connection with the EEO Act. Among other things, this means compiling evaluative criteria that apply to the substance of qualifications rather than their appearance. Tests, for instance, must emphasize basic capabilities of performing work and must subordinate the necessity for learned knowledge.

Placement

Internal employment, or the placement function, is the second part of the overall staffing activity. It relates to how well the company deploys human assets within the firm, and includes promotions, transfers, and reassignments. Correct placement of employees augments productivity by having people work at jobs for which they are best suited. It also serves to broaden and develop employees, thereby enhancing the firm's human assets as well as effectiveness.

Placement is one of a number of personnel activities that are pivotal in human resources management, for putting people in the right job is a direct and significant way of gaining a high level of productivity. A recruiting error can frequently be corrected by effective placement. Placement is critical to what will be described as operational training and development. Correct placement, both by promotion and transfer, can often precipitate motivation.

Promotion

Promotion of employees is of obvious importance to both the employee and the company. For the employee, it represents the opportunity to get ahead. For the company, it represents in a strictly business sense the upgrading or enhancement of human assets. Promotion includes movement to a distinctly different job of greater difficulty and higher value. Promotions include expansion of work responsibilities or growth in professional careers, either of which results in greater work status and greater value of the work being performed.

Promotion first involves the question as to whether to fill an open position by promoting somebody within the organization, or to fill the position by recruiting someone from outside the organization. This is another area in which human resources information can be an important input to the decision making of management. New-hire costs data can be compared rather precisely with the cost of filling a position by promotion from within: Screening costs are moderate and considerably less than those associated with recruitment. Furthermore, pay differentials are generally in favor of promotion. It should be noted in this connection that employees brought in from outside the company will be paid, on the average, less than persons replaced. Also, as a general rule, employees promoted to a new position will be paid less than employees brought in from outside to fill the same post. In fact, companies that do a great deal of promotion from within have found it appropriate to manage salaries at a lower-range position than those where promotion is an infrequent occurrence. Therefore, from every point of view, the cost aspects favor promotion from within as opposed to recruiting someone from outside the firm.

The effectiveness of persons recruited from outside versus those promoted inside the company is a more difficult area to evaluate. One factor that favors promotion from within is that the screening can be more effective in evaluating the qualifications of the person already working in the organization. In making these evaluations, the same screening techniques and practices are used for both in-house and outside candidates for a position. In addition, the company has had the opportunity to actually observe the candidate performing in work situations. The result is that the company has far more and better quality information to judge the qualifications of candidates within the firm. The future effectiveness of the work of any candidate is an intangible and one that can be only projected and never quantified. Present performance of the individual selected can be measured, but can never be compared with that of another employee or a candidate from outside the company.

On balance, the advantages of filling a post by promotion from within far outweigh those of outside recruitment in an overwhelming number of cases. Case studies suggest that even in companies with a heritage of home-grown talent, there are too many positions filled by outside recruiting. Key problems identified in achieving the correct balance of jobs filled from inside include the following:

□ The firm knows the defects of inside candidates; those of outside candidates are less visible.

□ Short-term operational needs, objectives, and expectations lead managers to be reluctant about giving up their star performers.

□ There is frequently an overemphasis on the need or desirability of filling a job with someone who has actually done that job or one very much like it, which tends to eliminate inside candidates.

□ There are political or cosmetic reasons why a firm sometimes tends to look to the outside. For intance, the "heir apparents" may not be suitable, and there is reluctance to cause relations problems by leapfrog promotion or filling the job with a candidate from another part of the business.

□ There is frequently a tendency to go prospecting in the labor market, in the hope that a superstar will be found. Once started in that direction, some jobs are filled from the outside by far less than superstars, almost by the momentum of activity.

□ There is a genuine problem of inbreeding.

Problems such as these are all manageable and when properly managed result in every known case with a far higher proportion of jobs filled by candidates inside the firm.

There will always be new hires. These should largely be at entry levels, or where specialized and advanced educational requirements are involved, or where there are needs for massive hiring due to growth or rebuilding of staff after cutbacks.

Promotions usually involve a number of job moves. The person promoted must be replaced; again, the company faces the choice of promotion from within or outside. Ultimately, a replacement must be brought in from the outside. A case study showed, on the average, that in the middle-level management positions, one promotion resulted in two or more job moves.

Proper placement of all types, including promotions, in most enterprises is far more complex than simply assignment of the best-qualified employee to each job. That simplistic approach suggests that the job is a "given," and people must be bent and fitted to the inflexible needs of each position. This is simply not the case, particularly in middle-level professional and managerial jobs. In these cases the total amount of work that is done and the configuration of jobs that can be designed to get that work done are many and varied. Therefore, the company that develops the capability of designing jobs to people as well as selecting people for jobs considerably extends its ability to promote employees within the organization to fill new jobs.

The ability and effectiveness to fill jobs by promotion from within is also determined to some extent by the excellence of the company's succession planning. All companies engage in some form of succession planning. Some have attempted to establish rather elaborate programs where organizational charts show every incumbent and position, and identify possible replacements for each position. Experience has shown, however, that such an approach is extremely costly and not terribly effective. Succession planning need not cover 100 percent of the jobs or the people. For one thing, many employees can be eliminated from succession planning because of age. Others can be eliminated because they do not really care to move forward, or because they have reached their career peak. Still others are in a position where the nature of their experience and background either confines very seriously the direction in which they might move or for practical reasons eliminates them from consideration.

Succession planning may be designed around jobs or around people. When designed around jobs, the company can establish logical career paths. There is seldom one single career path from a given job in the organization, but a number of paths. Succession planning built around employees analyzes individual abilities, experiences, and interests, and determines from such inputs which positions each employee might logically move to next. It is the combination of planning around jobs and career paths in terms of employee capabilities and interests for a limited number of critical positions and qualified employees that has been found to be the most successful and useful succession planning system.

Mise-en-place

In any firm, there are frequent job transfers, reassignment of work, temporary assignments, and special tasks, all designed to meet the operating needs of the enterprise. This includes the physical transfer of work or transfer of employees from one job to another as openings occur. Job transfer or job assignment change can also be an important employee development tool. Employees must be transferred or reassigned to different work in order to meet the needs of the business. Transfer can also be made with a second objective or concurrently dual objectives—employee development. To the extent that employees, by being transferred or by having work transferred to them, get experience or learn new skills that relate to company needs, the company is enhancing the asset value of its human resources as well as income values from proper deployment of these human resources.

Transfer of work or transfer of employees to new jobs may also be done for defensive reasons. The following two cases illustrate this point. A number of students of business have observed that the work life of optimum performance by management people is usually between 10 and 15 years.

After this length of time, productivity may decline even though experience increases. This may then call for reassignment of work or for actual transfer of top-level people. There have also been some very interesting studies that tend to demonstrate the presence of a boredom factor, or professional obsolescence factor, which affects people doing professional work for a period exceeding three years. When this happens, productivity may start to decline, and professionals become bored and restless, and eventually quit. This suggests the need to realign duties or actually to transfer professional persons to different types of work within their professional disciplines on a two- to three-year time cycle.

All these transfer and promotional movements, of course, involve the basic question of having people in the right place at the right time. It is part of what the French call *mise-en-place,* which literally means to "put in place." It must be viewed as a day-to-day continuing activity. Here again, of course, the individual supervisors and personnel staff close to operations must play the key roles. They must constantly be alert to and react to the needs of the organization. They must also be able to react to the needs of employees, both for diversity of work and for career growth.

Considerable emphasis should be focused on the placement function for a number of reasons. For one thing it is an area where employees give their employers low marks. Qualitative attitude surveys, in contrast to printed questionnaires, invariably show that employees overwhelmingly believe:

- □ Company policies are biased in favor of filling desirable jobs from the outside.
- □ Employees should have more knowledge about openings.
- □ The best qualified person frequently does not get the promotion or desired transfer.
- □ At best there is uncertainty about the basis of job moves of all kinds.
- □ Their employers generally do not pay enough attention to job assignments and job placements.

An opportunity to get ahead is high on the list of essential employee objectives. Dissatisfaction on this subject can lead to frustration and constitute a demotivator. *Qualitative* interviews designed to determine reasons for resignations also show invariably that placement questions are the number one or number two reason why employees leave, and particularly why the *best* employees start looking elsewhere. Placement work tends to lack glamour; individual success and failure tends not to be visible. Cumulatively, however, these elements have very great impact on both the capacity of the work force and its effectiveness. Most firms need to do a much better job in the area of placement, and *can* do it if the doing is done by first-level line supervisors and personnel staff people.

OUTPLACEMENT

The third part of the overall staffing function is outplacement of employees, which involves resignations (quits) terminations, and retirement. A great deal has been said and written about employee turnover, and considerable work has been done to reduce and control it. Most firms keep data and information with respect to turnover, although little of such information is usable in the human resources information sense of providing input for more effective planning and decision making. Quits of all kinds involve real cost, at least the expense of replacement, and this involves other employment costs for employees who ultimately replace them. To the extent that quits occur among highly experienced persons, the company is losing valuable assets, assets that may have been acquired and developed over a considerable period of time and at significant expense to the company. If the employee who quits is a high performer, then the company may have great difficulty in recruiting a replacement who is equally productive.

The management of turnover, of course, is an important part of the overall staffing job. It isn't simply a matter of keeping turnover to a minimum. It is asset retention and asset utilization. It involves the qualitative job of protection against loss of *key* assets, and the avoidance of loss of employee productivity. Here, again, information input as to the levels of turnover, viewed qualitatively in terms of the experience and performance of people leaving the positions, is critical to effective management of turnover. Determination of why employees leave and corrective action, where appropriate, are the ultimate objectives of turnover management.

Every company must also face the problem of terminations either for cause, for lack of work, or for the inability of the employee to perform up to standards. Termination for inability to perform up to standards is the most difficult part of this aspect of the overall staffing function. No company and no supervisor likes to face the difficult personal chore of terminating employees—particularly those who try hard and may, in every respect, be fine human beings—because they cannot perform effectively. Termination, however, of inefficient or unproductive workers is just as important to the overall productivity level of the firm as the employment or recruitment of productive employees in the first place. By being kind or generous or soft to the unproductive employee, the supervisor is being unfair to all productive employees, not to mention customers and stockholders. Furthermore the unproductive employee in a given job and company environment may be very productive elsewhere.

The termination action itself need not be harsh. Most companies provide severance payments, and employees are eligible for unemployment compensation. In many cases, firms continue pay or a high percentage of pay until a terminated employee relocates. This approach views severance payments as a bridge, assisting terminated employees until they successfully relocate. Some firms even provide outplacement assistance in finding a suitable position.

A few companies have carried out programs designed to enhance their human resources assets through a combination of termination and recruitment. A New England division of a major diversified electrical manufacturing company embarked on a program labeled "organizational enrichment." Each year it would identify, largely by performance ratings, the percentage of their employees who had the lowest productivity. These employees were then earmarked for termination. Termination was implemented by replacing these individuals with people recruited who had been identified in the labor market as having better qualifications, both near-term and long-term, and whose productivity was therefore judged to be superior. New employees were, in effect, brought in to replace less effective current employees in order to upgrade the productivity of the entire organization. This process of 5 percent managed turnover throughout the organization each year was carried on for a period of seven years. Through this one program alone, the company estimated that it had increased the productivity of its work force by 50 percent.

The whole purpose of retirement programs is to provide a reasonable and socially acceptable way of terminating employees when they are too old to continue working effectively. Actually, the point at which employees' productivity declines because of age varies with individuals. For administrative reasons, however, it is essential to establish a fixed date (usually tied to social security eligibility) for all employees except executives. This, as a business policy, is illogical because it frequently displaces employees who are more productive than employees who replace them. However, age is a universal criterion and there just isn't any other practical, reasonable, or tax-sheltered way to terminate older workers from the work force.

Some companies have concluded that, with respect to executive employees, they can be more direct and in some way more harsh by terminating those executives at any time when their productivity declines or another person can perform executive responsibilities more effectively. With a limited number of persons highly visible to directors, this is the practical thing to do. It is also practical to establish supplementary, nonqualified income plans to make sure that the job action, done for the good of the organization and overall productivity of the organization, does not have an impact on the income of the long-service, highly valued employees.

EMPLOYMENT MANAGEMENT FUNCTION

Most firms have an employment section or unit in the personnel department. The scope of its activities are, however, far more limited than the staffing function described here. Typically, the employment department deals only with the recruitment and screening activities. However, each of the staffing functions must be viewed as interrelated with the personnel selection activity, which contributes to greater employee productivity, as well as with certain other needed employment activities.

In terms of employee productivity, placement as well as recruiting and screening effects the degree to which the firm fully utilizes its human resources. Placement as a function is frequently not monitored or nurtured anywhere in the personnel staff; nor is it the concern of a number of areas. This suggests the desirability of expanding the staff role of the employment department to encompass all facets of staffing.

Line managers are accountable for staffing, but a staffing department would not do actual staffing any more than the compensation department makes pay decisions. The staffing group would provide central service and staff support, as they now frequently do in recruiting.

7

Manpower Controls

Among the traditional functional areas of employee relations, one that potentially has great impact on improving productivity, is the area of manpower control. Manpower control activities affect employee productivity, directly and significantly, because they involve the question of how many people should be in the firm. This, in turn, is the denominator of the productivity equation. Manpower control work indirectly supports productivity because it also deals with the question of what collection of knowledge, experience, and skills are required in order to accomplish the objectives of the enterprise. The subject of manpower controls is thus concerned with all those activities that determine the optimum number of persons and aggregate talent in the firm at any given volume of the business. Conceptually, therefore, at a given volume of business, manpower ratios are reciprocals of productivity ratios.

Manpower Levels

A number of students of business and some critics have publicly stated that businesses are generally grossly overstaffed. What's more significant is the fact that any number of surveys of management attitudes suggest that executives themselves believe their organizations contain more people than is necessary to conduct the affairs of the firm, though rarely is the opinion expressed that their business is *grossly* overstaffed. Studies and projects directed at developing and implementing more effective manpower goals invariably have concluded that manpower can and should be reduced, as little as 10 percent in a number of firms and as much as 30 percent in the case of a billion-dollar chemical company. It would not be necessary to have any study or survey, on the other hand, to conclude that top management of every company would perceive as a major enterprise goal the reduction of staff to whatever level is needed to run the business effectively. This seeming disparity between the facts of manpower and the intent of management is due primarily to the fact that managements lack the information, tools, and techniques to control effectively the manpower in their enterprises. They simply do not have the information guides or the technology to make ongoing decisions and judgments as to the appropriate level of manpower.

It is in some respects extraordinary that such information guidelines and technology do not exist. Companies have, over the years, devoted considerable resources and money to the development of rather refined and elaborate technologies in various fields of personnel administration. They have, for instance, developed quite elaborate and sophisticated programs in job evaluation. These, in effect, address themselves to the question of whether or not employees are in their correct pay grades. This usually means in turn that the technique of job evaluation typically helps to determine a 10 percent difference in cost in perhaps one of four cases. Such programs have value, but their cost is not insignificant. However, the subject of manpower controls, which have a far greater cost impact, has been largely neglected. Management has no plan, technology, or guidelines to judge appropriate levels of staffing.

Actually, companies do have information and guidelines, or can easily develop them, with respect to the number of operational workers needed to produce various levels of output on some specific types of jobs. Frequently, this information is quite precise. It is in the indirect, nonoperational positions where manpower control guidelines are lacking. For most firms, these areas represent a substantial part of the work force, typically one-third of employment and more than one-half of payroll. Furthermore, the indirect, nonoperational workers are becoming an increasingly large proportion of total employment.

The absence of usable manpower controls for these indirect and non-operational positions leaves unanswerable the question of whether there are surplus employees in a firm. Absence of control guidelines also leaves management in a difficult position in a number of respects. When business needs require reduction in expenses, manpower is cut intuitively or is reduced on the basis of financial inputs alone.

ECONOMICS OF MANPOWER CONTROLS

The economic importance of controlling manpower is almost self-evident, for enormous amounts of dollar costs are involved. Table 8 shows, for a sample of companies, the impact on bottom-line results of a reduction in

Table 8. Impact of 15 percent reduction in manpower on pretax profits (in millions of dollars unless otherwise indicated).

	Company "S"	Company "N"	Company "C"	Company "V"
BEFORE STAFF REDUCTION				
Sales	$98.5	$222.3	$842.3	$747.0
Expenses				
Employee	21.6	66.7	336.9	338.4
Other	72.3	143.3	459.9	315.3
Total Expenses	93.9	210.0	796.8	703.7
Pretax earnings	4.6	12.3	45.5	43.3
AFTER STAFF REDUCTION				
Sales	$98.5	$222.3	$842.3	$747.0
Expenses				
Employee	18.4	56.7	286.4	330.1
Other	72.3	143.3	459.9	315.3
Total Expenses	90.7	200.0	746.3	645.4
Pretax Earnings	7.8	22.3	96.0	101.6
Percent Increase in Earnings	70%	81%	111%	135%

Source: Company financial statements. Firms with approximately the same pretax return on sales were selected.

staff equal to 15 percent, on the assumption that the dollar reductions were proportionate to the numbers of employees reduced. In these cases the single act of bringing manpower levels back in line with operational and strategic needs produced a rise in company earnings from 69 percent to 135 percent in the four companies selected. Typically in industrial firms, a 15 percent reduction of payroll will double earnings per share of stock.

The cost of surplus manpower is, in effect, a double cost. The calculable first and obvious costs are payroll dollars and benefit costs of retaining excess workers. A secondary cost is the leverage effect on the economics of the manpower. As noted in Chapter 4, surplus people perform work that creates work for others. Some of this work created by surplus manpower is itself necessary work; payroll clerks for unneeded workers are just as necessary as payroll clerks for needed workers. Reducing levels of manpower has reverse effects in a number of indirect ways, such as curtailing the amount of communication required and simplifying organization.

There is a third element of cost associated with surplus manpower which is difficult to identify or measure. Surplus employees, or a group of employees who in the aggregate are surplus, may by the nature of their work become demotivated, dissatisfied, or bored. Where there is surplus manpower, there is also the danger that employees themselves will perceive all or some of their work as being peripheral and nonessential. Perhaps most important of all, surplus manpower conditions people to a less-than-optimum work pace. Thus, an individual accustomed to working slowly, who is suddenly required to increase his productivity rate, may find his job distasteful and excessively hard as well as unreasonably demanding.

Having unnecessary employees on the payroll does not always mean that they are not working hard, nor does it mean that some are not working efficiently. As a practical matter, where there is surplus manpower all employees may be working very hard and with great efficiency. By definition, however, excess manpower means either that some employees are working at lower-than-optimum productivity or that they are doing unnecessary work, or some combination of the two.

It is an oversimplification to view manpower control alone in terms of the number of people who are working in a company. What the business really wants is a much more results-oriented concept of manpower control. The enterprise objective in manpower control is really an optimum balance, or combination, of payroll control and employee productivity.

The economic objective is not to run the business with the least number of people or even the optimum number of people. The objective is to achieve enterprise goals. This in turn means obtaining the greatest revenue at the lowest payroll cost.

It isn't necessarily true that decreasing the number of people will effectively decrease the amount of payroll. There is obviously a relationship between the number of people and dollars of payroll, but it is not an automatic or fixed relationship. Fewer people, for instance, can mean more dollars of payroll if the work done by persons let go or on jobs eliminated is in fact performed by higher paid persons. This economic view of *payroll* control parallels the idea of dollarized productivity measures. The dollarized productivity measure is sales divided by payroll. Manpower control ratios measure payroll divided by sales.

Measurements of costs are not, of course, the only economic dimension of manpower control. A company cannot, for instance, operate at minimum manpower levels. For one thing, operating at the minimum manpower level would run the risk of meeting only the current year's operational needs and might sacrifice long-term values and strategic objectives. Also, companies cannot operate at minimum manpower levels simply because employees are not always at work. They get sick, they take vacations, they move to new jobs where time is needed for learning before they come up to optimum levels of efficiency. Moreover, people are never working at optimum rates for every hour of every day of every week of every year. All these economic circumstances require any enterprise to work somewhat above minimum levels of manpower.

Another important aspect of the economics of manpower controls involves the risk of inadequate manpower, of not getting vital work done at the appropriate time because the number of employees or those with required knowledge and skills are not available. This situation may cause the loss of an important customer whose order is not shipped on schedule or whose work is not finished when he needs it. It may mean loss of new business opportunities because insufficient time is spent in developing them. Then, too, there is the risk of having insufficient people to meet an emergency. Obviously, these risks and their possible costs cannot be quantified in a direct manner, as can the payroll cost of surplus manpower. But they represent real risks and therefore are potential costs to the enterprise. While they may not be quantified in a finite manner, analysis of the economic and operating characteristics of the business can provide management with some guidelines with respect to risks and costs of insufficient manpower. Such analyses are the responsibility of the risk-management element of the personnel function.

There are other economic and operating aspects of manpower control. For example, the rate of growth of a firm affects the manpower model. Rapidly growing firms need more of a margin of certain types of indirect or nonoperational employees. Highly capital-intensive firms also require such a margin. In any firm, positions that are critical to ongoing operations and require specialized training also should be assigned some margin between optimum and minimum manpower levels.

MANAGEMENT OF MANPOWER

Understanding the basic economic characteristics of management control is in many respects the first essential step toward effective manpower control. This must obviously be done within the context of the company's own economic and operating characteristics, and made an integral part of the company's own specific problems and objectives. Factually, there is no preprogrammed economic model for manpower control which fits all enterprises. A second basic step toward an effective manpower control program requires identification of management aspects that pertain to it. These are essentially general management matters or personnel policy matters rather than technical or procedural aspects. They include the question of incorporating manpower control in the general management structure; the degree of management commitment to manpower control; management's attitudes toward investment in manpower; and management's participation in resources allocation.

From the start, it must be recognized that there are a considerable number of basic general management policies, practices, and objectives which to a very large extent set the upper and lower limits of practical manpower control. General management devises the "game plan" and the strategies of the business. These strategies in turn affect practical limits on manpower controls. A strategy of growth through development of new products, for instance, requires higher levels of manpower. Management policies also set the tone for decisions with respect to the economic trade-offs inherent in manpower controls. Expense control versus risk management is a typical example.

Still another illustration is the fact that objectives of the company have impact on the practical elements of management control. High-growth objectives in one business requires one level of manpower; but another business may be run as a "gravel pit" in which very tight manpower controls would be appropriate. Finally, the specific managerial style in which the company's affairs are conducted must be considered. Very tight control, for instance, generally requires larger staff groups.

There is also the question of basic company commitment to manpower control. This is really not a simple question. Obviously, control of manpower is important to every company. But, *every* business subject imaginable is important to every company. Although the list of items or subjects of importance is unlimited, time and resources are not. Most firms are committed in some degree to manpower control, but the commitment is sometimes an abstraction. Commitment is really apparent when a company starts allocating resources and time, including the time of management to implement manpower controls. To do this profitably, management must weigh the relative importance and impact of manpower control activities against all other needs and priorities of the business.

The type of commitment also has relevance to effective management of manpower. A continuing concern and effort in controlling manpower communicates to all a very different commitment than harsh cuts when times are hard and earnings are down. Expectation of periodic cuts discourages careful conservation of manpower at other times and may encourage manpower excesses from time to time, which in turn may make necessary the periodic cuts. A policy of continuity in managing manpower is more humane, is certainly better balanced economically, and therefore more effective.

The analogy may seem incongruous but in many respects there are similarities between manpower control and physical inventory control. Generically, the subject of manpower control involves the question of how well the company is using its resources, which in this context refers to human skill and talent. Manpower control implies a humanistic view of optimizing return on a critical asset—the knowledge, skill, and effort of all employees. Inventory control, on the other hand, is distinctly materialistic and is concerned with how well the company uses such supplies and inventory. Nevertheless, both concepts involve a return on assets. While return on human assets obviously considers the critical question of human values, some of the analytic techniques and decision-making processes of inventory control have been found helpful in manpower control.

This line of reasoning has led to some recent investigation of manpower control which might be considered an investment approach. This work involves the development of an economic model of a business which identifies the minimum number of jobs and employees, and estimates the supporting payroll. Obviously, these facets of the model are clearly essential to the operational objectives of the firm, with due regard to the risk elements already identified, and represent the minimum employee costs. The current year's operations cannot be conducted without these positions in place.

Each additional position above the minimum number required is viewed as an investment. Since additional positions call for more people, there is therefore more payroll cost. For each item of cost there is then measured or judged the value of the work done by the incumbent of that position. Thus, in this approach, the number of people in investment positions create an expense that must be related to the income they produce. If the dollars of that income or revenue exceed the dollars of payroll invested by adding these positions above the minimum economic model, then the dollar returns of the enterprise increases.

There is another aspect to manpower investment. Many leadership firms have for years brought in college graduates in excess of their needs. Some have done the same in skilled worker categories. This is a selectivity exercise. The plan is to observe the performance of the trainees while at work. The best are retained and moved ahead. Others are not moved ahead, discouraged, or subject to outplacement. In many firms these trainees represent very substantial investments in terms of surplus manpower, both in direct and leveraged costs. The return on this investment must be necessarily measured over a very long period of time by very imperfect standards. Some experience in this practice suggests that at least part of the surplus manpower is really an expense, not an investment, and is indicative of imperfect personnel recruiting and selection procedures.

Another basic management consideration with respect to manpower control involves questions of resource allocation. Manpower control policies and practices should seldom be applied in a uniform manner throughout an organization. Most contemporary enterprises are engaged in multiple business areas. In each area, while every functional activity is important, there are some in which human resources management generally, and manpower control specifically, are more critical to continuing success. General management considers resource allocation on a regular basis, making decisions, for instance, with respect to the allocation of financial resources to different sections of the overall corporate enterprise. Part of this resource allocation job should involve manpower.

Generally speaking, the organization or the part of the business that has greatest opportunity for the future success should have priority for needed talent. It should be able to call on other sections of the enterprise for the human assets that will assure achievement of its objectives. There are cases where companies have planned growth in the very areas of the business which were already at dangerously low levels of manpower and where people were not performing adequately at current levels of activity. Human resources information can be an extremely important input to growth decisions for such reasons, and can indicate just how much talent must be redeployed or acquired.

INFORMATION GUIDELINES

In thinking about action steps to deal with manpower control problems, it is sometimes helpful to view them first in terms of informational guidelines, and then in relation to manpower control programs. In many respects, these guidelines involve the application of human resources information systems in the functional area of manpower control. Essentially, they define what manpower levels should be, or they establish standards for specific manpower decisions. Information guidelines provide general management with data as to what should be accomplished. It may then be the job of operational management throughout the organization to achieve these goals by various means: application of techniques and methods in some instances; review of work to be done; or assuring correctness of methods, the ability of people, and the efficiency with which employees work.

The simplest manpower control information guidelines involve the tracking of historic levels of manpower at various volumes of business. A simple index of employee census related overall to volume of work will tell the company what has been accomplished in the way of manpower as one basis for what might be accomplished in the future. Historic indexes can, of course, also be developed for different groups of jobs. Continuing indexes of manpower do not tell the company how well it is controlling manpower, but only whether it is doing as well as it has done before, whether it is improving, or actually whether manpower levels are increasing proportionally to the work being performed. Inflated levels of manpower are certainly symptomatic of declining employee productivity, and suggest an opportunity for increases in employee productivity and the reduction of employee cost.

In many instances the comparative indexes of manpower can be developed within the firm. The company with a number of retail outlets, for instance, can compare the level of manpower in one store against another on the bases of business volume, store size, and other relevant factors. This indicates which stores have the tightest control of manpower and which have the loosest. It also indicates what can be done, and identifies those operations having the greatest opportunities for reducing manpower levels. Examination of locations or units with the best regulated manpower may in turn represent a case, or a learning experience, for others.

External comparisons of manpower are also useful as information guidelines. Obviously, the firms or operations with which comparisons are made must have features common to the operant company. They must be similar in size, business type, and in economic and operating circumstances. Where this can be done, the company has not only historic indexes of manpower control to check its own performance, but also some measure of the appropriateness of its manpower levels, as indicated by the experience and practice of other firms. These peer-group comparisons are particularly relevant when they are tracked over a period of time. A given firm may, for instance, be higher in its manpower related to business volume than are the peer comparison companies. This may simply indicate that it is less capital-intensive, or it may merely reflect unique characteristics of the business. Tracked over a period of time, however, changes in manpower indexes *relative* to peer-group companies can provide insights into an improving or deteriorating manpower situation.

Manpower *ratios* can be calculated for either a short or long period of time. Ratios are the number of one group of employees divided by the number of a broader group of employees. Workers in a functional area, department, or unit can be related to another group of workers or to some other business data. The most frequently used, and most useful, manpower ratios measure the ratio of workers in a unit or functional area to all direct operational workers in production and marketing. Ratios may entail numbers of employees, but are more useful if dollars of payroll are used.

Lower levels of manpower, or better comparisons relative to peer-group firms, is probably, but not necessarily, better. Indexes are indicative only, *suggesting* a better or worse situation. They indicate the need for a more qualitative look, which in turn may require action steps. Lower ratios may, as noted earlier, mean that manpower levels are *too* low. Ratios supplemented by other guidelines are particularly useful.

Manpower ratios can also be used as information guidelines in a wide variety of functional areas, including accounting and finance, personnel, law, market research, industrial engineering, data processing, etc. They can also be kept according to organizational unit: division, department, section. Finally, they can be kept by location. Companies have, for instance, for many years maintained "personnel ratios," that is, the number of persons in a personnel department as a percentage of total employment. These ratios are improved if the "personnel employees" are carefully defined and if the numbers are related to total operations workers directly involved in marketing and production rather than to total employment. Similar ratios have been developed, particularly for research and development, and for financial employees. As is the case of indexes, the manpower ratios can be compared among units or locations within a firm. Peer-group comparisons are also useful. In the case of ratios of staff jobs, comparisons can be made with a wide variety of firms rather than peer-group firms.

The determination of operations jobs directly involved in the making and selling of the firm's products or services is critical to effective manpower information guidelines. This definition is not easy to deduce in the typical contemporary firm. They may or may not be direct employees as defined by cost accountants. They may or may not be nonexempt people as defined by the Fair Labor Standards Act. They are, however, invariably doing operational work. Use of indexes and ratios suggests that this core group for manpower control are those operational people exclusively in direct making and selling of the product. This group is a critical group, first because clear relationships of number of employees or dollars of payroll in relation to business volume can be established, and second because it frequently represents the greatest number of employees and dollars of payroll. Further, it is usually the group where cutback or increase in number of employees can be accomplished in the shortest period of time. Finally, the number of operational employees involved in the making and selling of products is the key denominator in manpower ratios.

These various types of information guidelines have led a few companies to develop manpower models, models of what manpower levels should be in various sections of the business at various volumes of operation, and under certain conditions. These represent top-down manpower control targets. They are similar to targets set in terms of sales, share of market, or pre-tax return on assets. They represent, in effect, optimum targets for manpower levels. These models indicate the ideal numbers of persons by job categories and by job levels in each area of the business.

Information guidelines have been used successfully by some firms as essentially the sole basis of a manpower control program. In these cases the guidelines, in terms of indexes, ratios, and models, are the goals or standards of performance for operating supervision and operating management. Top management delegates the job of building specific manpower tables. The work of devising the actual manpower control methods used to establish these standards is also delegated down through all levels of the organization.

Manpower Control Programs and Practices

Information guidelines indicate what is happening in terms of manpower levels, and perhaps identify what levels of manpower should exist.

Manpower control techniques and programs for reducing or controlling manpower specify how these goals should be achieved. The control programs and practices in this sense are quite limited, both in number of programs and in terms of their demonstrative effectiveness. In practice, these programs are usually a customized collection of reviews, studies, and actions, a few of which could be specifically identified with manpower control per se. The importance of the subject area and the absence of special technology suggests that this might be a fruitful area for developmental work by personnel staff.

The absence of manpower control information guidelines and technology obviously makes it difficult to manage or control manpower levels on an ongoing and consistent basis. The result has been that management actions with respect to manpower has frequently involved emergency cuts when business circumstances require. The trouble with emergency cuts is that they tend to be quantitative, not qualitative. The very emergency that precipitates such action usually precludes a thoughtful and qualitative analysis of the manpower situation. This in turn may lead to reducing the work force at the expense of human resources assets. By this action the company is in fact converting assets into income.

Emergency cuts also tend to be temporary. When the pressure for reduction of staff is removed, the need for employees returns. Frequently, then, rebuilding work forces results in more employees than ever, particularly in those areas where work has been put off during the reduction in force. Finally, there is some evidence that when companies repeatedly go through the emergency cut cycles, over the years they build up resistance to such emergency cuts. Thus, surplus jobs acquire a built-in status and work associated with them then tends to become viewed as essential.

Special studies to reduce manpower have been made with some success. These are qualitative as well as quantitative, and address themselves to the problems of where to reduce manpower, how to reduce manpower, as well as how much manpower should be reduced. Special studies are usually made by a project team, composed either of company personnel or outside consultants, or both. These teams have the time to make in-depth studies, are composed of members who bring special skills and/or experience to such work, and have objectivity. An interesting question, however, is whether line managers with equal time and support could not get equal results.

Special studies tend to be undertaken when there is time and money available for a thoughtful and comprehensive study. They represent one of many areas where "management of earnings" is appropriate, especially if the study is made when money is available and conclusions are applied when necessary. Not much of such investment work is actually done in human resources management. When the money is at hand, business activities are high and time is usually not available.

Reduction of manpower is an area of work that utilizes varieties of "expertise." One of these is the special knowledge, experience, and perspective of management engineers. This group includes the "efficiency experts" who are able to reduce manpower by applying various analytic and mathematic techniques. What they are apt to do is to reduce manpower from optimum levels to minimum levels. As a practical matter, much of the work of the "efficiency expert" is to find out from the line manager what work is postponable or above minimum levels, and then formulate their recommendations accordingly.

Management engineering is a broad area and some of the techniques of the industrial engineer have been applied in the factory and also in nonfactory positions. Work-flow methods, work layout, and even time-study techniques all have some applicability in manpower control for at least some salaried positions. Application of these techniques can contribute information that may result in greater efficiency and lower manpower requirements.

A variety of management engineering methods and practices have also evolved specifically for office positions and have been applied for many years to salaried jobs. These include such techniques as form design and records management. Management engineers have attempted to use such methodologies in analyzing exempt positions, but have had only varying degrees of success. Such technology has just as much applicability to salaried *operational* positions as they do to *operations* jobs in the factory or in the warehouse. When applied to management and knowledge positions, however, their usefulness seems to be restricted to questions of what work should be done rather than how the work should be done.

There are a few interesting cases where firms have established project teams on a continuing basis to represent their own collection of capabilities in the area of management engineering. These groups vary in their composition. There is a core group consisting of industrial engineering, office practice experts, personnel staff, and a cross section of line managers. There are also representatives for each major operating unit, who participate in the work of the project group whenever studies are done in their own organizational units. The members of such project groups collectively know operations well enough to eliminate work as well as methodize the work and improve the efficiency of people at their work. In these cases, the companies have provided line people with access to the knowledge and techniques of the management engineers, personnel staff, and other specialists. The project group has its collection of knowledge and has access to special technologies as needed. Firms have charged such project groups in various sections of their business to the ongoing job of assuring correct manpower levels.

The purpose of the most basic manpower control technique is to eliminate unnecessary work. Where manpower levels are in excess of needs, or greater than optimum levels, a limited number of variables are available to deal with reduction of manpower without affecting operations or exposing the firm to future imprudent risks. The correctness of the methods with which people work, their ability to do the work, and the efficiency with which they work are all variables. But these are variables related to the work which they are performing. If the work they are performing is not necessary to the accomplishment of goals or objectives of the enterprise, then there isn't much point in developing better work methods, or training people, or inducing them to work more efficiently. Removing unnecessary work is in many respects, therefore, the primary objective in manpower control.

Essentially, it is the line's manager's responsibility, aided by the personnel staff who are close to such operations, to assure proper manpower levels. They are the ones who know the operations, have the best knowledge of the jobs and amount of work done, and are in the best position to judge what work is essential. This is particularly true for work involving specialized knowledge and advanced technology. The greater the technology, the more the immediate levels of supervision must have responsibility and authority to control manpower. The maintenance of correct manpower levels and control must, therefore, be delegated deep into the organization.

Many policy statements and guidelines can be made available to the organization. Various types of audits and special studies are effective in bringing manpower to correct levels. Specialists in management engineering and personnel administration can be of enormous help. In the last analysis, however, it is the immediate supervisor who is close to, and has knowledge of, operations, and who must do the substantive job of controlling manpower. It is at this level of supervision where the knowledge exists as to what work needs to be done. At this level correctness of methods can be reviewed and established, people can be trained or selected for the job in the first place, and day-to-day supervision helps develop optimum efficiency.

Many companies repeat in each operations-planning period the process of constructing bottom-up manning tables. These consist of more conclusions than techniques. Each level of the organization, starting with first-level supervision, submits information about the number of employees in each job category and the amount of payroll required to accomplish budgeted levels of work. These summaries are typically reviewed by successively higher levels of management. Without manpower controls or guidelines, progressively higher levels of management would have less knowledge to use as a basis for approval, disapproval, or modification. Higher management, under these circumstances, tends to make manpower decisions largely on the basis of financial information.

An increasingly important aspect of manpower control is inherent in specialized knowledge jobs, which in terms of payroll dollars are a growing segment of most businesses. For these positions there is a crucial "make or buy" decision to be made. This is in many respects the same type of economic decision that companies have made for years when they decide to make or buy parts, supplies, or materials. There is, of course, a certain amount of outside help that must be hired for legal and fiduciary reasons. Public accountants are needed to certify company statements. Specialized legal counsel must be retained in order to make certain types of transactions. Beyond that, there are many make-or-buy decisions in research, finance, manufacturing, engineering, marketing, market research, and personnel. This may require hiring people on a part-time basis or using consultants because they possess knowledge and/or experience that does not reside in the firm. They may also be hired to accomplish special projects involving once-used knowledge, or to fill temporary vacancies. The quality of these make-or-buy decisions detract from or enhance the effectiveness of manpower levels and productivity.

8

Organization Structure

Organizational structuring deals with the question of how people work together to achieve the goals of an enterprise in the most effective manner. Organizational structuring represents the vehicle through which work is done. If that vehicle is awkward or cumbersome, it will inhibit or make difficult productive and effective work. An inappropriate organization structure also makes effective work between groups of people difficult. It is in these ways that organization structure primarily has an impact on employee productivity.

Some students of business feel that organizational structuring is the primary management problem in the area of human resources. The degree of change that takes place in company structures tends to support this view. By the more obvious standards of what interests management (that is, where management people spend their time), organization structure is not number one among human resources management subjects, although it has high priority.

This chapter focuses on organizational *structuring*, not organizational *planning*. Forecasting with any precision the nature and dimension of future organizations is another subject, and one that is less directly relatable to employee productivity. What is essential to companies in terms of employee productivity is an organizational structure that fits their needs, their operating and economic characteristics, their traditions, their particular working environment, and one that facilitates and encourages effective use of human resources.

TRANSACTIONAL ORGANIZATIONAL STRUCTURING

The literature of organizational structuring implies that such work typically involves well-organized projects designed to optimize effectiveness of work and to implement group dynamics. The plain fact of the matter is, however, that a great deal of organizational work is highly transactional. Some change occurs in the business and some modification is made in the organization to accommodate that change. Some problem occurs, and in working to prevent recurrence of the situation, some organizational change is made.

Opportune changes are typically modifications more than dramatic restructuring; each change or modification originating on a transactional basis is rather small. Cumulatively, however, they represent a considerable amount of change. In fact, studies show that very much of the substance of most organizational structures really at any particular stage has resulted from transactional causes or from reactions to specific situations, problems, and occurrences.

Even companies that are highly structured in their organizational attitudes and devote great amounts of time to organizational work have found that the net result of a formal approach is no more than a general sketch or overall outline of organization. Obviously, then, the transactional occurrences are what give body, substance, and detail to the organization. Frequently, a chart of actual company structure will reflect almost identically the formal organizational thinking. But the organization as it *really* exists and as it *really* functions reflects to a very large degree reactions to specific situations and problems.

A considerable number of informal organizational working relationships develop in any organization. These tend to evolve more toward the top of the organization than toward the bottom, although they can be very important at any level of the organization. What happens, of course, is that individuals or groups will themselves find the best ways of working together or of resolving and dealing with problems so that their joint interests are accommodated. As circumstances and as individuals change, these informal working relationships also change.

Organizational purists regret such informalities when they affect structure. They see organization changes resulting from reactions to situations or from the informal working relationships between individuals or groups as technical organizational imperfections. Their view may be correct, but what companies want, of course, is a functioning organization that induces effective employee work, regardless of its technical perfection.

There has also been concern expressed (in some cases legitimately) that transactional organizational changes and informal working relationships represent a business version of anarchy. Certainly, if transactional organizational changes and informal relationships *determine* organization without any guidance from the top, the company does have some combination of chaos and anarchy. But this does not in fact happen in well-managed companies because companies have shown no interest in describing in detail how work should be done or specifically how people should work together. This means that the top management or central staff does not prescribe exactly how people in the organization work together.

What is intended is that top management, with staff assistance, set only the general framework of organization, policies, and guidelines with respect to working relationships and key organizational questions. Frequently, transactional changes and informal relationships really are encouraged and actually reflect the delegation of authority and responsibility for organization structure to those who know best the nature of the work and are in the best position to devise methods for getting it done most effectively. This also reflects the realities of business; neither top management nor central staff can or should determine detailed work patterns and relationships throughout the organization.

Frequently, there is a question of how a company can constructively manage transactional organizational structuring and informal working relationships. This subject has not received the attention and thoughtful consideration that it deserves as an important determinant of the way in which the organization really works. A few companies have studied these key organizational structuring questions and have developed methods for management of transactional and informal organization. They have concentrated on the basic outline of the organization and have formulated guidelines that personnel at every level should use in developing working interrelationships. They have provided information briefs on the essentials of these relationships and have provided training to key people throughout the organization. They have not only permitted but also encouraged and expected that the detailing of organizational structure be done at the level where people have the specific knowledge of operations and specific accountability for work and working relationships.

Structuring the Organization

Organizational structuring in contemporary business is a very complex undertaking. It involves many considerations and many facets of work. Even in the initial steps toward organizational structuring, there is a need for a multiple approach. There are, for instance, four points or areas of focus in organizational structuring, each of which requires quite different attitudes, methodology, knowledge, and skills.

One of these points pertains to structuring the organization according to operational-level jobs. This is essentially a bottom-up type of organization, in which the structuring of bottom levels is quite independent of structuring at other points in the company. There is also a top-down type of organizational structuring, which is usually strategic in nature. This establishes the basic breakdown of the business and the basic positioning of key executives—classified to a large extent on their personal skills, on the principal problems confronting the business at the time, and basic strategic plans for the future.

There is a third point, which has really evolved as an organizational focal point in the past 20 years. It focuses on positioning the firm with respect to its markets and customers. This focal point is somewhere in the middle of the organization. It is a very pragmatic accommodation to the outside world.

The fourth focal point for organizational structuring is also in the middle of the organization. It is the first level of human resources management.

Tactical Organizational Structuring

Tactical or operational organizational structuring, as the name implies, has to do with how people are grouped and how groups are positioned, one to the other, in order to accomplish specific tasks. It seeks to establish the most appropriate organizational relationships in order to optimize effectiveness with given numbers and types of employees, facilities, resources, equipment, and stated tasks.

As noted, tactical structuring of the organization is the dominant approach for operational-level work. In these kinds of jobs there are orders to be completed, bills to be paid, material to be stored, and other very concrete and identifiable tasks that need to be accomplished. Tactical organizational structuring becomes less relevant as one goes through successively higher levels of the company hierarchy, and as one examines more and more that part of the organization dominated by knowledge workers rather than operational workers. It is in this sense that tactical organizational structuring is essentially a bottom-up activity. The very lowest level and then the next higher level are not really examined sequentially. Here "bottom level" refers to those areas of the organization that are structured by somewhat unique and distinct types of methodology and technology, and which to a very large extent are independent of the organizational thinking at higher levels of the organization.

Essentially, tactical organizational structuring technology utilizes the knowledge and technology of the methods engineer. At these levels, work to be done is quite concrete and identifiable and includes methods engineering techniques of determining the right methods of work, the correct work flow, and the appropriate positioning and interrelationship between work units. In one sense, tactical organizational structuring is like fitting pieces of a jigsaw puzzle together. There isn't one right way, but there are a number of ways in which employees and groups work more effectively together and thereby have a resulting higher productivity.

Tactical or operational organizational structuring to a very large degree represents design of the job and the work, and the fitting of employees to these jobs and to this work. As different people succeed in jobs, they do the same work and relate to others in essentially the same way. It is a very impersonal relationship—and frequently too impersonal. It considers first and almost exclusively the equipment and materials available to do the work, and the work to be done. Employees must then be fitted to that work and trained to do the work as prescribed.

Operational organization structuring can be usually directly left to supervisory management persons. They may be required and expected to use staff expertise. But the critical knowledge in tactical organizational structure is the work to be done and how facilities must be properly utilized. It is the direct supervisor who knows this best, and who is in fact accountable for getting work done. Companies have had success by periodically having impartial teams of experts and technical specialists do tactical organizational structuring studies. These people have experience and bring in specialized knowledge, techniques, or tactics for getting such work done. Companies that undertake such tactical organizational studies have found that the recommended changes must be implemented through line supervisors and maintained by them. Therefore, they should have a very major say, if not the final say, in just what results from such studies and special projects.

Operational or tactical organizational structuring in a typical industrial company affects the working relationship of between two-thirds and three-quarters of all employees. While it may be the least glamorous part of organizational structuring and the least written about in major business journals, it affects the productivity of the greatest number of employees. Furthermore, their work is clearly defined and the methods of performing it are also clear if not obvious. Bottom-level structuring therefore affects those where productivity, as opposed to productiveness, is the critial question.

Tactical organizational structuring is therefore a critical element of organizational thinking as far as employee productivity is concerned. Fortunately, it is an area where companies have the greatest amount of operational knowledge and by far the greatest amount of experience, where information and experience is available, and where companies know how to do the job.

Strategic Organizational Structuring

The second basic view or approach toward organizational structuring is strategic and top-down in nature. It involves how the overall business itself, rather than its component pieces, should be fitted together. It represents an organizational overview of the business. Strategic organizational structuring literally starts at the top of the organization and works sequentially through successively lower levels.

It starts by identifying what the chief executive officer or those in the office of the chief executive office can uniquely do, as contrasted with what they can do better than anyone else. The first step is to determine, therefore, what the chief executive officer will do. Having done this, then necessarily everything else will be the responsibility of those reporting to the chief executive officer. At the second level, therefore, the task is to sort out residue responsibilities and establish both the numbers of positions and the types of positions necessary to cover these areas of accountability. When this has been completed, then the next sequential level is examined in the same manner.

In a typical industrial organization, strategic organizational structuring covers only four or five levels of organization in an extremely large business; three or four levels in the billion-dollar industrial company; and as little as two organizational levels in moderate-size industrial companies at the bottom of the *Fortune* 1000 list. Strategic organizational structuring seldom applies in the industrial company to more than 5 percent of the total company census.

In nonindustrial organizations, the number of organizational levels where strategic organization thinking and practices are relevant is far greater. In the medical and clinical departments of a hospital that is only half the size of the smallest *Fortune* 1000 company, the number of organizational levels would be four to six. The same is true of a large law firm, or a public accounting firm. In some very large utilities, on the other hand, the number of levels covered would be two.

In the strategic organizational approach there are three basic inputs. The first is the basic operating and economic characteristics of the company, and what have been called the "critical success" areas. An understanding of what is really critical as well as what is really important or urgent is essential. This work requires an understanding of the business or businesses the company is in, and necessarily the businesses that it is *not* in. It also involves how different segments of the business interrelate and how they impact each other.

The second basic input involves the strategic plans of the company. This requires an understanding of the near-term and short-term objectives of the firm, the "milestones" of accomplishments necessary to reach those goals, and key problem areas in the future. Such areas are the foci of top management, and organization structure at the top must facilitate solutions applicable to them.

Thirdly, and very important, strategic organizational structuring requires an understanding of the skills of key people. In this category, organization is determined to a large extent by the philosophy of engineering jobs to people rather than people to jobs. Aside from the questions of what can be done uniquely by the head of the company and by other key executives, very much of the rest of the organizational structuring and the assignment of accountabilities must consider the particular backgrounds and skills of the individuals involved. At this level, therefore, almost by definition, the organization changes significantly whenever there is a change of personnel in key positions.

Strategic organizational structuring does not, therefore, apply many of the traditional organizational technologies. Basic understanding of that business, familiarization with the firm's strategic plans, and perception of the skills and abilities of key people comprise the elements of structuring. Aside from these tools, it is very much a matter of logically subdividing the overall enterprise. In this respect there are many possibilities, and the art of strategic organizational structuring is to establish from among a number of logical subdivisions those that best fit the business and which utilize the skills and knowledge of the key executives.

As mentioned before, executive functions involve productiveness rather than productivity, structuring the organization as a vehicle through which the proper and important things are done. Once these are firmed up, then key executives see that they are done efficiently. Of course, this influences the overall game plan and direction for the whole corporation and its supporting organization. It therefore has a leverage impact upon the effectiveness and productivity of all employees throughout the organization.

External Positioning

Enterprises do not exist as isolated entities. They exist to accomplish specific objectives that ultimately relate to an external environment. Therefore, organizational structuring must also address itself to establishing a structure that promotes and encourages compatible working relations with the outside environment. In effect, therefore, organizational structuring must be designed not only to optimize the productivity of people working effectively together within the organization, but also to promote effective working relationships with those outside the company.

Generally, the principal external positioning must be focused on customers. This merely reflects what is obvious: most businesses are in fact, or should be, essentially structured to serve their customers and be responsive to their customers' needs. But there are other external relationships that must be considered in organizational structuring. These include the government and the community. Generally, these can be dealt with by appendages to the organization. An essential element of organizational structure with respect to external environment is the marketing facility.

This external organizational positioning with the outside world occurs approximately in the middle of the organization. Obviously, it centers in the field sales organization—if there is one—either the individual salesman or the sales supervisor. The points of interface with the outside world are located in a number of internal areas, not just the sales activity. For instance, the engineering department in some firms works with customers to design products specifically adapted to those customers' needs. The external organizational focus is typically concentrated in middle-level management.

These areas of direct interface with the outside world are the focal points for positioning the organization to best accomodate its marketing needs. How these areas work, not only with the customers but with each other internal unit, is the primary key to the success of the enterprise. This dimension of organization may detract from productivity or add to it, depending upon what is required for marketing success. Either way, the external structuring of the organization is essential for enterprise success.

If there is a particular organizational technology that applies to external organizational positioning, it is a very pragmatic one. It simply involves an identification of what work is done in these areas that have the primary market impact, how that work is currently performed, and how it might be done more effectively. This is a very pragmatic organizational approach. It has some application at every level of the organization, but it is particularly useful in the area of external strategic positioning.

The first task of pragmatic organizational analysis is to simply identify exactly *what* is done—not what needs to be done, but what is in fact done. The second step is to determine *how* that work is being done, and what the results are, not only in terms of internalized company measures, such as efficiency and control of costs, but also from the customers' viewpoint. What is now done must then be reexamined primarily by those close to the scene and directly involved in the work. Out of such review comes ideas for how it may be done better.

Human Resources Management Structuring

The fourth approach or focal point in organizational structuring considers the lowest level at which personnel management decisions can be made effectively. Increasingly, effective personnel programs and practices require "human resources organization units." These must include a sufficient number of employees to make certain types of personnel policies and procedures practical. An example would be salary-increase budgets. Each unit must also be of a size and nature so that its supervisor is likely to allocate a sufficient amount of time so that human resources become a significant part of the management job. There are other requirements for a "personnel management unit," not the least of which is that its leader should be of high enough level to be delegated responsibility and authority commensurate with the importance and complexity of the area.

Frequently the personnel management unit will be the same as an organizational unit, say, the general foreman of the assembly department. Typically he will *not* be at the lowest level of supervision, such as foreman or assistant foreman. Quite often a number of units will have to be combined and the head of all these units will become the personnel unit head, without changing other organizational responsibilities of the units involved. In small divisions, the division manager may be the logical personnel unit head.

There are occasions when no existing unit can logically be a personnel unit. In these cases the organization must be modified. Thus, the approach toward human resources management organization is more than an identification process. It may be a determining factor in structuring parts of the organization. It is one important new approach to organization structuring, and is a critical element of improved management of human resources.

So much of what has been identified, and what will be identified, and which is required for improving employee productivity through more effective utilization of human resources, must necessarily be done by the supervisor. The list of these activities is very long, and includes complex matters that require knowledgeable and experienced managers who have considerable authority in carrying out these areas of responsibilities.

Top executives cannot fill these responsibilities because they simply do not know enough about the specifics of operations or people involved. Neither do many of the so-called first-level supervisors, those who oversee operations employees, have the knowledge or qualifications to carry out such activities. Managers at intermediate levels must usually be delegated such responsibilities.

The personnel unit manager approach is a new dimension of organizational structuring. It necessarily means the establishment of a multiple organization in even the most traditional type of businesses. The alternatives are to have successive reviews of personnel decisions by those higher in the organization, and/or procedures and institutionalized practices that provide simplistic, multiple-choice type answers to complex human resources man-

Figure 4. Organizational structure of the human resources unit.

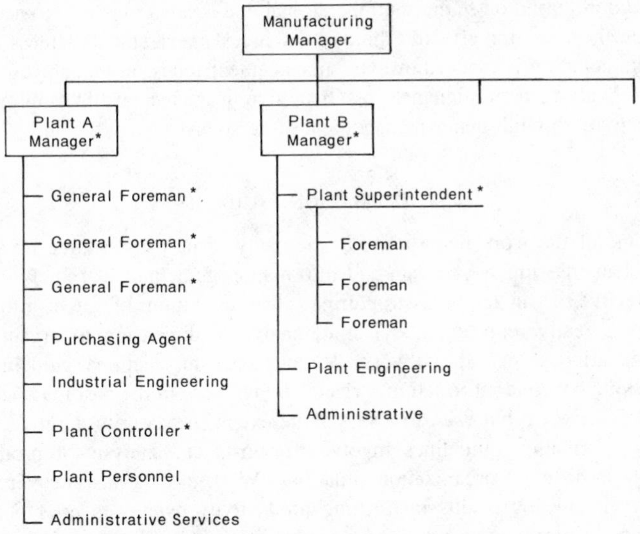

```
                        ┌─────────────────┐
                        │  Manufacturing  │
                        │     Manager     │
                        └─────────────────┘

   ┌──────────────┐           ┌──────────────┐
   │   Plant A    │           │   Plant B    │
   │   Manager*   │           │   Manager*   │
   └──────────────┘           └──────────────┘

   — General Foreman*          — Plant Superintendent*

   — General Foreman*             — Foreman

   — General Foreman*             — Foreman

   — Purchasing Agent             — Foreman

   — Industrial Engineering    — Plant Engineering

   — Plant Controller*         — Administrative

   — Plant Personnel

   — Administrative Services
```

*Human Resources Unit Managers.

agement questions. Neither is satisfactory as a method of improving employee productivity by better human resources management.

The unit supervisors for personnel management will vary a great deal between organizations and within organizations. In the manufacturing organization of a division, as illustrated in Figure 4, this unit manager may be a general foreman in some areas, the plant superintendent, or the plant manager. In some cases the unit manager might be a line foreman, but the scope and responsibilities of this management role would very likely be far greater than those usually associated with the foreman's position.

Generally, the three levels of human resources line management are unit manager, review management, and general management. In the same organization there may be from three to as many as a dozen operational organization levels, with the most likely number ranging from six to eight. This means that the reviewing level of human resources management may typically have overview of a dozen unit managers.

Identification of managers in the human-resources management organizational structure is a function of such things as the number of employees, level of employees, functional areas of work involved, physical location of employees, and existence of bargaining units. These are very different from the factors considered in operational, strategic, or external organizational structuring. They lead to a very complex human resources line-management organization with problems that are usually solved by modification of organization, based on traditional operational and strategic factors, to accommodate the need for effective human resources management. Unless this accommodation is made, however, management focus on human resources is not likely to be sufficient to result in significant increase in employee productivity through better management of personnel.

INFORMATION GUIDELINES

Some of the work being done in the study of human-resource information systems has uncovered data and information guidelines extremely useful in effective organizational structuring. The evolution of such information inputs really represent a dynamic, analytical dimension to organizational structuring, thinking, and work. Without these informational guidelines, and lacking concrete information, organizational work in the past may have been very analytical but was, to a very large extent, necessarily intuitive.

Information guidelines involve, for instance, analysis of productivity data in different organization situations. Work to date has uncovered some very interesting results in tracking productivity over even brief periods of time. In these cases, when an organizational change was made to increase productivity, the actual effects were measurable and the results have been most instructive. In one case, productivity did increase significantly when the organizational change was designed to improve work effectiveness. In two cases, however, productivity actually decreased significantly. In the others, the results were not significant enough to draw any conclusions.

Productivity data have also been useful in situations where organizational structure consists of a number of similar entities throughout an enterprise. Examples would be the branch offices in a machinery firm or the regions in a retail organization. In these cases productivity measures in all units provided some very valuable insights into the effectiveness of different organizational structures. By actually tracking productivity in different structures with similar operations sufficient analytic input was obtained to determine which organizational structures were most effective.

Another type of information input is how "similar" firms are organized. Here, again, the peer comparison group is critical and its characteristics must indeed be similar. This approach provides practical alternatives for the firm in its organizational work. When this knowledge is complemented by insights into *why* different organizational structures evolved in different firms, it is extremely useful. It's even more useful, of course, if there is also some additional insight into how different structures in these organizations do in fact work.

The number of organizational levels is another information input that can be very useful and instructive information. Whether or not the number of organizational levels are increasing or decreasing over a period of time can be even more instructive. Finally, comparison of the number of levels in peer-group firms is basic information input to organizational structuring work.

Another example of information guidelines is the ratio of supervised to supervisory employees. One firm found, for instance, that among exempt employees this ratio was less than three. Again, historic trends and peer-company comparisons can be very helpful guidelines. Where practical, internal comparisons are also useful. All such information inputs are really part of a human-resource information system that contributes to sounder management decisions in the area of human resources.

THE BUSINESS UNIT ORGANIZATIONAL CONCEPT

The business unit organizational concept emerged because many companies were operating in a number of discrete business areas, each of which required different management focus, business practices, and managerial style. The concept has been extended beyond this to define differing types of separate businesses, based upon the relative uniqueness, need for differing practices, and relative independence of the business unit. It has also been extended to organizational units that are not conceived as "businesses." The application of the business-unit organization concept is a key concept in many contemporary enterprises.

Increasingly, as businesses grow and become more diverse in their operations, and as they involve more and more technology, the executive management focus must be on criteria and overall performance measurement by units rather than on operation analysis or individual performance within the units. Therefore, the business-unit organizational concept has grown over the years from an accommodation to the realities of multiple business operations to a management technique or style that is more compatible with the complex multiactivity characteristic of the modern enterprise.

This concept has major relevance to fuller utilization of human resources. It has already been noted that techniques for increasing effectiveness of employee work must be managed at the firm level. Industrial or governmental groups can only observe and influence, for better or for worse, the levels of employee productivity. In a strategic sense, general management of each enterprise determines employee productivity, but in an operational sense, managers far down in the organization manage day-by-day employee productivity. The business-unit organizational concept, the adoption of personnel units in organizational structuring, and the emergence of delegative management (to be considered in Chapter 9) are all major influences on how well the job of operational productivity is carried out.

Generally, the categories included in the business organization unit concept are:

Operating companies
Business divisions
Profit centers
Operating units

Operating Companies

An operating company is a whole business in the sense that one can first answer the basic question of what business it is in. One can also apply the basic strategic planning processes and identify vulnerabilities and opportunities throughout the business, develop a strategic plan for accomplishment of business growth, and take specific action steps to achieve these objectives. The operating company as a whole business is well enough defined so that future emerging environmental factors can be evaluated for the purpose of identifying long-term business opportunities.

An organization entity is an operating company, or a whole business, only if it commands and controls all its own resources. It must have not only direct control of production, product development, and marketing, but it must also have completely organized and relatively independent staff services in such fields as personnel, law, and finance. Inevitably, there is a general management executive who truly manages that operating company in the executive management sense.

Operating companies have a high degree of independence within the overall corporate environment. They are not dependent, for instance, upon the operation of other units of the corporation for the achievement of their own objectives. Nor are they dependent upon other operating units for their raw materials or supplies. Generally, their sales may not be derived from the demand created by sales made in other business units of the parent corporation. The operating company is obviously not totally independent of the corporate office. It is subject to general policies, strategies, and guidelines originating in the corporate office. It usually must depend on capital allocations from the parent corporation, and must accept general management direction, and control and staff guidance.

Business Divisions

The business division fails to meet the criteria for an operating company in a number of significant respects. For one thing, while the business division must have control of production, product development, and marketing, it usually does not have primary control of staff services. In finance, for instance, the corporate organization does far more than set a chart of accounts, allocate funds, render advice for the corporate office, and audit. It has direct overview of controllership and accounting functions as well as auditing. Frequently, while the business division is independent of other businesses for its raw materials or supplies, some of its customers are also customers of other corporate units, so that a joint effort must sometimes be made or some of its sales must be made in conjunction with the activities of one or more other units in the corporation.

Many of the decisions of the division are interwoven with the decisions of the corporate office and/or other divisions. The corporate office may "orchestrate," for instance, the advertising budgets between divisions after budgets have been set. Or it may have direct accountability for such things as patents. The business division will frequently have common customers as well as an interdependent distributive system. Therefore, in these operating respects, the business division is not independent in critical decision areas but must make these decisions jointly with other business units or have these decisions determined by the corporate office.

Profit Center

Profit centers have variously been referred to as *business result* areas or departments. They fail to meet in a number of ways the characteristics of the business division. The actual operations of a profit center may vary a great deal, but the only thing that is a "given" is that each profit center produces a profit-and-loss statement that is in keeping with accounting practice. Using this statement, the company can identify the income it has derived from its operation and can identify expenses associated with it. Generally, however, the company does not have an independent balance-sheet accounting for the profit center.

Frequently, profit centers are really production or marketing activities. They may have some supportive staff and they may also have either control or a heavy degree of influence on products that are developed. Essentially, however, they control the profit-and-loss aspects of their operations, customer relations, or actual production and distribution of products.

Operating Units

These units are not amenable to profit-and-loss accounting. They are simply operating units where some statistical measure of performance can be established and where identifiable groups of people work together for the achievement of established goals. An operating unit may be a warehouse or a production department within a plant. Operating units have even been established for such areas as accounts payable or receivable, credit and collections, quality control, and computer operations. In an organizational structure set up along operating unit lines, the only characteristic necessary for its classification is that management can identify the unit and define it. Thus, operating groups can set performance criteria for the unit as a whole and measure accomplishments against those criteria. They can establish operational goals or objectives for the units and measure or judge progress against these goals.

ORGANIZATIONAL THEORIES

It has been said that just about all organizational dogma that existed prior to the 1950s have little relevance to organizational structuring in businesses today. The organizational principles and theories that existed and were applied prior to the 1950s may have had relevance then, but they don't apply very well to most firms today. Such basic yardsticks as span of control have had to be modified, not only because of the changing nature of enterprises, but also because of modern management methodology. Such long-cherished concepts as line-and-staff definitions simply do not exist in modern business. New basic concepts and approaches to organizational structuring, some of which have been identified, are emerging. As each of these new concepts evolve and are applied, other ideas and concepts surface and modify or support them.

It is not the purpose here to deal in great detail with organizational techniques and practices. It is the fundamentals of organizational structuring and its impact on productivity which have main relevance to better human resources management. Many companies have, however, had their organizations handicapped by the continuing application of old techniques that are no longer useful. Others, in the light of current needs and opportunities, have perhaps not been willing enough to deploy the resources or to initiate the newer, innovative organizational techniques that are needed to structure an organization so as to enhance and promote greater employee work effectiveness. Therefore, to provide some basis for comparison, some of the principal traditional organizational techniques and some of those that have emerged will be reviewed.

Span of Control

The principle affecting span of control is an example of organizational philosophy that has necessarily undergone great modification in the past 20 years because of the changing nature of business enterprises. Rules of thumb that existed not very long ago indicated that a manager could not really maintain effective supervision over more than six to eight persons. This guideline is no longer appropriate, and the reasons and rationale that led to such a conclusion are not relevant to the typical business of today.

Span of control today can vary appropriately from as few as 4 to as many as 24 employees. Just what the correct span of control should be is not a numerical question at all. It depends upon various factors: how much professional work or administrative work the manager must personally perform; the degree to which the supervisor must get involved in work in order to manage effectively; the type and diversity of technologies that are managed; the diversity of positions that are supervised; the number of relationships, other than supervisor-subordinate relationships, which the supervisor must maintain on a regular and continuing basis.

Single Reporting Relationships

One of the dogmas of organization, and one which is inherently suggested in all organizational charting, is that one person should have only one supervisor. Among exempt employees an individual typically has reporting relationships with a number of individuals. It is still true that for administrative persons, he must have a single identifiable reporting relationship—in effect, the business version of the "homeroom teacher."

A plant superintendent is an example. He must first have a reporting relationship directly to a plant manager, but he also receives very strong guidance, direction, and control from individuals such as the industrial engineering manager, the quality control manager, the labor relations manager, the personnel director, and a number of others. An actual analysis of some organizations suggests that while there are organizational lines of administrative reporting relationships, most exempt employees and many nonexempt employees report in a meaningful way to at least three persons.

Chain of Command

Traditional organizational precepts require each employee to follow the organization lines almost as though they were road maps. In theory, this means that the plant manager doesn't talk to a foreman, but relays his messages down the line. If a manager has a difference with an employee in another unit he is supposed to follow the prescribed organizational route. In today's complex organization, the enterprise cannot afford the time nor tolerate the time lag inherent in such procedures. A new ritual and protocol has emerged in order to have an effective and productive work force.

Line and Staff

For many years there have been very neat and precise definitions of line work and staff work. In the literature of business these words still are used to suggest distinct and separate types of activities. As a practical matter, however, there are four very identifiably different types of staff positions. Staff in the traditional advisory and informational sense occupies a minimum of nonline management positions in today's organization. Far more prevalent is a staff job that does some advising and information giving, and also has some direct areas of accountabilities of its own. An example would be the labor relations manager who has direct accountablity for the terms and conditions of the labor relations contract. There are others in staff-type positions, such as tax managers, who are actually carrying an area of business for the firm. The jobs they hold are far more like traditional line positions than traditional staff positions.

Matrix Organizations

As a practical matter the typical company is a multiplicity of organizations, one superposed upon the other. For example, a technically oriented company might have as its basic organization a functional line/staff grouping in the main area of its business. Superposed on this, however, and including some of the same people, would be an organization concerned with marketing of special products. Superposed on both of these levels may be an organization concerned with certain research and development activities. Finally, there may be a number of project-oriented organizations. Most companies today have at least two or three organizations superposed one on the other.

Project Organization

Project-type organization clusters key employees around specific objectives or projects. A technically oriented company may have a separate organization for each major program or project. Project organizations are typical of professional businesses; they are becoming more and more prevalent in staff organizations and, in some instances, line operations of industrial firms.

ORGANIZATION AND PRODUCTIVITY

No study known to the author measures the impact of organization on productivity or provides any known basis for such measurement. This is another of the many clear needs for developing human resources information for the purposes of information analysis and managerial planning, control, and decision making. It's difficult to imagine, however, any quarrel with the assumption that organization, the basis upon which people work together, has to be a major determinant of the level of employee productivity. Nor can there be much doubt that, until the past few years, the human resources management aspect of employee productivity has not been factored into organizational structuring.

Many firms struggle with organizational structure and organization analyses that are simply outdated and not suitable to the contemporary firm, which is complex, technology oriented, and multifaceted. Effectiveness of the enterprise is impeded by applying obsolete analytical methods to modern systems. The organizational structure of the modern enterprise must be better geared to facilitate the human resources management job, and this is particularly true when future productivity increases become more and more dependent on the effective management of these resources.

This chapter has reported the state-of-the-art of current organization work, which considers full utilization of the human assets of the business. Organizational structuring in complex businesses is inherently complicated, and the additional requirement of structuring to increase productivity makes it one of the more difficult managerial undertakings. Unless organizations utilize the new concepts of organizational structuring, they will lose a major opportunity to increase employee productivity.

The question of who manages organizational staff work is frequently asked. There was a time when a specialist in the field occupied himself only with designing and recommending organization structures, but in today's business world that is only a small part of the job. Within the various areas of focus, special consideration must be given to operational knowledge, human resources, and emerging technologies. It's difficult to conceive of any individual or group who could manage these independent elements of organizational structuring. The most the staff can do is to provide information input and advice, and otherwise play the role of "general contractor," leaving top level management as the decision maker.

9

Delegative Management

Delegative management is more a management style than a personnel technique. It is a managerial style specifically designed to increase the effectiveness of work. It essentially promotes greater productivity by removing restrictive or inefficient practices; by letting the best qualified person do the work; and by having work done at the lowest level in the organization where it can be effectively performed.

Obviously, managerial style or the practice of management must be tailored to fit many enterprise needs. These include the basic characteristics of the business and the problems and opportunities, both short term and long term, which confront an enterprise at any given time. It would be unrealistic, therefore, to think that a company would adopt a managerial style (and the systems, techniques, and practices that go with it) solely to improve or to optimize employee effectiveness. Yet, this is the purpose of the delegative management approach. It establishes *one* basic objective—optimum employee effectiveness to increase productivity.

DELEGATIVE MANAGEMENT DEFINED

In very general terms, delegative management sets policies, establishes objectives, articulates the criteria for measuring performance, sets the standards of performance expected, and establishes other types of guidelines and directives. Within these areas, it not only permits individuals and groups to do the work in their own way, but expects those accountable for the work to continuously devise special methods and procedures that improve the effectiveness of work.

This is a positive rather than a passive managerial style. It consciously sets policies that people can follow; it works to get people throughout the organization to accept responsibility not only by permitting them to "do their own thing" but also by expecting them to do so. Thus, it develops in people a high degree of willingness to accept responsibility.

Delegative management works to push work down in the organization where it can be done at the lowest level and where the details of operations are best known. It expects people to innovate and continuously find better ways to operate. This includes better ways to increase the effectiveness of work done by subordinates.

The focus in this managerial style is delegation of *authority*, as contrasted with delegation of responsibility or the fuzzy notion of accountability. The emphasis is not on what employees may do, but what they should do. Work is delegated to individuals rather than groups. Even when work must be done by a group, success is not credited to the group but to every member of it. Each member must strive to make every other member effective.

Clearly, delegative management does not lend itself to a neat, precise definition. It is an intangible, a way of work. In order to clarify what it *is*, it is useful to state what the subject *is not*. Delegative management is not anarchy. Individuals or groups do not select their goals, nor do they set policies by cases or precedents. Their latitude of action is within the framework of policies and guidelines; they must follow the game plan. There is nothing *laissez faire* about delegative management. It surely does not let people alone; it lets them do their work, but it expects them to do it well. Committees and assistants are rarities where delegative management exists. Committees *work;* and each member has an assignment. Committees function more like a project group than a typical committee. Assistants, where they exist, are part of a working team. For instance, a technician works with a design engineer.

Delegative management is not intended to make people happier or to develop a warm, friendly feeling among employees. Rather, its purpose is to give people control of their work and latitude of action with respect to the important elements of their work. Some behavioral scientists believe that this kind of environment indeed enhances the climate of work and provides for greater human satisfaction. That would certainly be a cherished by-product, but the objective of delegative management is to let its best qualified people design the methods as well as apply them. Within a structure of policies, guidelines, and controls, delegative management permits, encourages, and expects individuals and supervisors deep in the organization to plan and carry out their work with a high degree of self-supervision.

The organization that adopts this type of management has its rules, practices, and procedures. Companies moving in the direction of delegative management find they have fewer rules, but they do have rules. Requirements that accompany delegation tend to be confined to really critical issues and subjects, but within these boundaries they are vigorously enforced.

The Evolution of Delegative Management

Delegative management is not really a new idea, nor is it a discovery. In many ways it is the culmination of business ideas, managerial styles, and business experimentation over the past 40 years. It is, by and large, the logical result of experiences brought to a logical conclusion and precipitated in many businesses today by the urgency of increasing employee productivity by better management of human resources.

The history of employee relations has been a parade of human relations concepts and ideas over the past 40 years. One of the first of the new technologies in effectively managing human resources within the context of the contemporary business model was participative management. Oversimplified, the ideas of participative management were to permit those who do the work to actually participate in a meaningful, authoritative way in the determination of how the work should be done. This is, of course, very close to the core idea of delegative management, but delegative management simply goes further—it *expects* people to determine practices.

Viewed with the wisdom of hindsight, participative management had much to recommend it, but it failed and was soon discarded. Students of human resources management ascribe its failure primarily to the fact that it became a humanist device rather than a business practice. In fact, participative management became a social philosophy, preoccupied with enriching employees' work lives and making them happy. The results were higher costs and counterproductive incentives.

The techniques and procedures of participative management also became distorted. For instance, many of the procedures encouraged interference with the work of others, with some employees telling other employees how to do their work. It also involved techniques and methods of employee relations that may have validity in a clinical psychological environment but which did not work in the real world of business. For instance, participative management assumed that ''peer group pressure'' somehow contributed to people's ''shaping up.'' But, of course, people who do not respond well to supervisory pressure are not likely to respond well to peer-group pressure, and therefore the very process of peer-group pressure contributed to discord in many organizations.

Next came the X and Y theories of management. These represented an elaborate set of theories, ideas, practices, and case studies which aimed at striking a balance between management of things and management of people. Without seeming to oversimplify what were quite complex and very thoughtful investigations, one facet of these exercises aimed at a managerial style that explored and utilized the employees' interests, abilities, and inclinations.

More recently, organizational development has been the fad. This approach also recognized the inherent virtue of letting the best qualified person do the work and determine the work methods. Organizational development has largely failed because it retains the participative practices and the humanist views that caused participative management to fail. Furthermore, it has focused on the narrow issue of productivity based upon interpersonal and intergroup relationships.

Job enrichment is the most recent entrant in the parade of managerial development panaceas. It recognizes the desirability of direct worker involvement in determining how work should best be done. There is a compelling need for job enrichment, due partly to the fact that work has become so methodized and automated that it involves repetitive tasks that human beings cannot perform over a long period of time. Job enrichment also involves changing jobs to more fully utilize human talent, and in some cases this includes structuring work to include activities formerly done by higher-level persons and development of the most effective work methods. Job enrichment, however, is also now being permeated by humanist attitudes—jobs are being enriched because people will somehow enjoy their work life more. Once again a good idea is being warped in an attempt to gain psychological values and a more desirable social system. When this occurs, productivity frequently declines.

Open systems of management is another emerging managerial style which parallels the ideas of delegative management, but incorporates some of the concepts of participative management. Essentially, in open systems, the workers have as part of their individual and collective job the development of methods of work and working relationships. In fact, workers have a very real say in determining what the jobs are. Management still manages in terms of prescribing production requirements, purchase of equipment materials and supplies, and reviewing worker decisions. A very large part of the first-level supervisory job has, however, been delegated to the workers in an open-systems operation.

Common to all these theories and some lesser personnel practices is one underlying idea—the recognition that an essential element of human resources management is to have employees who do the work be a meaningful part of structuring the work. The delegative management process attempts to carry this to a new frontier of effectiveness, thus benefiting by the mistakes of the past.

ESSENTIALS OF DELEGATIVE MANAGEMENT

Businessmen have long talked about and practiced delegation. Most businessmen are inclined to delegate responsibility. Over the years, much has been learned about what delegation is and how it works. Certainly, one of the things learned is that, in most cases, responsibility must be matched by authority and latitude of action. Delegative management, however, accepts these lessons and attempts to extend them considerably. In theory, the essential meaning of delegation is that an employee has a task to perform and should handle it efficiently; that the employee has things to do and should do them properly. But all too often, it has also meant that employees must do tasks in a way that reflects the practices, thinking or rules of others.

As practiced in many large industrial and financial corporations, delegation has meant that an individual or group has been assigned a task or project, given very specific instructions in terms of objectives and milestones, and then must report back frequently and in detail. A very large and successful firm in the building materials industry got high marks in a leading business journal for the degree to which it delegated. Top management, however, when talking candidly, described the notion of "delegation" as ". . . we delegate a lot but follow very closely," and added ". . . our key people are free to take action but if it involves anything important, they are well advised to check with us first." These candid statements very accurately and realistically describe the real degree of delegation that exists in most "entrepreneurial" companies at this time.

All too often, employees are delegated authority but must check frequently. Authority, too, often means the freedom to do the right thing in a predetermined way, but freedom for just about everything is "subject to review." Actually, delegation of authority really means the right to do the right things in an approved way only.

The very low ratio of supervised to supervisory employees which typically exists in organizations today is indicative of the degree to which authority is, in fact, *not* delegated. Where one supervisor overviews two or three business units, that supervisor must obviously be following very closely the day-to-day decisions and actions of his subordinates, or he may have a very significant amount of work which he does individually and independent of the units supervised, or he has a very easy job. The fact is that when work is widely delegated, even in highly technical work, as many as a dozen people or units can be supervised effectively.

A few detailed and extreme examples will make the point that not much authority is really delegated in many enterprises today. One need only look to a couple of major issues in salary administration. Supervisors, of course, are (on paper) responsible for the pay of subordinates. But are they really?

In most companies, pay levels are set by the personnel department. This gives the supervisor a very finite range in which he may make pay decisions. When it comes to pay increases, supervisors also have a great number of restraints, all of which may be perfectly appropriate. Added to these are constraints such as budgets and guidelines and the condition that his decision must be then "reviewed." In one large company, pay slips for exempt employees, on the average, had eight authority approval signatures. If any one of these signees disagreed with the amount of increase recommended by the supervisor, which they frequently did, the whole matter was returned to him for further consideration. In any number of areas, therefore, supervisors who have authority allegedly delegated to them must get concurrence not only from their supervisors but from a number of other persons as well.

Under delegative management, it would be more appropriate for the supervisor first of all to decide the pay-level slot appropriate to each subordinate job. The supervisor would have to do that within the established salary structure and by comparison against guidelines such as benchmark jobs identified by pay relationships in the marketplace. For each supervised job, complete authority for pay increases would be vested in the supervisor, subject only to budgets and guidelines. Payroll slips would typically have three signatures: the supervisor, a personnel staff representative, and the human resources unit manager.

The lack of sufficient authority is one of the major reasons why an alarming number of middle-level persons are considerably disenchanted with their companies and their positions. Their day-to-day experiences suggest to them that they really aren't an important part of management. They know from experience that they really do not have the necessary latitude of action to do their work properly—they feel constrained and restricted. All this contributes to a considerable degree of dissatisfaction among key middle-level people within most organizations.

In delegative management there is a "prudent man" rule associated with this style of management. The "prudent man" rule has a number of facets. For one thing, it suggests that a supervisor should not do something different for the sake of difference. It suggests that he should learn the current system before improving on practices. It suggests that he must be always alert and careful in what he does in terms of how it impacts the work of others. And the "prudent man" rule also suggests that it is part of the responsibility and authority of a supervisor to turn to staff experts for advice and guidance in what he does.

Delegation of authority must be in the context of organization needs. There must be an awareness of what needs to be done, and a willingness to structure activities to deal with the tasks at hand. The exercise of delegated authority does not encompass a selection of basic chores, nor does it allow for decisions influenced by personal inclinations. One cannot do what is interesting or fun instead of what is necessary and supportive of company objectives. One cannot do what he is good at doing or what he feels comfortable in doing when those are not the things that need doing.

In many respects, delegative management reflects the French view of the law. To the French, if the law fails to say you can't do something, then you can do it. Delegative management does not mandate that you do what your job description says, but that you do what is appropriate unless established guidelines and constraints (possibly including job descriptions) specifically say that you can't do it.

It is important to note that delegative management doesn't necessarily have anything to do with centralization or decentralization. Logically, decentralization should facilitate delegative management, which itself should transfer important authority down into the organization. Decentralization is essentially a structural or procedural action, rather than one of basic managerial style. It deals, in any event, only with the relationship between executives of top corporate management and their immediate subordinates. All too often what happens under a "decentralized" operation is that a considerable amount of authority is delegated by the chief executive officer to some of those who report to him, and very little authority passes below that level. Decentralization, therefore, has frequently been a one-step process.

Institutionalization is the antithesis of delegative management. An institutionalized operation is one in which the systems answer questions, and where, at best, decisions represent choices from among multiple answers, and where judgments are dictated by approved alternatives. Institutionalized practices are designed, at least in part, to satisfy the company's desire to have work done effectively. They attempt to establish the one right method or the proven way. But at the administrative, middle-management, supervisory, professional, and top executive levels of the business, there simply isn't one right way. Methodizing the business at these levels can only result in inefficient work, caused by application of the wrong method in most cases. But worse, it creates a climate and an environment that inhibits work effectiveness.

Delegative management in many respects has its greatest impact on middle-level employees. The chief executive officer and other key executives reporting to him typically have a great deal of latitude of action. Constraints at the top executive level are, in fact, more often imposed from outside the business. A handful of top-level executives who work together can develop a confidence in each other and a close working relationship that makes possible a highly delegative style. Businesses have come a long way in devising practices that develop and encourage delegation of authority to those immediately reporting to the chief executive officer and other clearly visible higher-level executives. It is below this point, however, where delegation hasn't been very successful.

At the other end of the organization, in operations-level jobs in the factory and office, delegative management has limited applicability. Here the constraints or "givens" inherent in the nature of the work limit the latitude of action. There are specific tasks to be done, machines to be used, procedures to be followed. The work is controlled by the input and output at the work station. For reasons such as these, the degrees to which the ideas and principles of delegative management can be applied are limited. For example, they can be applied by involving workers in developing the correct methods and procedures, but after these have been implemented, the delegative working relationship is limited.

Some company experts suggest, however, that the opportunities for determination of work methods and work decisions at lowest operational job may have more applicability than has always been assumed. There are, for instance, many cases where expert industrial engineers developed their own best method of work, and then workers improved on that method substantially. An open system of work will at least give more insight to the question of the extent to which work decisions can be delegated to operation workers and how much such delegation impacts employee productivity.

It is in the middle-level jobs, those below senior executives but above operations-level jobs, where delegative management style clearly has its greatest opportunities and potentially its greatest impact on the effectiveness of work in most companies. The jobs at these levels of the organization very much determine actual productivity levels. Facilities, management styles, organization structures, and other areas such as those covered in this book, combine to determine a *range* of productivity level. Within that range, middle-management persons actually determine actual levels of productivity. The extent to which a delegative management style will increase the effectiveness of these people in what they do has an immediate impact upon the effectiveness of operation. In turn, this upgrading of operational performance has a leveraging effect upon employee productivity overall.

Many lessons have already been learned about delegative management, and doubtlessly, a great deal more will be learned. Clearly, however, from experience gained so far, delegative management means different things at different levels of the organization, *and* for different types of jobs, *and* in different types of businesses. For top-executive positions, both line and staff, authority can be delegated almost completely within the framework of such things as:

Legal constraints
Corporate policy

> Definition of the units charter and focus
> Specific objectives and standards, short term and long term
> Financial budgets

In middle-level jobs, goals and standards need to be more specific and rigid. Delegation primarily means authority to determine one's own method of work; to develop working relationships (for example, informal organization structure); and to give feedback relating to operational needs. In operational jobs, delegation is more applicable to adoption of established methods and work systems than to the determination of such matters.

In terms of jobs, the more the work involves discrete and advanced technology, unknown to general management, the more the delegation of authority is inherently necessary. In research laboratories management, for instance, overview is largely restricted to such things as allocation of funds and determination of new product objectives. Finally, of course, some types of businesses permit greater latitude of action and can tolerate greater delegation of authority than others. A small manufacturer has more latitude than a huge one; the local department store has more latitude of action in management than the local public utility.

FACILITATING CONDITIONS

Like any business style or personnel practice, delegative management does not work equally well in every enterprise. In fact, it does not work equally well in every section of any given enterprise. There are conditions or circumstances, some of which have already been noted, which experience clearly shows facilitates or makes more practical a delegative managerial style. One of these is the nature of the company organization. Decentralized organization, or the application of the business unit concept of organization, are conditions that contribute to delegative management. Delegative management obviously also works better where workers can control what they do. It was already noted that in operations jobs—particularly where procedures, facilities, and equipment are all fixed—there is little opportunity for the application of delegative management.

Operations that involve discrete technologies, on the other hand, represent an atmosphere in which a delegative managerial style is highly favored. Jobs in which *what* is done is as important as how efficiently it is done lend themselves to this style of management. Similarly, an operation that involves a complex and difficult cycle of work, and the people involved have an understanding of the interfacing with other units or elements, also represents a condition that facilitates delegative management.

Any number of personnel policies can affect the feasibility of a delegative managerial style. For instance, a company where workers participate in a reward system that pays significant amounts for improved results favors delegation. Rapidly growing, changing, or dynamic organizations also create an environment where delegative managerial style is favored, if for no other reason than company organization is too fast moving and changing to become institutionalized.

It is interesting to note that some of the conditions that facilitate delegative management are based upon the fact that a company has relatively little choice. It must delegate either because detailed knowledge is not possessed by people higher in the organization or because other circumstances make it difficult to have anything other than a delegative managerial style.

Other circumstances favor a delegative management style: A flat organization structure almost demands a high degree of delegation. The existence of performance criteria make greater delegation more prudent. An effective system of management audits, which do not interfere with authority but monitor results, also facilitates delegation. Much the same is true of various types of human-resource information systems.

One final condition most essential to effective delegation is a willingness to let subordinates do work in their own way even if it is less effective than the supervisor's way. That isn't always easy, but of course the important thing is that the work is done well. An even more difficult thing to accept is that higher-level persons must let subordinates do the work even if they do it less well. Assume that the supervisor could and would do it better. That isn't the point. Unless the subordinate does the work, he'll never do it better. And if the supervisor does the work that could be done at lower levels, then *his* work will be done less well, or not at all.

Certain elements of the internal environment of the business also have an extremely important impact on both the feasibility and effectiveness of delegative management. For example, anarchy can result unless there is also organization discipline. Organizational discipline doesn't mean "acceptance of, or submission to, authority and control" as much as it means the development of "self-control, character, or orderliness and efficiency." * In delegative management, the latter definition applies. This, in turn implies three essential elements of self-control, character, and orderliness:

Effective management of one's own time.

Conduct consistent with policies, guidelines and whatever restrictions or constraints exist.

A willingness to follow one's leader or leaders; and an ability to *listen!*

---

* All quoted definitions in this section from *Webster's New World Dictionary of the American Language,* College Edition.

Effective delegative management also requires a climate of organizational trust in the sense that each employee has a "firm belief or confidence in the honesty, integrity, reliability, justice, etc., of another person." To the extent that we might substitute "every person" for "another person" and add "ability" to the list of attributes, this definition would be descriptive of the climate necessary for effective delegative management. Initiative, or "the characteristic of an original new idea or method, the ability to think and act without being urged, 'enterprise'," is another key characteristic of employee attitudes if delegative management is to be successful.

Another element of climate in an organization which promotes delegative management is an expectation of excellence, in the sense that excellence is defined as "the fact or condition of excelling; superiority; surpassing goodness." Finally, companies where delegative management is successful have a high degree of organizational pride. Here, the word "pride" suggests "a sense of one's own dignity or worth—'self-respect' " rather than "an over-high opinion of one's self; exaggerated self-esteem; conceit."

These personnel and organizational characteristics are essential to effective delegative management. One of the arts or skills of nurturing this managerial style involves the development of such attitudes on the part of all employees. Its ongoing administration requires the kind of leadership that implants such thinking and attitudes throughout the organization.

It takes a certain type of individual to function well in the environment of delegative management. Those selected must obviously be very responsible persons, capable of conscientious self-supervision. Those who work in such an environment must be able to manage their own time well. They must be supportive rather than competitive in their relations with associates, sometimes being generous in their time as well as reasonable in their judgments. They must also be willing to *try,* even at the risk of making mistakes. Many people have such qualities; those who don't shouldn't be working in such an environment. All the rules and procedures won't likely help the misfits very much, and will in fact impede delegation of authority to others. In essence, the staffing function must choose those with the desirable personal attributes, and screen out others less qualified.

TECHNIQUES OF DELEGATIVE MANAGEMENT

If the essential characteristics and facilitative conditions for delegative management exist to a high degree, then there is not much need for techniques or methodologies to make it successful. These characteristics and conditions are essential "condition precedences." With a large number of such elements in place, real delegation of authority will happen to a very significant extent. Without them, no combination of other techniques or practices will bring it about.

The core techniques in the application of a delegative management style involve the systems management components of productivity—particularly organizational structuring, manpower controls, and the organization and use of personnel staff. Like most styles of management, the delegative type is based fundamentally on the attitudes of top executives and how they perform their work and their expectations. No technique can ever be substituted for these fundamentals.

The specific techniques that have been applied with some success in implementing a delegative management style have largely been adaptations of business practices and techniques used in various areas and activities of the business. At present, few unique techniques specifically designed for and exclusively used for delegative management are available. Most companies that have worked in the direction of establishing this mode of management have found that sufficient progress is obtained by utilizing basic management practices and techniques already available.

For example, one simple and effective technique sometimes used is that of time analysis. This involves various techniques or procedures for recording and feeding back to people how they spend their time, what they do, how they do it, and how much time they spend in each discretely identifiable activity. Analysis of this time deployment, for example, can identify major pieces of work or activities that can be more effectively carried out at a lower level in the organization. Simply the feedback of this information is usually sufficient to accomplish the desired result.

A form of job analysis has also proved useful in implementing delegative management. In this case, the analysis is applied to important, critical elements of key positions. The objective is to identify those activities of a distinctively lower value and which are not directly and inherently related to duties peculiar to that individual position. Those activities that can be disassociated are opportunities for delegation farther down the organization.

There has also been some experimentation in the use of the unit personnel-cost analysis techniques. Approximations of unit cost are established for each position in the organization. Elements of work are then analyzed to establish their values. This type of analysis also leads to identification of work that can be delegated to a lower level in the organization. Sometimes it is necessary to establish procedures and patterns of reviews to make this type of greater delegative style effective.

Delegation has the merit of potentially lowering costs while raising productivity, but it also has elements of risk. Therefore, some form of risk management analysis must be included in the work to increase the degree of delegation within an organization. Risk management in the human relations activity is its own reward in that it identifies major human resources vulnerabilities. It also facilitates delegative management by identifying those vulnerabilities associated with delegation of authority, and establishes the necessary audit and control points that minimize them. This identification process can in turn lead to practices that make even greater delegation more practical.

The art of leveraging knowledge is another example of a technique to promote delegative management. Leveraging knowledge relates to the use of high-level knowledge in a way that benefits less knowledgeable workers. The latter apply discrete and usable amounts of advanced technology in carrying out work that would otherwise have to be done by workers having higher-level knowledge. The leading tax expert in the firm, for instance, is in a position to interpret the critical and most intricate tax regulations so that he can transmit these to other tax persons throughout the organization. Thus, a limited resource, typically a high-level value resource, can be conserved while distributing its benefits in a wide range throughout the organization.

The essential step in all such procedures is to first identify the level in the organization where work is most effectively performed. Part of this analysis must, however, include time availability. Perhaps, for instance, the plant manager could perform every task of a managerial nature more effectively than anyone else, but he simply does not have the time to do all these tasks. The question then becomes which of these duties require his unique talents and which can be done by others, even though they may be done less effectively.

IMPACT ON PRODUCTIVITY

It is obviously extremely difficult to identify specific relationships between delegative management and productivity. Clearly the trade-offs involve efficiency of work, cost, and risk. Human-resource information systems have evolved crude methods of evaluating cost and productivity. The elements of risk, however, are still highly judgmental.

The data that have emerged from studies in the area of delegative management indicate what is already known. Delegating work to the level at which it can be effectively and least expensively performed must increase the effectiveness of work, or better use human resources. Data simply answer the question how much productivity is increased, or how much cost is reduced. These results must be weighed against risks and the overall result of the enterprise in terms of achieving its objectives.

Certainly, delegative management contributes to greater employee productivity by eliminating much work otherwise associated with developing procedures, rules, and practices designed to direct employees in terms of how to do work as well as what to do. It also eliminates work associated with enforcing the rules. Finally, it tends to eliminate learning time; that is, the time higher-level management or distant staff would take in a more institutionalized method of operation to learn key information and facts already known where the work is done.

Delegative management contributes to greater productivity by providing a more direct method for answering many daily operational questions. This is due to the fact that fewer persons get involved in specific decisions and actions. Table 9 illustrates the time spent on a sample of questions before and after a delegative style of management was implemented. The six cases are illustrative, but the hours expended represent actual data. The time saving, and therefore greater productivity, was leveraged in terms of payroll dollars of expense, since the review time spent was less costly than that of higher-level managers. This is a plus characteristic of the delegative managerial style.

Table 9. Cases of increased productivity under delegative management.

	Manhours of Work	
	Former Style	Delegative Style
1. Handling an employee grievance on work standards.	28	6
2. Determining annual salary increases for a group of ten employees.	19	11
3. Recruitment of office temporary typists over a six-month period in an organization of 25 workers.	62	9
4. Decision regarding the location of a company warehouse.	140	115
5. Decision with respect to a union campaign to organize technical employees.	132	52
6. Selection of point-of-sale display advertising for a single product.	96	80

There are also indirect values associated with delegative management. In some respects the delegative style simulates the environment of an entrepreneurial firm. Employees far down in the organization have an entrepreneurial attitude when they can indeed control just how their work is done and can see clear relationships between that work and overall results.

Another indirect value is that delegative management makes a firm look outward more than inward. More time is focused on marketing, customer relations, better quality, and greater responsiveness to customer service, and there is less preoccupation with administrative matters, procedures, and rules.

Above all, delegative management style indirectly promotes greater productivity because it motivates employees to excel. Employees work harder and more effectively when they have formulated their own work methods. Employees seek more productive work methods when they know that to be part of their job. Delegative management tends to promote alertness to the need for increasing productivity. Finally, it develops pride and a feeling of self-worth in people; many employees respond positively to a climate of respect and dignity.

10

Human Resources Development

Human resources development refers to all those educational, training, and developmental activities conducted by an enterprise. These activities have a definite relationship to employee productivity. If human resources development activities are not aimed at increasing the effectiveness of work, it is difficult to think of what other objectives might justify the expenditures necessary for such activities. The sole purpose of any human resources development activities is either to enhance the value of human resources assets or to make the talents and skills of people more effective in accomplishing enterprise objectives.

It would, however, be incorrect to assume that a company that has a great deal of human resources development activity, and which is itself technically sound, will necessarily achieve greater employee productivity. The effectiveness of people at work is obviously first a function of the talent and skills they bring to the job, whether they apply knowledge and skills vigorously, and whether such efforts are applied to the correct activities. Given these fundamentals, it would then be reasonably correct to assume that appropriate and needed training and development activities will enhance employee productivity up to the point of sufficiency; that is, to the point where employees have enough knowledge and skills to work at optimal efficiency.

TYPES OF HUMAN RESOURCES ACTIVITIES

Human resources development is, of course, a very broad term encompassing all activities designed to get employees to work more effectively within a given organization and with the methods, products, and people that are then within the organization. There are a considerable number and variety of training and development activities. No company could possibly utilize all the training and development programs, practices, and techniques now available. The first objective, therefore, is one of identifying needs. The second is the selection of the activities in the area of human resources development most appropriate in meeting those needs. For most companies, even needed training and development activities yield an unrealistic commitment of time and resources. This overall list must then be reviewed, priorities decided, and schedules set.

Building an effective human resources development program is made more difficult by the fact that many people in the field use the same words to mean quite different activities. There are also differences of opinions among experts as to which techniques work and how any one of them works in a given situation. There is such a variety of training and development activities that it is even difficult to have an organized way of thinking about training and development.

Except for those who are practitioners in the field, there isn't really very much value in cataloging the various types of training and development activities. Certainly, the field could benefit by more precise definitions and a standardized terminology, but again this doesn't have much to do with general management or with the subject of increasing employee productivity. For purposes such as those set forth here (developing an organized and thoughtful way of increasing the use of human resources), perhaps the most useful way to view human resources development is by first focusing on basic management practices used in training and development, and then on some of the more important and more publicized techniques of conducting these activities.

TRAINING AND DEVELOPMENT: MANAGEMENT PRACTICES

Three areas of human relations development are basic to any organized effort to increase productivity or maintain a high level of employee productivity. These areas are so firmly integrated with the managerial process that they are frequently not identified as specific training and development activities. The first of these comprises work-oriented communications. The second consists of a "training" specifically designed to give employees the information and the skills they need in order to do their job. The third is human resources development, labeled here as "operational training and development," the type of training and development that occurs during the normal course of work or as a direct result of work experience.

Communications

Communications with employees about job duties expectations, how to do their job, and other work-related information is the most elemental form of training. Work-related information obviously communicates to the employees exactly what their job is. This may or may not be a written job description. The critical thing is that employees know *what* work they are to do. Work-related instruction tells *how* to do the work. This does not necessarily mean explaining specific methods, but may be merely statements of required objectives, standards, and general guidelines.

Communications as a part of human resources development also conveys management's ideas of what is expected and of specific things that need to be accomplished. It also serves as feedback to inform employees of how well work is done, how it needs to be done better, and what areas of work need to be improved. Feedback is not dependent on formal appraisal or objective programs. In fact, even where such programs exist, communication of this type should be an ongoing part of supervision. Work communications in many cases also involve understanding of the degree of responsibility or accountability, the limitations of authority to carry out work, information about priorities, the policies of the company, and the urgency or priorities assigned to different subjects and activities.

Direct verbal or written communication is clearly the most elemental form of human resources development. When information is properly communicated, it provides the crucial knowledge an employee needs to work effectively. Effective communication is also the primary instrument in other activities designed to develop human resources. If employees do not know their jobs, the most sophisticated forms of management by objectives or the most elaborate training systems will have no impact, and may in fact detract from employee effectiveness. There isn't much point in training a person in terms of how to do his work better and more effectively unless he knows what that work is.

For most companies the greatest opportunity for increasing the effectiveness of work through more effective communications is among middle-level employees. Communications at the operations level is usually adequate because of the very nature of the work being performed. It is also usually adequate at the top of the organization, simply because of the limited numbers of people involved and their close and continuous interaction. It is at the middle-level, however, as studies have shown, that employees do not understand their jobs well, are uncertain about standards of performance, the criteria by which they are to be judged, or what they should do to improve the effectiveness of their work.

These most elemental forms of human resources development don't involve very glamorous work and generally are not much fun for those in training work. These aren't the things that are much talked about at the meetings of the National Association of Training Directors. Unfortunately, they are also not the types of activities for which people involved in training get very high marks within their own organization. But work-related communications is one of the cornerstones of effective human resources development, and it represents a very high percentage of the contribution that training and development can make to greater employee productivity.

Training

Any use of labels in the field of human resources development inevitably contributes to semantic confusion. The word "training" is used here mostly in the sense of "business education." It involves giving employees the knowledge and skills they need to do their work. Such needs are quite identifiable and specific, and usually have a high order of priority and urgency. While such distinctions are never precise, training also tends to focus on knowledge and skills necessary to do currently assigned work; "development" relates more to preparing employees for future assignments or new experiences.

All persons in a given trade or occupational category need to have certain knowledge and skills in order to be proficient. Specialized skills and knowledge may be characteristic of certain classes of jobs in a company. As a result, training is one area of personnel administration where the use of preprogrammed courses of instruction are useful and appropriate. There are many examples of such training courses.

Precedents and available programs for training operational-level persons are numerous, either in trade or occupational groups or in specific office or factory job categories. These include available programs for factory machine operators, assemblymen, inspectors, and other production workers; programs for skilled tradesmen; programs for office workers, from file clerks to secretaries; and courses of instruction for such key technicians as computer programmers and draftsmen. These courses are well developed and are used widely. Many are available to all firms.

Experience has indicated that preprogrammed instruction for middle-level people can also be extremely useful. For example, a number of supervisory training programs have been developed for application in a wide variety of company situations. Such programs are possible because there are certain core skills and core areas of knowledge that all supervisors must possess in order to do their jobs effectively. All supervisors, for instance, make decisions. There is a methodology and basic skill in effective decision making, and a one-day training session has proved to be very effective in increasing the decision-making skills of first-level and intermediate-level supervisory personnel.

Interviewing skills are also inherent in the work of supervisory people, who may conduct hiring and internal selection interviews. Moreover, they are constantly interviewing employees with respect to grievances, questions, or work appraisals. A one-day preprogrammed session has been most effective in increasing the basic interviewing skills of supervisory people; in this instance, through the use of tape-recorded interviews that illustrate the basic principles and techniques of effective interviewing. Every supervisor also has to have skills in such activities as appraisal, communication, equal employment opportunity (EEO) compliance, pay decisions, and grievance handling. Here, again, one-day sessions on supervisory skill development, which have broad applicability in many fields, have been developed and can be adapted to specific company situations.

Training in all these areas enhances the quality of supervision. Quality of supervision, particularly at the personnel-management unit level identified in Chapter 8, is very critical to effective management of human resources. Training in core areas of knowledge and skills is essential for most firms in developing a high quality of supervision.

A limited number of these supervisory skill sessions, usually six or eight, are generally sufficient to summarize the basic core skills and knowledge needed by supervisory people. By using already developed sessions, a company benefits by spreading the considerable developmental cost, by using proven communication techniques and teaching methods, and by utilizing a great deal of accumulated experience and feedback from a wide variety of sources. Once the basic course is given refresher sessions need to be conducted only about every two to four years. This means that total core skill and knowledge training need involve, on the average, only three mandays of time for each supervisor per year.

Another important feature of training sessions and training activities as defined here is that results are measurable. Frequently, the results of training sessions can be measured by immediate change, by production indexes, by observed differences in work output or behavior, and frequently by testing. In this area, therefore, there is a way of measuring the results of training, the investment in training, and the return on such investment. These activities can therefore be treated like any normal business investment expenditure.

Operational Training and Development

Operational training and development is difficult to define. It covers the day-to-day teaching of fundamental knowledge and skills, and how to apply them to work effectively. It also includes training and development that reflect learning from actual experience. Such activities have not been treated as discrete areas of activity in human resources development. However, a great deal of the training and development that really occurs in a company is done in the normal course of the operations of the company.

Work-related communications has been described as a basic training activity. Any periodic or formal communication is supplemented, refined, and clarified in the course of day-to-day operations and events. A formal communication, such as a job description, represents only the framework or general guideline in terms of each employee's duties and responsibilities. These must be explained, amplified, and related to specific activities in the course of operations. These daily communications about duties become the body and substance of understanding of jobs. Therefore, operational training and development (OTD) is the essence of work communications, which in turn (as already noted) is a basic part or prerequisite of effective human resources development.

Such programs as appraisal, management by objectives, and standard setting are only the formal and visible parts of such activities. Employees are being appraised and reviewed against objectives continuously in the course of operation. How well these day-to-day appraisals and feedback of work qualities are being conducted is really the heart of such programs. It is in these ways also that operational training represents a cornerstone of effective human resources development.

Teaching, coaching, and counseling in the process of operations is another part of OTD. It is the supervisor's job to show employees how to do their work and to explain what they do not understand. It is the supervisor who should advise them in their work problems and working relationships. This aspect of OTD also involves encouragement, when appropriate, and firmness when needed. This is the role of the operational leader, or coach.

In operational training and development, every important work event becomes a learning experience, or what has been called the "critical incident method." A supervisor reacts continuously to events, incidents, or situations at work in the normal course of operations. How these are handled and the degree to which each event becomes a learning experience also represent the essence of OTD.

By the very nature of operational training, a considerable part of this key activity is necessarily done by the immediate supervisor. This is why, in turn, supervisory training is such a vital part of an overall human resources development program. The excellence of this supervisory responsibility is determined by such considerations as:

Ability and experience
Attitudes
The extent to which OTD work is perceived to be a basic part of supervisors' responsibility
Time sufficient to do such work

Support and advice received from higher-level management and personnel staff

The key in evolving an effective OTD activity is the ability of supervision at every level of the organization to carry out his role. Effective personnel staff, when available and close enough to operations, can support the supervisors in OTD not only by their advice but also by actually doing some of their activities. The human resources unit manager *manages* and monitors such activities and assists or counsels immediate supervisors in special cases.

Considerable OTD involves either development of the potential of some employees for future assignments or relates to training experiences outside the experience of the immediate supervisor. In these cases the human resources unit manager or central personnel staff must conduct the OTD. In fact one of the criteria for identifying a human resources unit manager is his capacity for doing or managing operational development activities. Therefore, while much of the operational training work occurs in the course of day-to-day work and is conducted by the immediate supervisor, part of the operational development work requires attention from higher-level management and a great deal of it is done most effectively by group activities.

Much of the group operational development work is simply centered in learning by experience. This learning need not be limited by the personal experience of individuals or groups. Every employee does not have to learn by his or her own experiences, but can also benefit by and learn from the experiences of others.

There is an emerging body of knowledge and experience in the area of centralized operational development methods. One of these important techniques or procedures is what might be labeled "developmental experiences," which may be simple group sessions conducted for a number of employees who have common developmental needs. These sessions may also be held to identify critical experiences among a group of people with common jobs or common job responsibilities, or to communicate experiences of a few people to many other similar situations.

A computer manufacturer, for instance, with a very large branch organization conducted a series of discussions about developmental experiences. The first step in this program was to identify the critical success areas in branch operations, such as the selection of new sales personnel. Then results among hundreds of branches were analyzed, and the branches that had the best record in these success areas were chosen for further study. The people responsible for the course then visited these branches to see how their managers had handled these critical operational areas. After this, the "best experiences" were described and analyzed by the staff, reviewed by higher-level management, and fed back to the branch managers who had these experiences, who then proceeded to further refine and improve their methods of hiring. Once this was accomplished, a program was built to present these best practices to all regional managers, who in turn conducted similar training sessions in the normal course of their overview of their assigned branches.

Another approach to operational development on a group basis involves the "case method." This concentrates on the evaluation of a company's own specific problem cases. In a large diversified firm that had experienced common trouble spots, the first step was to identify the causes and suggest opportunities for eliminating basically unsolvable problems or unanswered questions. Those responsible for the training program then wrote up these problem areas and presented them as case studies. Of course, this task was rather simple because the case writers did not have to invent a company, or describe fictitious key people, or invent basic data. They had a real case, that of the company conducting the developmental exercise.

After the case studies had been written, a group of participants was selected, composed of middle-management persons who were judged to have very high potential. The subsequent case sessions had a number of valuable results. For one thing, they gave top management a measure of the general managerial capability of the participants. Most importantly, they provided development based upon experience in that particular firm, and also led to a number of useful suggestions for the solutions to real company problems.

A third type of operational development program is the "extensions" session. This activity is so labeled because its contents are really by-products of other programs or activities conducted for specific purposes. An example is the developmental by-product obtained in the course of administering compensation plans. Outstanding individual employee success or failure cases covered by an incentive compensation plan can be analyzed to identify developmental needs or opportunities. More directly, the very feedback related to an effectively administered compensation plan could be a developmental process. Similarly, many personal activities may have developmental by-products. Such multiple results enhance the cost/effectiveness of any personnel activity.

Operational training and development programs are low-cost or no-cost activities, and are usually closely and immediately related to operations work. In this respect they have a direct if not measurable impact on employee productivity. Just how positive and how much OTD impacts productivity is a function of how well it is managed. Management of this human resources development activity is extremely difficult because most of it involves a great number of singular experiences, each with a relatively small inpact.

OTD can be managed, however, if the following requisites are included in its framework: selection as well as training of each level of supervision, proper organization structuring, effectiveness of the human resources unit manager, an effective personnel staff at operations levels, and a well-conceived and properly administered OTD effort, supported and guided by higher-level personnel staff.

INDIVIDUAL DEVELOPMENT

The basics of human resources development—communications, training, and operational training and development—clearly have the greatest impact on employee productivity. In combination, they will likely represent more than one-half of the training and development that really occurs in any firm. In order of impact on productivity, the individual employee's development is the next most effective activity. This is true because the individual is still the unit of production insofar as human-resource assets are concerned. It is the individual who does things or decides things. It is the individual who has attitudes, personality traits, perceptions, and feelings that manifest themselves in work.

There is a great variety of individual development techniques and procedures. Three that have particular merit and have been widely applied are appraisal of performance, self-development, and management by objectives.

Appraisal of Performance

Appraisal of performance is a basic personnel technique used in business for many years. Appraisal programs are part of the formal process for evaluting the work of individuals. Sometimes this evaluation is made for the purpose of drawing conclusions and arriving at decisions. In other cases, evaluation provides feedback to the individual as a means of training and development, or is used in development programs for individuals who need upgrading.

Conclusion ratings, or appraisal for the purpose of making decisions, is an important part of human resources management. Appraisal techniques designed to obtain personnel conclusions can be quite simple. In many ways it's only necessary to ask the question, "How well is each employee performing?" The answer to this is known in the organization. Such conclusion ratings can be made with a high degree of validity on a five-gradient scale. A number of field tests indicate a very high degree of validity in such ratings, as long as they reflect judgments of performance, made in no more than five gradients, and require only conclusions.

The problem with employees' conclusion ratings in many firms lies in getting such information to some central point (such as the corporate office) for the purpose of reviewing and controlling supervisor decisions and actions. If a system can be devised so as to pass on information obtained at the work place, without having it adulterated by subsequent corrective inputs, very simple and valid systems can be used.

Conclusion ratings are extremely valuable. For one thing, they should be the basis on which *supervisors* make certain key personnel decisions. In merit pay increases it is the performance conclusion ratings that largely guide these supervisory decisions. Performance conclusion ratings similarly guide promotion, transfer, and other actions affecting personnel. The key to their proper use is that they should be the exclusive guide for judgments made by immediate supervisors and human resources unit managers, and should not be perceived as a higher-level management or central staff control device.

A second value of conclusions ratings under an appraisal program, which has emerged in the past few years, is that they have become a basic source of data or information in a human-resource information system. As noted in Chapter 3, knowledge of performance levels in each of the business units of a company has in itself a great value. When such information is related to turnover, employment experiences, and other data in a human-resource information system, it can be extremely valuable.

Techniques of appraisal designed to assist in the development of personnel are rather broad in scope. They attempt to help managers analyze performance, and these systems of evaluative appraisal are generally quite complex. Since the actual procedures used are unimportant, some appraisal experts argue that the best employee appraisal form is a blank piece of paper. Their point is that the important thing is that supervisors periodically do some hard and objective thinking about the performance of each employee and each working group or project team. In the practical world of business, however, most supervisors need some criteria or guidelines to help their thinking in the appraisal process. To help them in this there are a considerable number of forms and processes, but no one is particularly better than another, and all are imperfect. In fact, one of the best methods for appraisal is to make available a number of distinctly *different* types of appraisal processes and let each supervisor have the authority to choose whichever appraisal process best helps him.

Experience has indicated that there are a number of sound appraisal approaches and basic principles for effective evaluative performance appraisal. These include:

Trait ratings such as cooperativeness, intelligence, length of experience, and amount of education must be avoided. All of these are but symptoms of performance (and probably in violation of EEO).

The appraisal process is judgmental; therefore it should not measure such things as absenteeism or production, which are factual.

Something in addition to words must guide ratings. This may be comparative judgments, one employee against another, or comparisons against preset standards of performance.

The process must be flexible enough to permit supplemental appraisal factors unique to each individual job and work situation.

The evaluative appraisal process is diagnostic rather than conclusion oriented. Evaluative appraisal is a means to an end—the improvement of employee performance.

The appraisal process is highly supportive of the basic areas of human resources development: work communications, job training, and operational training and development. It encourages, and frequently requires, that at least some periodic communications feedback be made to individuals so that they know how well they are doing in their work and how they might improve their performance. The appraisal process also helps identify group business educational or training needs as well as group operational training and development needs and opportunities.

Evaluative performance appraisal (as contrasted with conclusion ratings) can affect performance of employees in three ways. The simplest way is to tell employees how well they are doing. This is a "mirror on the wall" approach. The logic is that if the employee knows his strengths and weaknesses, he will himself exploit those strengths and work to correct his weaknesses.

Performance appraisal also provides a sytematic method of determining specific training and development programs that will increase the knowledge, skill, and productiveness of groups of employees. This input is indispensable if productive training and development *programs* are to be accurately geared to real needs rather than perceived needs, or to activities presumed to improve effectiveness of work. The evaluative performance appraisal process should be the primary basis upon which company training and development programs are built.

Most importantly, however, the evaluative performance appraisal process is a diagnostic tool that leads to judgment of the strength and weakness of each employee, and thereby to cumulative appraisals of groups of employees and project teams. That inventory of strengths and weaknesses then makes practical the design of an individual program or plan for improving the performance of each person, group, and team. Each performance improvement plan should be quite simple. At any point, or in any operating period, it is usually practical to work on only a single strength or weakness, or a very few, if substantial improvement is to result.

Eventually, this type of appraisal pays off, as illustrated in Figure 5, when it culminates in a performance improvement plan. It need not be a sterile intellectual exercise that produces no more than an unused inventory of knowledge. That knowledge of strengths and weaknesses should yield a plan for performance improvement by building on strengths and/or improving weaknesses. When implemented, performance will improve unless some part of the process is faulty. If performance improves, then productivity improves; if it doesn't, then performance criteria need to be reexamined. Finally, as noted earlier, if employee productivity increases, then business results improve; otherwise, employees are effectively working but are doing the wrong work.

Self-Development

Many employees want to improve their performance; they do take pride in their work and want to go home knowing that they have done a good day's work. Further, they want to keep their jobs, and they want to get ahead. All these are conditions that motivate employees to improve their performance. If these assumptions are correct, then (given the proper conditions) there will be some important degree of self-development on the part of employees. Proper conditions must include the work environment (discussed in Chapter 5) and some of the financial incentives mentioned in Chapter 11. The self-development process is also aided if the employees are given some concrete information, which may be substantiated partially by an appraisal program, of how well they are doing, areas in which they have demonstrated strengths in the minds of their supervisors. They also need to know the areas in which they need to improve their performance.

In rapidly growing companies where there is little time for formal training and development, self-development typically occurs a great deal. Growth companies tend to hire people who are not only qualified to do the job they are first assigned to do, but who also have the potential for growth. The very nature of a growth company provides opportunities for promotion and therefore provides strong incentives for self-development. In fact, in many growth companies, employees have to work hard and grow quickly just to keep pace with the growth of the company. Some of the not so rapidly growing companies have worked hard to "simulate" growth in order to achieve a number of objectives, one of which is to encourage self-development.

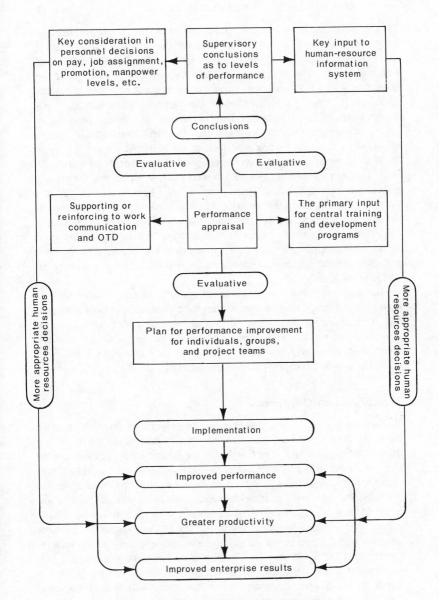

Figure 5. Objectives of performance appraisal.

The basic question a company faces is how it can nurture self-development. For one thing, improvement from self-development *must be recognized* by the company. Self-development takes an employee's time and effort, and it is hard work. Employees can be very easily discouraged if they think that improvement resulting from genuine efforts has gone unnoticed. Secondly, of course, self-development that improves performances should be rewarded by salary increases and, where there is a bonus program, by higher bonuses. Improved or newly acquired capabilities should also be rewarded by promotion when opportunities are available.

If at all possible, a company should attempt to channel and direct self-improvement efforts so that they align with the firm's interests. In terms of current job effectiveness, self-development must be selective so that new knowledge or capability will contribute to improved performance. Continued development efforts are more difficult, but no less important, to channel. This guidance frequently cannot be well provided by the immediate supervisor. Whenever possible, self-development that is truly geared to employee and company needs should be supported. Tuition refund programs are an example of such support.

In many enterprises, even moderately well nurtured self-development makes an important contribution to improved productivity, both near term and long term. For most firms it should be emphasized throughout the overall human resources development activity. Usually, self-development is a very low-cost or no-cost activity so far as the company is concerned, but it can yield significant improvement in productivity.

Management by Objectives

While some executives regard management by objectives (MBO) as a recent discovery, the first MBO experience was actually recorded in history during the days of King Arthur. The Knights of the Round Table rode out into the fields at the beginning of each month and told the serfs which field to plough and what was expected. At the end of the month they rode out again and rewarded the serfs with grain or punished them by cutting off their heads. Since that time the goals or objectives have become far more subtle and are generally less related to individual needs. The rewards are somewhat more generous and far less harsh. Although the relationship between rewards (or punishment) and results may be less compelling, the principles are the same.

Management by objectives is essentially a managerial process rather than a personnel technique or practice. It is a process really designed for application to a limited, but important, group of employees who are generally the highest 5 percent of the work force in an industrial firm. MBO relates more to productiveness than to productivity because it focuses attention on high-priority versus low-priority activities, and induces employees to structure their work to be supportive of unit or business objectives. MBO programs may also contribute to greater employee productivity by setting specific "stretch" goals, and thereby high levels of known expectations.

Management by objectives contributes to the training and development of employees only indirectly. Such programs can be a source of identifying training and development needs, but the objectives themselves generally include areas of required improvement in personal performance. Even without specific training and development plans, MBO goals encourage self-development. The objective-setting process itself also focuses employees' attention on the important and the relevant.

There has been a great deal of experience with programs in management by objectives. A lot of it is very bad, but from it has come a number of criteria or requirements for an effective management-by-objectives program. These include:

☐ The process must be essentially top-down. For instance, the objectives of the chief executive officer are the stated objectives of the company. The objectives of all subordinate executives—those reporting to the chief executive officer—must first support the objectives of the chief executive officer; secondly, they must reflect problems, opportunities, and resulting objectives set for the sections of the business which represent their own areas of responsibility or functional cognizance.

☐ An MBO program can never attempt to identify every objective. This is impractical, and any attempt to measure more than a half-dozen or so major objectives in each position increases the cost and decreases the effectiveness of the program almost geometrically.

☐ The programs must be structured to avoid setting objectives that are visible and dramatic; nor should they reflect the interest of the individuals.

☐ Whenever possible, goals should be quantified, even if the measures are gross or are projected approximations of accomplishment.

☐ The goals set must include certain norms or standards for performing regular job responsibilities.

☐ Management-by-objectives programs must not be directly related to pay decisions or job assignment decisions.

Standards of performance may be an integral part of a management-by-objectives program as they might also be a part of appraisal programs. In setting standards of performance, there is a necessity for identifying both the criteria by which performance will be measured and the measurement system itself. Obviously, standards are most effective when they can be quantified. Except in the most automated operations position and top-executive positions, it is seldom possible to quantify all performance standards for any position. Standards of performance are best set when they directly relate to position description responsibilities. That is, each major area of work is identified and then standards of performance are set to reflect either satisfactory or target levels of performance in each major area of responsibility.

ORGANIZATION DEVELOPMENT

The particular approach to training associated with "organizational development" (OD) focuses on interpersonal dynamics that occur within a group or between groups. It is actually an offshoot of laboratory psychological studies in group dynamics, and it focuses strongly on techniques such as "T" group meetings. It presumes that results of the application of such techniques will be a more open working relationship, a stimulation for personal growth, an environment more personally rewarding, and somehow more effective work.

The assumption of programmatic organizational development is that organizations are not more effective because they have unsatisfactory interpersonal or intergroup relations. Actually, experience shows that there is perhaps only one of one hundred cases where the number one need for improved effectiveness is interpersonal relation deficiencies. Much of the disappointment in programmatic organizational development is therefore not related to the appropriateness of the technique or to the lack of the practitioners' professional skills, but simply to the facts that answers are forthcoming for questions that don't exist or because high-priority activity is given to a low-priority need.

Frequently, organizational development practitioners are selling knowledge based on characteristics of "unhealthy organizations," which are symptoms to some degree of every organization. Businesses have invested enormous amounts of money on programmatic OD, but like so many preprogrammed activities, they present answers and specific methodology known only to practitioners, who assume that every company has the question that matches their answer.

Programmatic organizational development applied by skilled practitioners certainly will get people to work more openly with each other, but if they are already working openly enough, this does not contribute to enterprise success. The concept of sufficiency in human resources management demonstrates repeatedly that if there is enough of quality, more of it does not contribute to more effective results. Where there is a sufficiency of openness, more of it can, in fact, reduce the effectiveness of relationships, and this has happened in many companies.

Programmatic organizational development may or may not contribute to personal growth, but the key is whether it contributes to the type of growth in people that is most important to their future development and whether OD growth increases the effectiveness of the organization. Experience again demonstrates that the need for better or more open relations does not have high priority in personal growth in one of a hundred cases. Resources devoted to a low-priority activity—in this case, improving interpersonal relations—diverts resources away from higher-priority items, and this inhibits both individual growth and the success of the enterprise.

Organizational development sessions can also be a lot of fun and in this sense are personally rewarding. It is, in fact, a form of group therapy, another interesting experience. But again there is a great deal of evidence that making work more fun or the interjection of interesting experiences does not necessarily increase the effectiveness of work. In fact, this particular form of group therapy can be highly frustrating, and has been a shattering personal experience to some.

The primary technique of organizational development is the "T" session, which means "training" session. This in turn pivots around "team building meetings." These meetings involve a group that sits down, usually outside the work environment, to discuss themselves. The meetings usually last two or three days and are guided by a third party, the clinical psychologist, and aim at reaching a high degree of candor. Normally, team building involves four steps. The organization first sets objectives on a joint basis. They then set agenda. The third step involves the meeting itself, which is a lot of discussion and feedback and which hopes to arrive at some conclusions and establishment of priorities. The fourth step then is to decide what to do with the decisions that came out of the meeting, if any.

The second basic technique of organization development is the formation of intergroup meetings. In these, the same steps occur, but the meeting is attended by representatives of a number of organizational units that have frequent interrelationships and are interdependent on each other for results. Each group has had their own "T" group session, after which they presumably understand themselves and can now reach out to understand others.

The third tactic or practice involves the organizational mirror. The main purpose of these group meetings is to obtain feedback, to let each person see how others view him and how everyone sees each other. This is supposed to promote more openness and better understanding, which in turn, is intended to result in more satisfying, and perhaps more effective, work relations.

The themes that are pervasive in programmatic organizational development are in fact really as old as organizations. Paraphrasing the practitioners themselves, the process really aims at:

Opening up communications
Bringing the involved parties face to face

Dealing directly with problems
Enhancing collaboration in contrast to competition
Developing a problem-solving atmosphere
Placing the emphasis on diagnosis in identifying questions

The problems are first and foremost what has already been identified, namely, that interpersonal or intergroup relations are rarely the primary cause of less than optimum productiveness. Organizational development is another form of participative management and involves all the problems associated with it, not the least of which is that people tend to render judgments or decisions on subjects they don't know much about. Organizational development leads to soft organizations at the expense of productiveness. As a process, it is extraordinarily costly and can raise the expectations of people. It also aims at changing the balance of power within an organization, which necessarily means downgrading the role of the supervisor, loosening controls, and lowering organizational discipline.

Development of Future Abilities

What has been described with respect to training and development has focused on improving effectiveness of work on currently assigned jobs. These activities result in near-term improvement in productivity. There is a second dimension to human resources development. This involves developing employees to fill future needs and areas of responsibilities, which is actually asset development.

Development of employee potential is a complex and difficult undertaking. One of the problems is that the company is undertaking development when there is at least some uncertainty as to exactly what positions people are being developed to perform. Another problem is the fact that techniques and methods deployed for future development are at best imperfect, and are frequently unproven. Thirdly, it is extremely difficult to measure the results or the value of future development of employees. It is almost never possible to measure such results in absolute terms such as improved work output or test results. Furthermore, the results of development may not actually manifest themselves in the work situation until a very considerable period of time has elapsed.

Development of future abilities is a part of human resources planning. Such activities are designed to determine capabilities needed in the future and the action steps required to meet these needs. Human resources planning must, of course, be derived from strategic plans of the enterprise and from forecasts of future employee relations environment.

Future developmental activities should never represent a program for all employees. Operations jobs need not generally be included. In jobs at this level, each move to a new job represents a discrete or finite movement, either vertically or horizontally. In operations jobs the first requirement in meeting future manpower needs is that the employment process should create a reservoir of talent able to assume higher-level responsibilities. From this talent a selection process for promotion from within or reassignment needs to be managed effectively. Then it must be recognized that, once people are moved to new positions, there will be need for training and development. Finally, for many operational-level positions, future needs can be readily filled by outside recruitment if the internal placement process cannot do it.

In professional jobs, growth occurs generally within a discipline. Much the same is true with respect to many "staff" areas, such as accounting and finance. In these cases, future as well as current needs are met by the type of "professional development" activities outlined in the next section of this chapter. In addition, some employees or groups of employees can be eliminated from consideration for future development activities for other reasons. For those nearing retirement age, for instance, the future is now. Also, not every employee seeks or desires substantial job movement. Still others are not willing to make the time or effort investment required for developing knowledge or skills that qualify them for substantially higher-level or different types of work in the future. Finally, at any time, some percentage of the work force has reached its career peak, and are unable to assume significantly higher-level responsibilities in the future.

When each of these factors is considered, a future development program should be considered typically for only 5 to 10 percent of the total work force. The identification of these positions and the employees appropriately covered by a future development program is another critical step in future development activities.

One of the key activities in a program to develop personal capabilities requires the appraisal of future potential. This is a form of performance appraisal, but focuses on future potential abilities rather than effectiveness in performing currently assigned duties. Knowledge, or at least insight, of those with high potential is another area of information that exists in any organization. Those with really high potential at every level are known to just about everyone in the organization. The identification of those with high potential therefore requires drawing conclusions. These can be deduced by applying the five-gradient rating system already described with respect to current performance conclusion ratings.

The more difficult process then involves dealing with the questions of "how much" potential for personal growth—in what way can high potentials be developed most effectively, and how would this relate to enterprise needs. This process virtually involves case studies. Certain basic human qualities, such as intelligence and ambition, must be assessed. Just how these qualities have been demonstrated in the recent past is one way of evaluating them. Psychological assessment can provide an enormously helpful professional input to appraisal of such basic personal qualities.

Employee preferences and interests form a second vital input to future developmental planning. Their identification is not a simple process. Most employees do not have a well thought through and realistic set of personal career goals. Finally, the evaluative appraisal of potential must extrapolate past and present performance to predict future potential. This process is also very difficult and leaves much room for error. Essentially, in such performance forecasting the focus is on demonstrated successes and strengths and how these might be utilized.

Such evaluative inputs must then be the basis for constructing a plan for each individual. This plan must relate the potentials to enterprise needs, and must include certain action steps for necessary future personal development. The entire process takes a great deal of time, time of higher-level persons. Each case will require from 5 to 15 man-days of work. Few companies have found it practical to follow this conceptually correct and essential process. Most have felt it necessary to cut back on the number of persons whose potential usefulness has been appraised, or to shortcut the system, or both.

Programs and activities for training and development of future potential are numerous. Proper job placement and rotation to provide the rounded background necessary for future assignments is one effective activity highly useful in implementing future development plans. Careful selection of outside courses, seminars, and lectures, and participation in industry, trade, or professional organizations are also helpful. Participation in special assignments or project groups to provide new exposures and opportunities for further assessment are other training and development activities aimed at meeting future needs. The real difficulty in such future development plans is that each person is a unique case. Therefore, even with sound strategic plans and operational forecasts, the developmental objectives are at best imperfect and usually quite unclear. Moreover, developmental activities cannot be programmatic or proceduralized, but must be subjected to careful and continuous monitoring of discrete cases. Development and implementation of that kind of activity is the real art of future development management practice.

SPECIAL HUMAN RESOURCES DEVELOPMENT

In every organization there are some employee groups for which the human resources training development activities outlined do not meet the needs of those involved. The needs of such groups are unique, or the nature of people and/or jobs are such that none of the foregoing activities is sufficiently productive in either increasing employee productivity or enhancing human assets. In such areas, special training and development activities must be used. Two such groups, common to many companies, are executive development and professional development.

Executive Development

Training as a basic human resources development technique is rarely applicable to executive-level positions. These positions are not filled by trainees, but by those who have demonstrated sufficient knowledge and skills to perform their work effectively. There are rare exceptions. When firms were computerizing records, for instance, some training of executives was needed in the basics of computer technology, but this was mostly geared to understanding how this technology was used and managed.

Future development certainly has no applicability at the executive level. For top executives, as for retirees, the future is now! Appraisal techniques have application in other executive positions, but even in this area, the needs and applicable techniques may have to be modified. Appraisal of individuals in executive positions is seldom structured, proceduralized, or recorded. The focus of appraisal is quite different at the top-executive level. The orientation is very much focused on business results, actual short-term results and proxy evaluation of progress toward long-term objectives. In every executive position, business and personal performance are highly correlative. Management by objectives is truly a style of management with very little, if any, human resources development by-product at executive levels.

Executive development practices are unique, and don't fit well into the human resources development categories. Most executive development practices would fall in the category of "operational training and development" and "self-development," if anywhere. They are almost exclusively oriented to business results and are aimed at increasing productiveness, not in increasing productivity of efficiency.

Companies that have had success in "executive development" are rather secretive about their experiences, viewing their success as valuable proprietary information. It would be no breach of confidences, however, to *illustrate* executive development. Three selected activities will serve this purpose: case studies, counseling, and peer exchanges. These represent a cross section of practices that have been successfully developed and implemented.

While every firm is unique, the problems and opportunities it faces are seldom without precedent. A form of human resources development at the top-executive level first identifies through business research the precedents relevant to actually existing company problems. Their applicability to these problems are then examined through research. When possible, discussions are held with companies named in the studies to determine what the situation of each was, what they did, why they followed a particular course of action, and how it worked. This process rarely uncovers an answer, but the body of knowledge and experience gathered is useful in deducing reasonable solutions. This is a kind of operational training and development, but it is based upon experience in other firms rather than internal experience. It's really an executive problem-solving and decision-making process, and that's what executive development is all about: improvement planning, decision making, and resources allocation.

A classic executive development activity is coaching and counseling. Board members can be helpful to the chief executive officer by acting as his sounding board, and by sharing their experiences and the experiences they observe in other situations. The chief executive in turn "counsels" top-level general management and staff executives, frequently whether they want it or not. A reading of some literature published by leading firms shows that they have often sought counseling from outside consultants. Some executives feel that this is a most productive use of outside consultants as well as key persons in their legal firm, public accounting firm, and advertising agency. This is an auxiliary executive development activity that can be organized and structured for maximum usefulness.

A third contribution to executive development is information exchange among peers. The "who" and "how" of these intercompany activities is critical. Peers who are competitors aren't likely to be helpful; attorneys worry a lot about that kind of information exchange. Exposure on the basis of commonality of club membership is a chancy way of gaining peer-group interchange; casual and informal discussions are not likely to be a productive use of executive time. Conscious selection of peers and structured interchange of information and experience have proved to be the most effective executive development technique.

These are only illustrations of the unique types of developmental activities that have been evolved to meet the special needs of executives for "development." It is a very new area for exploitation in human resources development. It is, of course, directed at a very few jobs and individuals. But time costs are modest, and the leverage effect on enterprise results and overall employee effectiveness, even with moderate success, is enormous.

Professional Development

Human resources development in professional units of companies or in wholly professional enterprises is different in a number of important respects. Many of the activities described for human resources development are really not applicable to professional work. Others have narrow usefulness and are applicable only to the administrative part of professional jobs. In other cases, there are unique or special types of developmental activities which are an important part of the development of professional people, but these are not applicable at all, or are of minor value and importance, in the development of nonprofessional employees.

It should be recognized that human resources development among professional people has a special significance because it represents not only increasing productivity or effectiveness of operations, but also assets building. In fact, when we talk about human resources among professional people, we are talking about them as the assets of their group.

Essentially, the way in which people are developed in a professional operation is very largely a function of the operation of the enterprise or unit itself. It is, for instance, very much a matter of the strategic focus of the organization and the distribution of its products or services. Development is determined to a very large extent by the level of professional work undertaken by the group. It is also influenced to a great extent by the quality standards the firm or business unit sets for itself. The level and type of work done very much affects the professional growth of professional people. Finally, the management style is a major determinant of the nature and extent of all professional development.

Another important factor in the development of key professional people is the continuation of their formal education. By definition, professional enterprises sell their collective professional knowledge to either a number of customers or to "corporate" customers. Level, scope, and depth of their professional knowledge is critical, therefore, to the success of the professional unit or company. In all professional enterprises—those working in traditional academic disciplines and those related to business technologies—the expertise of the staff represents the assets they sell. It is therefore vital that the professional staff keeps up to date with the technological advances in its field. Otherwise, "technological obsolescence" is inevitable.

The problem of technological obsolescence in the physical sciences has been well demonstrated. Most of the important technical breakthroughs have been made by scientists within ten years of graduation from college. This is true not only in the physical sciences field, but also in many business disciplines, such as marketing. It is difficult to believe, however, that people somehow acquire intellectual hardening of the arteries after age 30. The problem is, rather, that they do not keep abreast of their professional fields.

There are various things which companies do to deal with the problem of technological obsolescence. These include:

□ Sending professionals to courses in established universities.
□ Suggesting programs of self-study, particularly if they result in some form of "recertification."

☐ Permitting or encouraging professionals to engage in teaching their subjects.

☐ Having in-house academic programs, although this is possible only in very large research organizations.

☐ Permitting or encouraging participation in professional societies.

Many of the day-to-day developmental techniques associated with the increased use and knowledge of professional persons are also outside the mainstream of the traditional training and development activities. Most of the effective learning experiences occur in the process of work; in effect, learning by doing. This, in turn, requires a structured and organized method for the acquisiton of skills and the managing of knowledge. It involves learning by the experiences of others as well as learning by one's own experiences.

A very considerable amount of the development of professionals is implemented through career development assignments. These can be both vertical and horizontal—vertical by assuming higher-level scientific and professional responsibilities, and horizontal by assignments designed to provide a broadening of knowledge. Learning by other people's experiences is possible only if other people's knowledge and experiences are available. This means that human resources development programs in the professional organization must include in their learning system the access to a reference library. Professional organizations practically always maintain some system for the input of knowledge and experience from a central depository that has an effective retrieval system.

HUMAN RESOURCES DEVELOPMENT PROCESS

The procedures used in human resources development have a significant impact on the success of such activities. The first principle is that there be few canned answers in human resources development. The justification for time and money expenditures on human resources development is that they improve enterprise results. Improvement, however, must depend upon the nature of the enterprise and its particular problems and objectives. There just aren't any two identical enterprises. Therefore, except for a few types of training and development programs that have been identified and which address themselves to the needs common to groups or classes of employees, human resources development activities must be customized.

The key to successful resource development, therefore, is highly dependent upon the appropriate assessment of needs. There have been too many human resources development "experts" selling and preaching what they know, which usually turns out to be generalities instead of specifics. Rather than start with somebody's stock answer, a firm should begin with an identification of its questions, problems, and opportunities. Relatively little knowledge and skills have evolved on how to identify human resources development needs. This is partly caused by so much attention being focused on the development of programs and by accepting ready-made answers. The result is, of course, that unless needs are effectively identified, there are innumerable techniques, programs, and activities available which are specific in nature but nonspecific in application.

The last step in the process involves analysis and evaluation of cost/value relationships. In a hard practical sense the elements of any proposed training and development program or activity should be: identification of objectives; articulation of how the achievement of these objectives will contribute to improved utilization of human resources; cost estimates; *and criteria as well as methods for measuring results.* Without these elements and methods for measuring return for time-cost investments, there should be great reluctance to undertake any human resources development activity.

Development of human resources is a business proposition. The appropriateness of that proposition must first depend upon the correctness of its assumption and that is proved by identification of needs. Ultimately, however, it must also depend upon the chances of its success—what it contributes to enterprise progress or what positive results it produces relative to income. This can be done only when the objectives of the program are identified before activities are undertaken and when some system for evaluating the results is established in the first place.

Much of human resources training and development is a form of maintenance expense. New people are constantly being hired and must be indoctrinated and trained. Experienced productive employees leave the company for many reasons, such as retirement, and are replaced by those who need training and experience. Operations or circumstances change, or new problems confront the business, and employees must be prepared in the broadest sense to meet new conditions, problems, or opportunities. All the training and development required for these events merely maintains productivity; they are defensive tactics. Therefore, elimination or reduction of these activities, for any reason (such as reducing this year's expenses), contributes to lower productivity and higher expenses in succeeding years. Some training and development may be or can be strategic in nature; that is, designed to obtain fuller utilization of human resources and thereby increase rather than merely maintain productivity.

11

Incentives

Both financial and nonfinancial incentives are critical parts of any organized effort to achieve and maintain a high level of productivity. Incentives provide motivation to do what is required, and to do it effectively. There is a direct and frequently measurable relationship between many incentive plans or programs and the productivity of workers.

Incentives alone, of course, will not bring about higher productivity. Some companies have erred in the past by assuming that incentives would, in and of themselves, increase productivity. Incentives obviously are not a substitute for management; rather, they are part of a management system's approach toward obtaining high levels of productivity. It is equally incorrect, however, to assume that there could be an effective work force or a high level of productivity without having incentives of some type.

It has been said that some people will work just as well without incentives as they would with them. Usually, such views are expressed when a company is contemplating supplementary incentive pay plans. Frequently, these views are very personal and moralistic—good people don't *need* incentives! The assumption is that employees don't respond to motivation, but this reflects a serious lack of knowledge with regard to the instinctive human qualities of the average employee. These anti-incentive views simply do not square with psychological research.

Incentives should be applicable to *all* employees of an organization. There are a great number of different incentive plans. Generally speaking, quite different incentives are appropriate to different groups and levels of employees. There is also a considerable body of experience and precedents. Thus, firms have a great variety of cases, as well as a number of different types of plans, to examine before developing and implementing incentive plans in their own organizations. Experience proves that incentives must be not only tailored to the individual needs of each company, but also adapted to the overall management style and practices of the firm.

NEED FOR INCENTIVES

Incentives are not designed to get hard-working employees to work harder. Their objective is to induce employees to extend proper and reasonable effort. Effort itself needs to be defined if work (input) and value (output) are to be analyzed. Effort may be interpreted as partly elapsed time or hours at work, which to employers usually means hours on the job. But employees sometimes perceive it as hours away from home. Effort may also mean hours *working,* as opposed to hours *at* work, or may mean simply *activity,* that is, how much energy is expended while working. Incentives influence the amount of time employees spend working and how much effort they expend while working.

Effective work in any enterprise means far more than just hours or activity. Faster motion or more frenzied movement does not necessarily mean more effective work. Productivity of employees depends on more than reasonable effort and work pace; it also depends on the employees' willingness to do things in a positive way, which they would otherwise choose not to do, not think to do, and occasionally, dislike doing. Incentives, therefore, represent a business expression of the psychological concept of stimuli. As long as people seek more in the way of material rewards and higher standards of living, compensation incentives to a very large degree will be a key part of the overall stimuli essential to obtaining full utilization of human resources.

Any enterprise that needs to create an environment and motivate employees to behave in a way not of their own choosing must consider incentives of some sort. Part of the overall motivation system must consist of financial reward. Incentives of this kind are compelling persuaders in getting people to work in a way that would not be their natural inclination. Actually, they are used to manipulate employees, but in a constructive manner by inducing or motivating them to do things that promote optimum productivity.

Frequently, incentive plans affect productivity dramatically. In operations work, studies show that productivity is typically 20 percent higher under incentive plans, and there have been cases where employee productivity doubled when an incentive plan was installed. Incentives don't always show dramatic results in short periods of time. Studies of plans covering top management and professional employees show that changes in behavior and increase in effectiveness typically occur gradually over time. Sometimes they result only in a small increase in productivity, perhaps 5 or 10 percent.

But the leverage effect of that increase of, say, 10 percent, has considerable influence on effectiveness of work in a management group. There is a limit to how hard employees can work or should work. If employees perceive that the incentives are forcing them to work beyond reasonable limits, then the incentive system will have a negative effect. It may, for instance, motivate people to work hard to loosen up on standards or take shortcuts in the system. Incentives, as a part of the management of human resources, aims at a delicate balance between employee effort and work expectations. The general relationship between hours at work plus effort expended during those hours on the one hand, and output on the other is illustrated in Figure 6. There is a level of input which represents inadequate input. Most employees are likely to choose a level of effort or work pace in the range of inadequacy. Incentives, in part, motivate employees to expend greater effort and work at the optimum range of effort illustrated. Once employees get used to the optimum level of effort, most find it more satisfying than an inadequate work pace or level of effort.

Incentives must not, on the other hand, motivate employees to expend effort beyond the optimum level. If they do, the work pace and effort becomes physically and/or emotionally overdemanding, and only incremental output occurs. This is the high-risk level of effort, and is distasteful and perhaps harmful to employees, and of marginal value to the enterprise. Additional effort is excessive; most employees cannot endure such a pace except for very short periods of time, after which total output declines.

Properly structured incentives also motivate employees to work smarter as well as working harder. They represent a positive way of motivating employees to order their priorities properly, focus on the important work, and

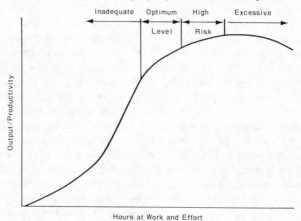

Figure 6. Effort and productivity.

follow the most effective methods. This purpose of incentives is particularly important in worker-controlled production, in jobs that apply technical or professional knowledge in areas that should not be methodized or institutionalized, where output cannot be quantified, and where the concept of "productiveness" is critical to work effectiveness. Worker-controlled production is becoming common in an increasing number of jobs. Even a growing number of factory production jobs have one or more of these characteristics.

The management art is the design of more incentives which, in totality induce people to behave and work in a manner that contributes to optimum accomplishment of enterprise goals. No single plan or program can accomplish this. No set of plans, programs, or practices in combination are appropriate to all companies, nor can any combination in a single enterprise ever achieve such an ideal goal. Furthermore, the best set of programs and practices must be complemented by the day-to-day actions, attitudes, perceptions, and behavior of the individual supervisor's acting within the constraints of the firm to satisfy individual employee motivational needs.

Essentially, the subject of incentives provokes such questions as: What makes people "run"? What turns them on? Knowing the answers to these questions, as they apply to individual employees or to groups of employees, is a key part in effective management of human resources. Studies conducted on this subject show a number of important factors. First, there is never, or almost never, a single factor that motivates people. Secondly, for most employees, money is the number one motivator during most of their work career. Thirdly, and obviously, people tend to be motivated to get things they do not have or do not think they have. Employees in low-paying jobs will put money high on the list of their ambitions. People in insecure positions tend to value security relatively higher than will those in very stable work environments. One of the basic tasks in building effective management systems, including incentive programs designed to utilize human resources effectively, is to answer this question of what motivates people. And part of the effectiveness of day-to-day supervision is to know the answer to this question for each employee.

Incentives of all types also have their costs. These are time costs and usually some expenditures of money. There is, therefore, in the management of incentives a cost/value variable, which reappears in so many of the considerations involving human resources management. The enterprise goal is to have the values of the greater productivity from incentive plans exceed the cost of such plans. Thus, the structuring of incentives must represent the appropriate balance of motivating people to perform at optimum effort on the right things at a cost that justifies improvement in operations.

Incentives must also be first examined and then designed and implemented in the context of an overall motivational system of the firm. This must include consideration of nonfinancial matters such as job security and overall work environment. It must consider positive incentives and negative incentives, and the removal of deterrents. Finally, the overall motivational system must include financial incentives, including promotion pay practice and performance salary increases.

DISINCENTIVES AND NEGATIVE INCENTIVES

If it is correct that incentives can be stimuli that get employees to change their behavior, their attitudes, and their performance, then it is equally true that both financial and nonfinancial plans that motivate people to do the wrong things are deterrents, or *disincentives*. Anything that motivates employees to work less effectively as a disincentive. Financial incentive plans, for instance, that cause negative work attitudes because they are perceived to be unfair or unrealistic, or because they come into conflict with other basic employee values, may be disincentives.

Over the years a considerable amount of research has been done on both the nature and effect of disincentives on productivity. The result has been a rather long list of potential deterrents, and some insights into the relationship of various practices and their negative effect on productivity. Rather precise information exists on incorrect financial incentives, which, if anything, motivate people to violate standards, avoid the system, work effectively on the wrong things, or work by the wrong methods.

In addition to incorrect financial incentives, there are a variety of other types of disincentives. Promotion based on favoritism or seniority, rather than ability, represents a disincentive to improve performance. Failure to deal with employee questions or grievances in a timely and constructive manner can be a disincentive. Some company action that seems rational may turn out to be a disincentive. For instance, some companies have urged employees to work out better methods of work, with the result that fewer employees were needed. Paradoxically, some employees who helped work out the better methods got laid off. In this context, the incentive for better work was to lose one's job, and that is clearly a disincentive.

There is also some evidence that a highly authoritarian style of supervision creates dissatisfaction among workers; indirectly, this is another disincentive. A salary system that rewards people for something other than effectiveness of work will necessarily stimulate people to behave in whatever way the rewards system is geared and will not increase the effectiveness of their work. Pay increases that come automatically with time motivate people to stay in their job, and this may be due to a desire to get along and survive rather than to work effectively.

Part of the process of building incentives into a company must necessarily be to identify elements of disincentives. A formal personal audit includes identification of disincentives followed by appropriate action plans, which may result in a greater net motivation by removing demotivators. Frequently, it is appropriate procedurally to identify and remove or neutralize disincentives before positive steps are taken to adopt or improve positive incentives. Presence of disincentives may make difficult or impossible the establishment of positive incentives.

No one particularly likes to talk about them, but there are also negative incentives in an overall motivational system. In a broad sense, there are two distinctly different ways to motivate employees: positive motivators, such as financial incentives, where an employee is rewarded for achievement; and negative incentives, where an employee is penalized for failure to achieve. Ideally, of course, a company always strives to build nothing but positive incentives, but as a practical matter, negative incentives are to some extent a necessary part of every overall motivational system.

Some form of fear or concern for loss of job, downgrading, or other types of punitive personal action are negative incentives. The blatant use of power is simply not an accepted social behavior for business. Furthermore, such conduct by the enterprise is a two-edged sword. Actions by the enterprise which represent arbitrary discipline or improper use of authority incites reactions from employees, either as individuals or in groups. The company that operates under a constant environment of confrontation is not a very productive enterprise.

The use of the negative incentives need not be punitive; they are more appropriately structured as being corrective. Corrective personnel actions may be passive in that the poorer performers get more moderate salary increases or no salary increases, that their bonus awards are small or zero, or that they are not considered for promotional opportunities. To be effective, a corrective approach towards negative incentives must be accompanied by effective communication. Employees must know what is expected in the first place, and they must be told how they failed to accomplish what was expected. If employees are to perceive these actions as fair treatment, they must receive assistance from the supervisor in correcting deficiencies.

Negative incentives, passive or direct, must not be so strong that they create an environment of fear. This may retroact and motivate people to be ultraconservative so that they lose the incentive to try. Stringent negative incentives also discourage what is sometimes the important inclination of persons to take unpopular positions on issues, which experience may later prove were correct and in the vital interest of the firm.

While negative incentives are inherently disagreeable, they do have their positive side. Corrective action with respect to the employee who is not measuring up, or who performs in an inappropriate or improper fashion, may seem harsh to that individual, but it is the essence of fairness to other employees. Inappropriate or improper action by one employee detracts from job opportunities and the work environment of others. Management, of course, must take the enterprise point of view and represent the interests and aspirations of the majority of employees. To permit inappropriate or inadequate work on the part of a few at the expense of many would be the essence of inequity.

NONFINANCIAL INCENTIVES

Consideration of incentives is sometimes confused with financial incentive plans and pay practices alone. Nonfinancial incentives are a part of the overall motivational system for any firm. Generally, nonfinancial incentives are neither as strong or as reliable as financial incentives but cumulatively, they are important. For some firms they are, in fact, a major part of the motivational system.

Some nonfinancial incentives have already been discussed in Chapter 5. This dealt with environment of work and identified a number of important elements which in effect represent nonfinancial incentives. These include physical work environment, the nature of the company work, and the image of the business in the eyes of the employees. Even such work environment characteristics as the expectations for excellence represent a form of nonfinancial incentive. There are, of course, a considerable number of nonfinancial incentives. In fact, when all nonfinancial elements of rewards to employees are listed, the list is very long. A few of the principal elements of nonfinancial incentives can, however, be illustrative and be the basis for considering some of the characteristics of nonfinancial incentives.

Certainly, the job itself can be an important nonfinancial incentive. It is generally true that people work harder, more diligently, and with more enthusiasm when they are doing work they enjoy. For some, whether or not the job is interesting and diverse can be an incentive. For others, the degree to which the job is routine and uninteresting represents a nonfinancial incentive—they prefer less taxing work. Whether the job itself builds an individual's self-esteem can be a nonfinancial motivator. This is but one of the ways in which placement is such a key part of effective human resources management.

How employees are treated by their supervisors and their coworkers is an important element of job satisfaction and is therefore an indirect, nonfinancial incentive. This relates to day-to-day treatment by supervisors, how instructions are given, and how much help the supervisor and others are to the employee in doing work. It includes also how well the employee's questions are answered or how well problems or grievances are resolved. The quality of supervision and the role of the human-resources unit manager thus influences the effectiveness of nonfinancial incentives.

Job security is an important element of job satisfaction and therefore a nonfinancial incentive to many people. To others, the degree to which the job represents a learning experience can be a critical nonfinancial element of work satisfaction. At different stages in their careers, many professional employees are far more motivated to broadening their knowledge and increasing their personal asset values than they are in moving ahead.

Also, the status of the job and the recognition that is given to its occupant can be an element of nonfinancial incentive. Companies, of course, are constantly dealing with the problems of title, location of office, where one gets to park in the parking lot, etc. Each of these elements may be small, but they can be important benefits cumulatively, for they very much affect employees' attitudes and the effectiveness of work.

These nonfinancial incentives have many important characteristics. Some are "givens" and are not manageable. For example, a company cannot change its business in order to create more favorable nonfinancial incentives, nor can it tailor side benefits to fit the views of the recipients. Status may be very important to one person, but embarrassing to another. Some people may covet security very strongly, and others may even consider it demeaning to be concerned about security.

The cause-and-effect relationships between nonfinancial incentives and productivity are very obscure and unclear. There has been enough experience and evidence to indicate that these relationships are real and cumulatively important. They cannot, however, be quantified, and it is very difficult to find a measuring stick that measures their effectiveness.

Some nonfinancial incentives can become disincentives. Titles and other symptoms of stature are a good example. If overemphasized, employees can strive for the trappings of success rather than the substance of success. They work hard and structure their thinking and activities to *seem* important, but they do not work productively. Therefore, the management of nonfinancial incentives as a way to gain greater productivity is tenuous and difficult, and demands great sensitivity to differences in people.

FINANCIAL INCENTIVES

A great deal more concrete experience has been gained with respect to financial incentives than to nonfinancial incentives. Experience has not only been greater but more observable. Much of this experience can be generalized to provide ground rules for effective incentives. There are a number of general principles or yardsticks for evaluating financial incentives. These apply to almost every type of financial incentive. They also apply to every level of position which may be covered by a financial incentive plan. Some of these are:

Employees must know what the goals are and what the rewards are. This means that they must know exactly what comprises the performance criteria area, and what the measurement system is. They must have this information before the start of each planned period.

The goals must be understandable. This means that the performance criteria must relate not only to things that employees perceive and understand, but must be also clear enough so that those covered by the plan are well aware of how that plan works.

The goals must be attainable. This, of course, means that they must be attainable in the eyes of the employees as well as in the eyes of management.

There must be a very distinct and direct relationship between what an individual accomplishes, or what a group of employees accomplish, and the rewards they receive.

The rewards must be significant. In other words, the race must be worth the running.

There must be a reasonably short time span between recognition of employee accomplishments and the time the rewards are received.

The reward must be irrevocable. It must not be subject to future jeopardy.

An employee must have the tools or the facilities to accomplish work expectations.

The incentive system cannot be in conflict with other employee vital interests. It may not, for instance, be in conflict with basic security needs of employees.

The financial incentive system must be compatible with overall job requirements, work environment, and the general management style of the firm.

SALARY INCREASES

Before considering extra compensation systems as a form of financial incentive, companies are well advised to first pay attention to their basic salary administration system. In fact, sound extra-compensation incentive plans superimposed on chaotic salary administration can result in greater chaos and perhaps disproductivity. Very important financial incentives can be built into the companies practices through the use of sound salary administration alone. Employees can be motivated financially in two ways: first by promotional increases, and second by true merit increases.

Almost all companies grant increases to their employees when they are promoted to distinctly higher positions. To be effective, the promotion increase must be immediate, and it must be significant. Certainly, the employee must do better financially after a promotion than the increases he or she would have received without being promoted. Companies must also deal with promotional increases for those employees, such as professional employees, who do not experience promotions by going from one job to a distinctly different job, but rather get "promoted" because they achieve a new level of professional competency or because they have received added responsibilities.

Most companies have mastered the rather simplistic problems of promotional pay increases. Particularly in rapidly growing companies, these can represent extremely effective and strong financial incentives. In one of the most successful growth companies today (a machinery manufacturer), exempt employees in the past five years received a promotion and a promotional increase on the average of every 15 months. This company, interestingly enough, would say that it has no financial incentive plan, but the frequency and size of their promotional increases alone are very strong financial incentives. This is particularly true when one notes that the average salary increase, including promotional increases, for all of their employees exceeded 18 percent, compounded per year, during the period of study.

Companies have had far greater difficulties in creating salary incentives through "merit pay increases." It's difficult to argue with the basic logic of the traditional merit-increase concept. This says, in essence, that employees whose performance is bettered should receive larger increases and should receive more money for a given job. The theory is that if we pay people more for better performance, their productivity will increase. And if productivity increases, business results will be improved.

Most merit-increase programs have never fulfilled that objective. From the very beginning, salary administrators found problems of measurement. How do we determine through performance appraisal or merit rating who is performing better and how much better? First attempts at measurement were made by identifying traits of behavior, such as attitude, education, and experience. The measurements were then improved to develop more direct measures of performance on the job, including the identification of critical success factors, the setting of standards of performance, and the evaluation of achievement in relation to goals or objectives. But even here, the problems of developing forms and systems that would collect information about performance, which could be the basis for salary increases, and transmit this information to some central point such as the corporate office presented insurmountable problems.

The second problem, one that has really never been resolved, is a basically incorrect assumption of many merit-increase programs that the *only* reason for granting salary increases should be the performance of individuals. Actually, salary increases must reflect a number of important considerations. Performance is one of them, but the change in the cost of living, pay parity with other employees (particularly those covered by union contracts), pay relationships between employees, and other factors must also be considered. Some of these obviously have nothing to do with performance.

Over the past few years, some companies have dealt with these problems and have introduced a new generation of effective merit-increase programs, but the measurement problem is still in a state of flux because designers of salary systems are still pursuing the idea of some central point for information that is already known locally. As noted in Chapter 10 with reference to conclusions appraisal, supervisors at the unit, section, or location level can identify the outstanding performers, the marginal performers, and the intermediate-level performers. A number of tests have demonstrated clearly that people who have observed the performance of a sample group can rate performance with fair accuracy. These conclusions ratings, as pointed out in Chapter 10, are all that is needed for approving or disapproving performance salary increases.

A second key feature of the new generation of merit-increase programs is the recognition of the basic limitations of the conclusions performance appraisal mentioned above. First of all, it is not possible at most job levels to make more than five distinctions with respect to performance. Human judgment is simply not capable of pinpointing more discrete distinctions with respect to observable work performance. Therefore, if discrete distinctions in excess of five gradients are indicated, they reflect something other than performance.

In terms of the practicalities of salary administration, this means that salary increases granted for improved performance may not be less than about 7 or 8 percent. Specifically, a salary increase for performance must be in the range of 0, 7, 14, 21 percent, etc. Of course there may be small variations in this scale, but certainly no single individual should be granted an increase of, say, 9 percent in recognition of better performance when other individuals receive a merit increase of 7 percent.

Another lesson learned, and which is reflected in the new generation of salary increase systems, is that salary increases based on performance should not be commingled with pay increases for other purposes. If, for instance, all employees are to be granted increases of 6 percent for economic reasons, then an employee receiving a performance increase should get at least 13 percent. It is essential that the employee receiving this percentage should be told that 6 percent is for economic reasons and 7 percent is for improved performance. It really does not matter too much whether the total increase is granted at one time or separate amounts at intervals.

These types of merit increase and effective performance increase meet all general requirements for the sound incentive program already outlined. Over a period of time, such systems can distinguish very dramatically between employees who perform effectively and those who perform at marginal levels. These distinctions represent very strong financial incentives for employees to work at optimum levels.

There are some other important aspects of this new approach to performance pay increases. Some companies do not budget them because in their opinion the increases that reward higher productivity represent investment spending and not expenses. The yield from such investment spending is high, since there is no capital committed and the investment is made only after the yield is realized. In companies that place no limit on improved performance or greater productivity, there should be no limit on performance pay increases. Furthermore, withholding performance pay increases actually earned by improved effectiveness might become a legitimate grievance.

INCENTIVE PAY PLANS

Incentive plans for operational employees, particularly those performing repetitive factory jobs, have existed for many years. There are many well-proven and highly effective incentive plans available for these types of jobs. Actually, the number of operational employees covered by these plans has been declining for almost 20 years, and the percentage of total factory workers receiving these benefits has also been declining. This trend is not due to any lack of interest on the part of management in providing financial incentives to operations workers so that they will achieve objectives and optimize output. Nor does it represent any inherent defect or flaw in traditional incentive compensation plans for production people. Rather, the declining number of persons represents fundamental changes in the nature of production jobs, which leads to factory jobs characterized by technical knowledge, worker-controlled methods, and operations performed by groups. Such work characteristics make difficult the application of traditionally established factory incentive plans.

There is, at the present time, some concerted effort by a few leadership companies to modify traditional incentive plans and develop new plans. These modifications attempt to preserve the basic concepts of incentives and to reward individual employees or groups for higher quantity and quality of production. But they do so by designing plans suitable to more technically oriented, diversified factory positions. It is simply too early to draw any conclusions as to whether or not these efforts will be successful.

The number of direct sales employees covered by incentive plans has also been declining over the past 20 years, and for basically the same reasons. Increasingly, sales involve diversified and complex products. The job of salesman now is to sell greater volume and the more profitable products in the line. He must also provide service to customers, and information inputs to the home office. The result of this is that an increasing number of sales compensation plans are salary plus bonus usually based on quotas or goals. Frequently, the quotas are based upon multiple criteria of performance. Also, an increasing number of sales incentive plans are geared to profit by product line.

It has been widely assumed that incentive compensation plans are not applicable to professional persons. As a practical matter, about 5 percent of the *Fortune* 1000 companies have such plans for professional employees somewhere in their organization. In addition, a number of professional businesses have incentive compensation plans. One study of a sample of companies in the pharmaceutical, electronic, and chemistry industries is particularly instructive: The six most successful companies, in terms of their output from research and development (R&D), were identified, and the six that had extremely poor track records in the same terms of effectiveness were also identified. Each group was then studied to see if there were characteristics common to the successful firms which were lacking in those that had been unsuccessful in their R&D operations. This work showed that all successful companies had four characteristics that were lacking in the unsuccessful firms. One of these was the presence in the successful R&D operations of an incentive compensation plan for professional people.

Over the past 25 years, incentive compensation plans for management personnel have been developed to a fine art. Originally these incentives for management people were basically profit-sharing plans, but as companies developed into multibusiness multiunit organizations, profits of the firm overall became a poor measurement criterion for the achievement of business unit management.

To meet this problem, goal-oriented plans were introduced about 15 years ago. Essentially, these programs set profit goals at the beginning of each year, or other measurement period. All participants receive awards, based first upon how well the business performs against the preset targets, and secondly upon personal contribution to the overall achievement.

The difficulty with such plans has been the requirement to establish goals before the measurement period begins. The theory is that goals set for each year should represent equivalent management achievement in the light of economic and other circumstances that exist at that time. Such a system has the virtue of providing incentive for management to excel in difficult years as well as in favorable years. It provides equal incentive for management to excel in business units that are essentially less profitable or experiencing difficulties. But, of course, the critical problem is establishing goals before the year begins.

A "new generation" of management-incentive compensation plans has evolved during the past few years. Among other things, such plans resolve the problem of goal-orientation. Under these plans, the principal quantifiable criteria for measuring managerial performance in each business unit are determined. These criteria may involve such measures as return on investment. As few as two and as many as five criteria have been established. For each of these criteria, rational economic standards are set for target, for minimum, and for maximum achievement. Then the standards are described and accepted as permanent unless there are basic changes in the business or the economic environment. The numbers themselves, of course, may change as conditions change, but the standards remain constant.

The newest development in incentive-pay compensation plans applies to middle-group employees, and represents new technology. But even though experience with them has been limited, there has been enough to indicate, first, that the plans for employees in this group can be developed successfully and implemented, and secondly, that there has been sufficient experience to develop some principles and guidelines. Essentially, three types of plans have evolved and have been successfully applied to middle-group employees. These are goal-oriented, discretionary, and special award plans.

The key task in a goal-oriented plan is to establish performance criteria. This requires answers to several questions. First, what are the factors that substantially measure performance in the business unit where the incentive plan is being applied? Second, what standards or targets must be established with respect to each of these performance criteria? Third, what system for measuring performance against these standards must be developed? The process of setting targets and standards is extremely difficult and can best be done by human-resources unit managers. An incentive system for middle-level positions must also provide a system for higher awards for achievement in excess of goals and lower awards for failure to achieve goals. This is seldom done on a straight formula basis. Finally, plans sometimes provide variations in actual payments for individuals, based on how they contribute to the overall group achievement.

Discretionary plans are essentially the framework for granting to some individuals the discretion, and therefore the authority, to pay awards. This includes the discretion or authority to communicate or not to communicate the basis on which awards are made. These plans should obviously not be arbitrary, but inherently they allow considerable latitude to a manager in the application of corporate policy and guidelines. In one case, a large financial institution, the company set a budget of 3 percent of salary to be paid as bonuses to middle-group employees. Each of the departments and units established for administering the plan were advised of this allocation. Corporate staff provided guidelines, policy outlines, requirements, and information to inform and assist managers in developing the specifics of their own incentive programs. Within these very general guidelines, each department then had the authority and responsibility to develop specific performance criteria, the methods of measuring performance, and the system for recognizing individual work contributions. Each year the corporate staff reviews the plan, audits the results, and discusses the audit with the people covered by the plans.

A third type of incentive plan for middle-group employees is the special award plan. Some of these have been in effect for a long time. The idea of special awards programs is simple. Those who have made extraordinary achievements or accomplishments in their jobs are eligible for awards in the year in which they make the achievements. Typically under such a program, individual supervisors may recommend any of their people for such an award. There are no limitations in the number of recommendations they may make; the only requirement is that the achievement be extraordinary. These recommendations are reviewed by higher-level management until they are finally reviewed and approved at top corporate levels. The key to success of special award programs is obviously the definition of what constitutes an extraordinary achievement.

IMPACT ON PRODUCTIVITY

As in the case of all activities that impact employee productivity, it is difficult to establish with any great precision either the actual or the potential improvement in productivity which would result from the adoption of incentive plans. There simply are not at present the types of information systems that make this kind of quantifiable documentation possible in most firms. But in the case of incentive plans, there are at least some cases and special studies that give some quantitative insights into this problem.

With respect to incentives for production employees, a great number of cases have been the subject of considerable study and some documentation, all of which demonstrate that under the right circumstances, incentive pay plans contribute to greater employee productivity. With respect to management incentive compensation plans, there have been two rather comprehensive studies of business results in bonus and nonbonus paying firms. Both studies concentrated on a comparable group of bonus-paying and nonbonus-paying companies. Both showed that by any measure of business success, the bonus-paying firms were more successful than nonbonus-paying companies.

Perhaps the most persuasive evidence of the usefulness of incentive plans in increasing productivity are the views of management people in companies that have such plans. Practically all believe that incentives make a positive contribution toward more effective employee work. In fact, it is hard to think of any reason why a company would adopt incentive plans unless it did believe that one of the results would be higher productivity.

It is interesting to note that employees themselves generally favor incentive pay plans. Many favor them because they believe that under such plans they will earn more money. This is in the company's interest if the greater money earned reflects greater productivity. Many employees, however, also have expressed the view that under an incentive pay plan the better performers are the better paid employees.

There is, in total, sufficient information and input to know that incentive plans, properly structured, *can* contribute to greater employee productivity. In all areas of personnel administration, it takes a considerably greater amount of data and experience to *prove* a point than to know that it is true, and there may not be sufficient data to really *prove* to a doubting audience that incentive plans actually contribute to greater productivity. At the very least, incentives of all sorts must be considered in any organized effort to fully utilize human resources.

12

Personnel Management of Productivity

Not every activity or possible program that impacts employee productivity has been covered in previous chapters, but those that have been represent for most firms the principal opportunities for better management of human resources. In those areas alone, most firms should be able to select a sufficient number and variety of specific activities, tailored to their own particular needs, to undertake an organized and formal program for increasing the effectiveness of people at work.

In the management of this program, three other important questions must be dealt with. The first involves personnel planning. Obviously, the activities of personnel administration generally, and those particularly pointed toward improving productivity, must be planned in order to effect the objective. There is also a need for developing long-term personnel plans and incorporating them into the strategic plans of the business. Besides their impact on employee productivity in future years, personnel plans have immediate relativity to ongoing operations. Another important element of personnel management is the use of personnel staff. It is the job of the personnel staff to provide information, advice, and support to management in bringing about the full utilization of human resources. Obviously, the way in which that group is organized and structured, how it is staffed, and how it operates must have a major influence on subsequent efforts to increase employee effectiveness. There are, finally, some specific procedural and administrative questions that must be answered before attempting any organized effort to increase productivity. These are important hardware questions, which can impede productivity improvement if neglected.

PERSONNEL PLANNING

A study was made a few years ago of business planning activities in a number of leadership companies. In half of the written long-range plans of these firms, there was no specific planning with respect to employee relations or the use and management of human resources. In a dozen firms that had some personnel information in their strategic business plan, it was largely confined to census and payroll cost data. For projection of future personnel policy, this information was extrapolated literally without any qualitative evaluation. Obviously, such an approach assumes that the future will be the same as the past, which is the only assumption known to be incorrect. In none of these plans was there a separate section devoted to human resources, although there was ample attention paid to such subjects as type of furniture to be used in retail outlets, contemplated changes in bookkeeping practices, cost of office supplies, and details of a warehouse to be built three years later.

If "people are the most important assets" and if (as suggested in the introductory chapter) future increases in employee productivity will be more and more dependent upon effective management of human resources, then it is hard to avoid the conclusion that management strategy must include thoughtful and rather comprehensive planning with respect to employee relations. This would seem to be essential to the effective management of human resources, and is particularly important because every indicator suggests that factors affecting human resources management are not only changing rapidly but also becoming increasingly complex.

If personnel planning is not considered in the strategic plan of a company, there is danger that near-term personnel actions may be taken in order to increase employee productivity. This may in the long run create new forms of unproductive practices or may otherwise make more difficult the management of productivity in the future. The absence of long-range planning and a planned orderly transition to new environmental factors will likely make later management of productivity more difficult and perhaps result in a decline of employee productivity. It is reasonable to conclude, therefore, that despite the oversight of personnel input to strategic plans in the past, the dynamics of modern organizations demand this vital input to the strategic plans of every company.

Employee relations planning, like all elements of business strategy, is in effect a bridge to future operations. Employee relations input to strategic planning impacts the current year's productivity hardly at all, and next year's productivity very little. However, personnel planning has a cumulative effect on each subsequent year's productivity. The introductory expenses associated with strategy organization may be significant, but those associated with employee relations tend to decline in subsequent years. As with other areas of the plan, the start-up cost is always more than yearly sustaining expenses.

Subjects or Areas of Personnel Planning

A number of relevant areas or subjects in strategic or long-range personnel planning are critical to the business process itself, and also have very direct relevance to increasing employee productivity in the future. Naturally, the planning process, like all facets of employee relations, raises unique questions for each business. These questions relate to the business itself, its industry, and its basic objectives. On the other hand, a considerable number of important subjects are applicable to businesses generally. These principal areas of general business importance are outlined below.

Profile of the work force: Most companies have seen unprecedented growth over the past ten years in the number of middle-level positions, particularly specialized knowledge workers. Those who anticipated this growth fashioned personnel policies and activities that would meet this need and would contribute to higher productivity in specialty jobs. The question now is "what will be the work force changes in the future?" The answer can be found in known current trends and developments.

Census projections: On the basis of changes in the profile of the work force, anticipated changes in business, and other factors, it is quite practical to make rather accurate projections about the future work force both by basic position categories and for various areas of the business. Such projections have obvious importance to the business overall. They also tell the company such simple things as space required to provide a reasonable work environment for employees and what should be done to determine and plan future organization. Such projections are direct input for anticipating human resources development activities. All these planning data have direct relevance to future productivity.

New positions: When organizations are examined over significant time spans of 10 to 15 years, many positions that do not presently exist will be needed. Some of these will be critical to achievement of enterprise goals, including productivity goals. These projections will also have value in anticipating changing roles or new areas of responsibility and involvement in established positions. Identification of such changes, particularly in leadership positions, is vital to the planning process and has direct relevance to employee productivity.

Succession projections: As do many personnel planning inputs, succession planning appropriately starts with a limited number of critical positions.

Identification of succession needs for such positions and proper planning for them can be built into the strategy planning of the firm.

Labor demands and supply projections: Labor-demand requirements of the firm can be matched against labor-supply projections available from published economic information. This combination of supply and demand inputs, in addition to information with respect to the company's own projected growth areas, provide important insights into staffing, succession, and recruiting needs. In some cases such projections can identify major potential problem areas in achieving planned company-growth strategies.

Staffing cost: Future recruiting requirements plus knowledge of cost of new hiring make it possible to prepare realistic projections of staffing costs. These projections also provides clues as to how the company must in the future restructure its recruiting practices.

Organizational models: One of the problems in many existing ways of planning the personnel population is that they inherently assume a static state of the company's organization. Part of the planning process should, in fact, build likely organization models for the future. These need be only organizational sketches, which then lead to transition planning that will facilitate transition with minimal disruption.

Human resources development requirements: It is usually only necessary in the personnel planning process to identify the major areas in which significant amounts of development will be required, the time at which such development activities should be initiated, and the general types of development needed to meet company goals. When these areas require extensive investigation and a wide spread of activities, then the cost of human resources development can be built into the long-term cost projections of the firm.

Compensation levels: Projected compensation scales should be forecast in multiple parts, each based on a different rate of inflation. They should also recognize the variable rates of compensation growth in different job or occupational categories, and should include contemplated increases in benefit costs. Only in this way can realistic compensation forecasts be made.

Payroll cost projections: Given the forecasted employment census population, compensation and benefit levels, and changes in compensation benefit practices, it is then possible for the company to forecast with reasonable accuracy the total dollar payroll in the future. This forecast may also give important insights into what the company must do to improve dollarized productivity levels.

Labor relations: A number of vital elements with respect to labor relations must be considered in the plans of the company; some of these have specific relevance to employee productivity. The growth of "new unions" in the field of public employment was, for instance, anticipated as far back as 1950. Future emergence of unions in other formerly sacrosanct areas is almost certain and has equal importance. Changes in the union environment and the impact that it may have on bargaining postures represents another area of strategic company planning. Finally, anticipation of expansion in major contract provision issues should not be neglected.

Management technology: In every long-term business cycle there will be changes evident in management technology. Computer processing is an example. The evolution of human resources information systems and changes in human resources technology may well bring important changes in management technology in the future, including considerations of changes in basic management practices. The emergence of delegative management would be an example of a major change in practice that might be crucial in the planning process and have significant impact on employee productivity.

Environmental conditions: Increased portability of pensions was predicted and, on the basis of that forecast, some firms changed their pension practices to conform with that likely event. On the other hand, such forecasts are not always so accurate. A few years ago there were many companies who assumed that the four-day week would become a widespread reality, but that is a projection largely unfulfilled. Nevertheless, this type of forecast should be contemplated and treated as an alternative with respect to personnel inputs in the business plan. All such possible environmental conditions should be anticipated and where they might have major relevance to the management of the company or to the management of its work force, they should be considered as alternatives and should be the bases of specific plans for changes in personnel policies and practices if they should be adopted generally.

The Process of Employee Relations Planning

Some general guidelines, based on experience, for effective input of personnel considerations into the strategic business plan and supplementary personnel plans are available. The initial guideline is that the personnel planning period is essentially a 10 to 15 year cycle. It is within this time frame that fundamental changes affecting employee relations generally occur. This far exceeds the typical business planning cycle of five years. The need in personnel planning, therefore, is to identify fundamental changes occurring in the personnel cycle and then to establish from that the likely changes that will occur in the time cycle of the business plan.

It is also necessary in many areas of personnel planning to benefit from basic research conducted by large financial institutions, the government, "think tanks," and other outside sources. Typically, it is beyond the resources of any one company to undertake such fundamental research. Some have joined together in an industry or group effort to pool their resources in gaining such basic knowledge in the personnel planning area.

It is generally not necessary in personnel planning to do a 100 percent sampling in any subject area in order to extract basic personnel inputs to strategic plans. Rather, focus should be on major changes, on factors affecting critical positions, and on those personnel subjects that are either comprehensive in the economy overall or have particular relevance to the specific marketing and business plans of the company. It is also important to recognize that personnel planning will never have the statistical precision of financial and market forecasts. It will always involve some fundamental judgments.

Hunches or fantasties of emerging personnel environment should be avoided. The correct way to plan personnel is to identify changes that are now occurring and which, unless reversed, will inevitably result in situations that have significant impact on the management of human resources. This approach emphasizes the use of known changes as the bases for planning. And, of course, if facts in the future indicate even further changes, then personnel plans can be revised accordingly.

It was noted earlier that in many respects strategic business planning, including personnel planning, is a bridge to the future. Some companies have developed and started implementing the idea of building a "second bridge" in their strategic planning. The second bridge technique reverses the typical planning process that starts with identification of major environmental factors in the future and suggests major business opportunities 10 or 15 years ahead. These are then examined in the light of the company's current capabilities to see which (if any) might represent meaningful opportunities, and what steps, actions, and investments would be necessary to cross the bridge.

A few companies have used human resources capabilities as a basis for building strategic plans. This process examines the question of whether or not existing human resources in the business can be the basis for growing new businesses in the future. One area in which such a process was utilized successfully was among companies heavily involved in government contract work in the 1950s. As government contract business declined, many of these companies had to plan for commercial activities. A few were very successful in identifying core technologies of their existing professional staff and in planning how this collection of knowledge could be deployed in the commercial world.

ORGANIZATION AND USE OF PERSONNEL STAFF

The personnel department represents those employees who assist line executives, managers, and supervisors throughout the organization in human resources management. They are "staff persons" who, among other things, support management in improving productivity through more effective utilization of human resources. Because it is their area of staff specialization, they should possess much "how to" knowledge and technology so as to provide counsel in activities that promote better use of human resources. They keep abreast of new technologies that support advances in productivity, and should be involved in day-to-day decisions and actions designed to improve it.

Role of the Personnel Department

The degree to which the personnel department effectively carries out its basic assignment in supporting the line organization in human resources management, including management of employee productivity, depends to a very considerable extent on the role or the charter of the personnel staff in the first place. The primary role of personnel should be to support the basic management objective of effective human resources management; that is, to assist management in bringing about the full utilization of the company's human assets. In effect this could be labeled the "operating" personnel activity, which works directly with managers and professional people at every level of the business on a day-to-day basis to help them become more productive in their work. It also involves the day-to-day activities that help supervisors throughout the organization to bring forth the best effort and the most effective work from their subordinates.

Necessarily, the personnel department performs a number of other activities that reflect different or additional roles. These include:

The rapprochement role: This means, in a unionized organization, collective bargaining. In groups of employees not represented by unions, it means the establishment and implementation of those personnel policies that substitute for collective bargaining contracts; including the handling of grievances and complaints.

Knowledge accumulation: This simply involves the accumulation of needed knowledge in the specialized areas of personnel. It includes intracompany knowledge and knowledge about people within the company and their talents, their abilities, and their experiences. It also applies to the academic disciplines that make up the personnel field, such as psychology, sociology, economics, and law. It consists of knowledge with respect to experiences, both good and bad, of other companies. Finally, it is the know-how or specialized expertise required to implement given programs and activities.

Centralized administrative services: This is the area of centralized recruiting, centralized record keeping, processing of administrative forms and information, etc.

Employee services: Such disparate activities as management of the cafeteria, the parking lot, employee publications, and recreational activities are among employee services.

Compliance role: Increasingly, some major part of the personnel department's activity must be deployed to assure that the company is meeting the requirements of government regulations.

The personnel department: Finally, some members of the personnel department are assigned the role of effectively managing the Personnel Department.

Performance of all these roles requires considerable time and effort. Most are occupied by recurring work, which must be handled continuously or has urgency. The needs for centralized service, compliance, employee service, and union relations are all highly visible. There is the danger that the less visible or urgent, but in many respects more important, roles of personnel relations with nonunion employees, knowledge accumulation, and the operating personnel role will be neglected. These are the vital personnel activities that assist in full utilization of the human assets of the enterprise.

Organization of the Personnel Function

Organization of the personnel function is important, not only because it structurally facilitates or impedes the effectiveness of personnel people, but also because it can actually influence what they do and how they focus their attention. Organization of the personnel function is important for an even more basic reason—the company's personnel effort is carried out by personnel people *and* operating managers. The critical interaction, therefore, is how that structure coordinates the performance of the total personnel effort. Therefore, the interrelationship of the personnel staff and operating managers is critical. This suggests that the basic organization of the personnel function must reflect the basic organizational philosophy of the line organization it essentially serves.

Personnel organization should focus on its basic mission, assumed here to be the full utilization of the human resources of the company (the operating personnel role or activity). In addition, it should be such that its usefulness as well as its costs can be rationally monitored. Finally, and in many ways most important, the personnel group must be organized so that it is most readily utilized by its *customers,* the line organization. Traditional organization of personnel departments does not meet these criteria very well.

Traditionally personnel organizations have been structured around functional areas of activity. This means that the basic breakdown of activities is usually made for employment, training, wage and salary administration, benefits administration, communications, and labor relations. The logic of this pattern is that the personnel field involves diverse and complex bodies of specialized knowledge, and that (at least within the personnel department) it makes fairly clear and understandable that salary questions go to the salary department and employment questions go to the employment department. Unfortunately, while the traditional functional organization of personnel staff may be simple and clear to the personnel group, it provides a very complicated and confusing organization to line managers. These managers tend to view questions as "personnel questions," without the discrete functional distinctions that are comfortable for the personnel specialist. Furthermore, functional organization, if anything, tends to overemphasize technology; in other words, it promotes or encourages art for art's sake. The salary administrator tends to place all personnel problems in a salary administration context; the training specialist tends to classify training as the critical human resources management issue. Functional specialists also are inclined to focus their attention and gear their activities to the activities of their peers in their field of specialization, as well as to their customers.

Functional personnel organizations seem to promote technically sound answers that may not meet the needs of a particular organization or unit. They concentrate too much upon technical excellence of programs and activities, and pay too little attention to questions of whether or not the programs will work. The goal of personnel activities is to develop what is most appropriate and useable, and not necessarily what is technically excellent or sophisticated.

The functional organization also tends to contribute to institutionalization of personnel decision making. The centralized specialist develops procedures in which excellence of his knowledge or techniques may outweigh the line supervisor's knowledge of the individuals and circumstances involved. Centralized direction based upon functional categories has an inherent tendency to require institutionalized practices. In some respects, functional organization concentrates too much on practices, procedures, and controls designed to preserve the purity of systems rather than to promote more appropriate personnel decisions.

Because of these considerations, personnel organizations increasingly tend to be organized, at least in part, around operating personnel activities more than functional specialties. Both traditional functional and operating personnel organizations, are illustrated in Figure 7. The focus of the operating personnel organization is the operating personnel unit; this follows in each of the significantly sized business units throughout the organization. The operating personnel managers work for, or closely with, one or more line human resources unit managers. It is this organization that is specifically charged with the job of assisting management to optimize the use of human resources.

Under the operating personnel concept, the personnel department is first organized by activity rather than by function. Essentially, the operating personnel people are the focal point of the organization. They are located physically with the organization they serve. Record keeping, administration, service, and other similar personnel activities are centralized as much as possible. These activities usually serve all units or at least all units in a location. The work also tends to benefit by centralization, by mass operations, by methodization and mechanization, and by computerization. Here, of course, one of the key issues is cost effectiveness of operations.

Knowledge areas are centralized, although not necessarily to the same

A. Traditional Functional Organization

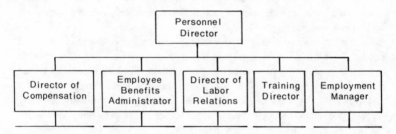

B. Operating Personnel Structure

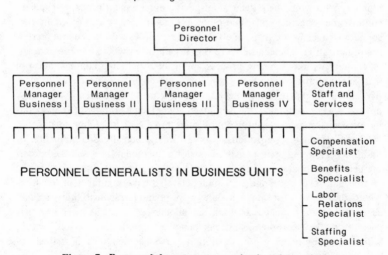

Figure 7. Personnel department organization alternatives.

degree as the record keeping and administrative service activities. The central knowledge areas tend to be structured along functional areas. It is important to note, however, that under the operating personnel concept, knowledge does not reside exclusively in people who fill these positions. A great deal of personnel technology comes, for instance, from the operating personnel units.

It is the job of the knowledge expert in various functional areas of personnel to be the central depository of special functional knowledge. He should have a higher level of technology and expertise in his particular functional area, but he does not possess it solely. In fact, he gets much of his technology and knowledge from operating personnel people and managers throughout the line organization. He also relies very heavily on getting knowledge from outside sources, from the experiences of other companies and from consultants.

A well-trained operating personnel manager can serve the total personnel needs of as few as 200 or as many as 1,000 employees. This is possible because the operating personnel manager utilizes the central services of the record keeping, administrative, and service organizations. He also relies on and uses the knowledge of the centralized knowledge departments. In many respects the operating personnel manager serves as the personnel director for the operating unit manager where he works, and for other supervisors in the same organization.

Such an organization provides a complex multigrid framework for personnel people. For instance, in hiring it would be the operating personnel manager who would help determine specific employment needs, job specifications, man specifications, and other job requirements. The operating personnel manager would then, in effect, place an order with the central recruiting organization. The central recruiting organization would then prepare ads or contract with an agency, process applicants (including administration of tests and preliminary interviews), and perform other work necessary to identify sound candidates who meet the requirements specified. When these processes were completed, the candidate would then be referred to the operating personnel manager, who would screen him for his operating managers.

The personnel organization in some firms is actually a combination of traditional grouping of responsibilities along functional lines and the operating personnel structuring. In a large food company, for example, each of the section unit-level corporate staff members also have a number of locations where they have operating personnel-coordination responsibilities as well as corporate staff functional work. In another case, a chemical firm has each of its key corporate staff personnel also perform "liaison" work, which includes many of the operating personnel activities described for some divisions of the firm.

Use of the Personnel Function

The degree to which the personnel department truly contributes to greater productivity is very much a question of how the department is used as well as how it is organized. To be really effective, operating personnel managers must be involved closely with the operations they serve. This, of course, is one of the basic principles of the operating personnel concept. It is not possible, for instance, for company personnel people to do a good job of determining personnel needs or to work closely with management throughout the organization in solving day-to-day personnel problems (which, cumulatively, so much affect employee productivity) unless they are involved in operations. Only in this way can they, in a timely and effective manner, bring their knowledge and experience to bear in helping management deal with these situations. Only in this way will they ever gain the confidence of both the supervisors throughout the organization and the employees so that they can make a positive contribution to the solution of problems.

The personnel organization, particularly in the operating personnel units, must be permitted or required to take an active rather than a passive role in operations. Activities should be structured so that personnel staff is engaged in activities not only useful in their own right in a programmatic sense, but which will make it possible for personnel staff to have an understanding of the feelings of employees in different units of the company on major issues. Among these issues are ambitions and aspirations, complaints and disaffections of individuals, and what motivates individual people as well as employees collectively. In a really well-functioning personnel organization, attitude surveys of a conventional nature are really not necessary. If it is important to know what employees think about a specific issue, the operating personnel manager should be able to advance very accurate insights. If he does not really know how employees think about an important issue, then he should have enough rapport with employees to find out, by asking them!

The operating personnel people should be tracking individual career growth. They should be well aware of developmental needs for individuals and for groups. They should be closely involved in operations so that they are aware of the existence of obstacles that impede effective productivity.

Administrative Questions

For those firms that find themselves in a position where they cannot increase productivity in the future sufficiently by the use of substituting machinery for people or by increased methodization of work, the better management and more effective use of human resources must necessarily be a major business activity. The whole process of how this activity can be managed is an important administrative question. The magnitude of the investments involved, the complexities of the issues, the scope of activities, and the potential returns to the business, all suggest the need for some organized systems approach toward improved productivity.

An organized system logically involves some distinct personnel administration questions and some matters of process or procedure. These include the assignment of the responsibility for such work, business assessment in order to determine just what needs to be done and how it should be carried out, methods of reviewing or monitoring work in this area, the actual measurement of progress in improving productivity, and continuous administration or operational planning of future activities.

Any subject as important to an organization as increasing employee productivity should logically involve the assignment of responsibility for such a project to a systems manager, or perhaps to a group of persons who will carry on this systems management job. Obviously, line management is responsible for the productivity of employees, but line management is responsible for everything. There is also, as in so many areas of business, the need for coordinated staff advice, information input, and monitoring activities. This is the area of great need for systems management.

There is no single background or functional skill that could hope to get the job done by one person or by a unit. To a very large extent, the systems manager in the area of productivity is very much like the business planner; both are general contractors who pool from various sources inside and outside the company the skills, knowledge and experience necessary to support management in getting the job done. They must provide the leadership in identifying work that must be done, coordinate the activities of all participants, and distill and synthesize the work already accomplished so that management may review and continuously monitor the productivity.

Some companies have considered establishing a new functional job or department, the productivity department. Most such attempts have been unsuccessful, primarily because they involve a duplication of staff areas already in existence. While the systems management responsibility can be assigned to a number of places, depending upon the background of individuals, the organization, the structure, the company, and style of management, the most logical place would be the personnel department because essentially we are talking about the productivity of employees.

Part of the support job in improving productivity involves business assessment. Productivity is important to every company, but it does not have the same priority for every business. Obviously, any number of subjects determine business success or business survival. At a given time, the relative priorities of increasing productivity in an overall business sense must first be determined.

Even when productivity has a high order of priority, then it is necessary to assess in each given company situation those areas that affect productivity and which present the greatest opportunities for that firm, at that time, to increase productivity. For some companies, continued substitution of machinery for people might be the key for continued improvement of employee productivity. More likely improvement will be realized in a number of areas or activities, but certainly not in all those available or even all those identified in this book.

In short, it is essential for any successful program to increase employee productivity that it focus on those areas that have the greatest possibilities. No company has such great resources or such overwhelming needs for improving employee productivity at a given time that it can in a meaningful and substantive way work in every category and major area. Prioritization of the areas selected is thus a second step necessary to the business assessment of employee productivity.

To the extent that the business assessment indicates that employee productivity must be accomplished at least in part by better management of human resources, then some form of business personnel audit must be conducted. The objective is to identify, among a great variety of personnel subjects which impact productivity, those subjects that at a given period of time represent the principal opportunities for that company.

As a practical matter, many leadership companies today recognize that they need to audit the effectiveness of human resources activities, just as the accountants audit the use of physical assets. Personnel audits have many values, such as spotting personnel problems before they reach major magnitude. Personnel audits identify human resources vulnerabilities that need to be dealt with. Audits are also used as an ongoing tool of management, both as a measurement of business effectiveness and as a basis for management decision making. Thus, the personnel audit serves a broad purpose, but it is a vital step in an organized system for increasing employee productivity through better management of human resources.

Once specific activities in the area of employee relations have been identified through the personnel audit, then there is obviously a need for operational planning to get things done. Planning must include, as it usually does, what is to be done, when, what resources are to be committed, and who will do it. For productivity improvement, it should also include declarative statements of the criteria by which results will be evaluated, set milestones to measure accomplishment, and provide timetables and schedules.

13

Responsibilities of the Personnel Unit Manager

Increasing employee productivity, or making fuller utilization of human resources of the company, is indeed a systems problem in the sense that it involves many subjects, many sections of the business, and many individuals in a coordinated effort to increase productivity by better management of human resources. The cornerstone, however, and the ultimate point at which efforts to improve employee productivity fail or succeed, is geared to the degree to which personnel unit managers, as defined in Chapter 8 in the first instance, and supervisors generally carry out their responsibilities.

These personnel unit management people are typically deep in the organization; there are many of them, and human resources management is only a part of their overall responsibilities and therefore receives only a part of their time and attention. They are not typically trained professionally in the techniques of personnel administration, yet they play the critical role.

The accountabilities of supervision for increasing employee productivity is pivotal and involves a considerable list of specific activities and responsibilities, all of which have been identified in previous sections of this book. But the nature and key role of supervision, and particularly of unit managers when they exist, become apparent when all these diverse activities and responsibilities are summarized.

The personnel unit manager, first and foremost, is the key person in communicating a company philosophy of full utilization of human resources. Written communications and formal announcements by top management will serve to state the official policy, but verbal, reinforcing communication occurs when the unit manager discusses and describes that policy and makes decisions that implement it.

Most of the human resources information developed at this stage has been used by higher-level management and top staff personnel. As information systems continue to develop, however, similar information will become available for use by unit personnel managers. When it becomes available to them, they have the responsibility to use the information guidelines and data. As human resources developmental work continues, unit managers have an added responsibility to provide feedback to top management concerning human-resource information needs and implementation problems of those centrally responsible for the system.

The unit manager is also the true first line of company compliance with government regulations and of the success of affirmative action programs. Currently, this responsibility particularly applies to EEO and the Occupational Health and Safety Act. If there is a union, the unit supervisor is actively involved in contract administration, if not in bargaining. Finally, in the last analysis, it is the unit manager who must see to it that unproductive practices—whether self-imposed or inherent in the organization—are identified and eliminated wherever possible.

Another responsibility of the unit manager is the effect on employee productivity of the environment surrounding the company. If employees have personal or home problems that manifest themselves at work, it is the unit manager who must see to it that the employee is helped to the extent possible and that appropriate personnel actions are taken to insure optimum productivity. Where general social environment manifests itself in the work place, line supervision must deal on a day-to-day basis with work manifestations of such environmental situations. It is also the line supervisor who sets expectations of excellence, who emphasizes quality of work and high standards, and who through his day-to-day attention develops employee attitudes to the point where they expect excellence of themselves.

Higher-level management and central staff rely heavily on supervisors at every level for essential inputs in evolving and implementing appropriate personnel policies. When the policies are implemented, it is the unit manager who must communicate these policies to all employees and see to it that they are properly applied.

In the area of staffing, either the unit manager himself or the other supervisors under his jurisdiction are accountable for determining recruiting needs in their own organization. They are also accountable for final screening and selection of employees. Frequently, the unit manager will also play an important role in applying the evaluative criteria for screening employees for the long-term needs of the company, in addition to meeting specifications required to do the job being filled. Similarly, it is the unit manager who has the basic responsibility for appropriate placement, which for various reasons is one of the pivotal personnel activities that influences levels of employee productivity. These responsibilities include selection of persons for promotion, necessary transfer to meet operational needs and to effect development of people, proper design of jobs, and generally seeing to it that the right person is in the right job.

Much of the work with respect to manpower controls has to do with setting guidelines, and otherwise determining appropriate levels of staffing under various operating circumstances. Within these guidelines, however, it is the unit managers, where these exist, and in varying degrees all supervisors plus personnel staff close to operations that essentially have the job of controlling manpower. They are the ones who have the essential knowledge of what work needs to be done, and they are the ones who actually prepare manpower forecasts and recommend manpower requirements.

Employees throughout the enterprise develop informal organizational relationships, but these are sanctioned by supervisors and, when they exist, the human resources unit managers. It is the supervisor's responsibility to see to it that informal relationships not only contribute to greater employee effectiveness, but also concur with the framework of enterprise organization policy and are consistent in managerial style. Supervision also plays a major role of developing as well as implementing operational organization. Supervisors do more than contribute to organizational relationships at operational level; essentially, it is staff experts who contribute and line supervisors who decide and implement operational organization.

The whole objective of delegative management is to structure the organization in such a way that human resources management decisions can be delegated to the lowest level. That lowest appropriate level is the unit manager or a line supervisor. It is the whole purpose of human resources management organization structuring to establish the unit manager positions as the appropriate lowest level in the organization where real managerial authority for key decisions in the area of employee relations can be delegated. It must also be noted that many of the facilitating conditions described as being essential for effective delegative management are influenced by the supervisors.

The three basic areas of human relations development, identified in Chapter 10, are the responsibility of supervision. While much of work training and operational training and development may be programmatic, supervisors conduct some of the human relations development work, select those eligible for programmatic training, and provide essential inputs of the needs of programmatic training and therefore the type of training to be conducted.

In the area of individual development, supervision again plays the key role. Supervisors at every level are the only ones who can make conclusions appraisals. Supervisors and the personnel staff that supports them also make the initial, and the essential evaluative performance appraisals. The amount of self-development that results is due to many factors, but the supervisor contributes heavily to this important facet of human resources development also, and actually nurtures self-development. Finally, at each level of the organization, supervisors set the objectives for subordinates when a management-by-objectives program exists.

Only human relations unit managers and higher-level managers can conduct, direct, and monitor future development. For this important activity, these levels of supervision conduct evaluative appraisal and contribute heavily to actual developmental activities. Furthermore, supervisors at every level influence long-term development of employees by handling job moves of all types.

Supervisors also have major responsibilities in the area of motivation and incentives. They determine, implement, and control many of the nonfinancial incentives, such as how employees are treated by their superiors. They influence in one way or another other nonfinancial incentives such as the work individuals perform and how they perceive their opportunities and their security. In many ways, supervision affects the existence and nature of disincentives and negative incentives.

In any firm, supervision has some effect on employee salary levels and salary progress. In firms practicing some degree of delegative management, supervision determines or has a major impact on employees' salaries and salary progress.

Typically, supervision has less responsibility for pay under incentive plans and only indirect impact on benefits. Under incentive plans, however, they frequently are involved in setting standards, making recommendations about such matters as plan participants and individual award variations. For both incentive pay plans and benefit plans supervisors have a communications responsibility.

It's very surprising that nowhere in the literature of business could the author find a well thought through and detailed discussion of supervision responsibilities for the management of human resources. There are infinite numbers of statements or assumptions that management and supervision are responsible for employees' work and for the effectiveness of their work. Such expressions are inconclusive and are no more accurate or useful than the statement that a supervisor is responsible for costs.

Supervisors play an important role, and have major responsibilities for human resources management and for the full utilization of the human resources of the enterprise. These responsibilities are not vague peripheral parts of the job of supervision. They need to be detailed and clearly understood. If supervisors are to be held responsible for their human resources management job, they should be supported in this work, and trained and developed to do it effectively. This is the cornerstone of increased employee productivity through more effective human resources management.

Index

appraisal of performance, 153-156, 157
authority, and delegative management, 131, 135-136

benchmark data, 39-40
bureaucracy, employee reaction to, 74-75
business
  divisions, 124-125
  economics of staffing, 81-84
  image, and employee effectiveness, 77-79
  productivity and results, 12-15
  see also business unit
business unit
  business divisions, 124-125
  operating companies, 124
  operating units, 125-126
  organizational concept, 123-124
  profit center, 125
  see also business

capital substitution
  economics of, 22-24
  future use of, 21-22
census projections, 188
chain of command, 127

climate, and delegative management, 140
coaching and executive development, 166
collective bargaining, unproductive contract provisions and practices, 28, 57-59
communications and training, 146-148
community environment, 71-72
compensation
  financial incentives, 177-178
  incentive pay plans, 181-184
  levels of, 189
  salary increases, 178-181
compliance role, personnel department, 193
conclusion ratings, 153-154
control
  payroll, 101
  span of, 126-127
  see also manpower control
cost
  of human resources acquisition, 82-83
  of incentives, 173
  of new hires, 45-48
  of recruiting, 85-86
  of staffing, 189
  of surplus manpower, 100-101
cost information, human relations information system, 43-44

cost/value relationships, human resources development, 169
counseling and executive development, 166

defensive information, human relations information system, 43
delegative management
    defined, 130-132
    essentials of, 134-138
    evolution of, 132-133
    facilitating conditions, 138-140
    and productivity, 142-144
    techniques, 140-142
    see also management
demethodization, and productivity, 26
development
    executive, 165-166
    of future abilities, 162-164
    individual, 153-160
    operational training and, 149-153
    organizational, 133, 160-162
    see also human resources development
discretionary incentive pay plans, 183-184
disincentives and negative incentives, 174-176
disproductivity, 55
    and trappings of affluence, 77
    in union contracts, 59

earnings, management of, 78
economics
    of capital substitution, 22-24
    of manpower control, 99-102
    of staffing, 81-84
economy, productivity data, 7
employee(s)
    capital investment per, 20-21
    development of potential, 162-164
    effectiveness, and business image, 77-79
    and home environment, 69-71
    investment per (1975), 23
    productivity increase, 15-16
    reaction to bureaucracy, 74-75

employee relations planning, 187-191
employee services, 193
employment
    defined, 84-85
    management function, 97
    mise-en-place, 93-95
    placement, 90
    promotion, 90-93
    recruiting, 85-86
    screening, 86-88
    strategic needs, 88-90
environment
    business image, 77-79
    community, 71-72
    employee and home, 69-71
    and expectations of excellence, 75-76
    general social, 72-73
    government, 73-75
    and personnel planning, 190
    personnel policies, 79-80
    physical conditions, 76-77
Equal Employment Opportunity Act (EEOA), 63
evaluative information, human resources information system, 44-45
evaluative performance appraisal, 155-156
executive development, 165-166
expectations, and employee effectiveness, 75-76

factors, human resources information system, 42-45
full utilization
    commitment to, 2-4
    productiveness, productivity, and, 2
    questions about concept, 4-6

goal-oriented incentive pay plan, 183
government
    as environmental factor, 73-75
    and unproductive practices, 28, 61-64
group therapy, 161

human resources
    acquisition cost, 82-83

effective use of, 28-31
full utilization of, 2-4
human resources development
   activities, 145-146
   individual, 153-160
   process, 168-169
   and productivity, 31-32
   requirements, 189
   special, 164-168
   and training, 146-153
human resources information
   availability of, 35-37
   work types, 37-38
human resources information system
   analysis procedures, 52-53
   defined, 34-35
   factors, 42-45
   factor information and guidelines,
      45-50
   guidelines, 38-40
   management decisions, 40-42
   multiple indicators, 51-52
   organizational structuring information
      guidelines, 122-123
   survey information collecting and reporting, 50-51
human resources management, structuring, 119-122

image of business, and employee effectiveness, 77-79
incentives
   financial, 177-178
   need for, 171-174
   negative, and disincentives, 174-176
   nonfinancial, 176-177
   pay plans, 181-184
   and productivity, 184-185
   salary increases, 178-181
individual development, 153-160
information exchange, and executive development, 166
information guidelines
   manpower control, 105-107
   organizational structuring, 122-123

information system, 34-35
   see also human resources information
      system
institutionalization vs. delegative management, 136
interviews, allocation of time for, 87-88
investment approach to manpower control, 104-105
investment spending and human resources
   information system, 49-50

job analysis, and delegative management,
   141
job enrichment, 26-27, 133
job satisfaction, as incentive, 176-177

key productivity index, 48-49
knowledge
   accumulation, personnel department,
      192
   leveraging, and delegative management, 142

labor, supply and demand projections,
   189
labor relations, 189-190
line and staff, 128

machinery, as substitute for people, 20-24
management
   decisions, and human resources information system, 40-42
   of earnings, 78
   of manpower control, 102-105
   open systems of, 133
   participative, 132, 133
   theories X and Y of, 132-133
   training and development practices,
      146-153
   union contract restrictions on, 59
   of unproductive practices, 66-67
   see also delegative management; personnel management
management by objectives (MBO),
   158-160
management engineering, 109

management technology and personnel planning, 190
manpower
  levels, 98-99
  ratios, 106-107
manpower control
  economics of, 99-102
  information guidelines, 105-107
  investment approach, 104-105
  management of, 102-105
  and productivity, 31
  programs and practices, 107-111
matrix organization, 128
measurement information, human relations information system, 44
merit increases, 179-180
methodization and productivity, 24-27
motivation
  and incentives, 171-173
  and negative incentives, 175
  and productivity, 32

new hire costs, and human resources information system, 45-48

objectives, management by, 158-160
Occupational Safety and Health Act (OSHA), 63
operating companies, 124
operating units, 125-126
operational training and development (OTD), 149-153
organization
  business unit concept, 123-124
  external positioning, 118-119
  models, 189
  personnel function, 193-197
  personnel staff, 191-193
  planning vs. structuring, 112
  and productivity, 128-129
  theories, 126-129
  see also organizational structuring
organizational development, 133, 160-162
organizational structuring
  business unit concept, 123-126

and external positioning, 118-119
human resources management, 119-122
information guidelines, 122-123
operational, 115-116
and productivity, 31
strategic, 117-118
tactical, 115-116
transactional, 113-114
see also organization
outplacement, 95-96
output, union contract restrictions on, 58

participative management, 132, 133
pay plans, incentive, 181-184
payroll
  control, 101
  cost projections, 189
people, substitution of machinery for, 20-24
performance appraisal, 153-156
  objectives, 157
personnel function, organization and use of staff, 191-197
personnel management
  administrative questions, 197-199
  and productivity, 30, 31-33
personnel planning, 187-188
  areas, 188-190
  process, 190-191
personnel policies and employee effectiveness, 79-80
physical conditions of environment, 76-77
placement, 90
productiveness, 2
productivity
  administrative questions, 197-199
  company data, 9-10
  and delegative management, 142-144
  and effort, 172
  employee, 15-16
  general data, 7-9
  and government, 73-75
  and human resources information system, 48-49

improvement methods, 19-20
improvement opportunities, 10-12
and incentives, 184-185
levels and trends, 6-7
and manpower control, 31
and methodization, 24-27
and motivation, 32
and organization, 128-129
and personnel management, 30, 31-33
potential impact, 12-15
productiveness, full utilization, and, 2
as systems problem, 18-19
transactional approach, 17-18
and turnover, 83-84
and unions, 59-60
and unproductive practices, 27-28
and work methods, 24-27
productivity bargaining, 60-61
professional development, 166-168
profit center, 125
project organization, 128
promotion, 90-93
and salary increase, 179
and transfer, 93-95

rapprochement role, personnel department, 192
recruiting of employees, 85-86
reporting relationships, single, 127
responsibilities, personnel unit manager, 200-201
retirement, 96
risk management and delegative management, 141-142

salary increases, as incentives, 178-181
screening of employees, 86-88
selection and productivity, 31
self-development, 156, 158
skills training, 148-149
social environment, general, 72-73
span of control, 126-127
special award incentive pay plan, 184
staff
and line, 128

personnel, organization and use of, 191-197
staffing
business economics of, 81-84
cost, 189
employment, 84-95
employment management function, 97
outplacement, 95-96
standards, and employee effectiveness, 75-76
status, as incentive, 177
strategic information, human resources information system, 44-45
strategic needs, and employment, 88-90
strategic planning and personnel planning, 191
structure, *see* organizational structuring
succession planning, 92-93
succession projections, 188-189

tactical organizational structuring, 115-116
termination, 95-96
"T" groups, 161
theory X and theory Y, 132-133
time analysis and delegative management, 141
training
and development, management practices, 146-153
operational, 149-153
and organizational development, 160-162
in supervisory skills, 148-149
transfer and promotion, 93-95
turnover and productivity, 83-84

unions
and productivity, 59-60
and productivity bargaining, 60-61
unproductive contract provisions and practices, 57-59
unproductive practices, 27-28
collective bargaining, 57-61
and government, 28, 61-64

unproductive practices (*continued*)
   management of, 66-67
   self-imposed, 64-66
   types, 55-57
utilization, *see* full utilization

work, developing better methods of, 24-27
work force profile, 188
work types, human resources information, 37-38